COUNTER-IMPERIAL

CHURCHING

for a

PLANETARY GOSPEL

COUNTER-IMPERIAL

CHURCHING

for a

PLANETARY GOSPEL

Radical Discipleship
for Today

Timothy Murphy

PROCESS
CENTURY
PRESS

ANOKA, MINNESOTA   2017

Counter-Imperial Churching for a Planetary Gospel: Radical Discipleship for Today

Process Century Press
RiverHouse LLC
802 River Lane
Anoka, MN 55303

Process Century Press books are published in association with the International Process Network.

Cover: Susanna Mennicke

VOLUME III: THEOLOGICAL EXPLORATIONS SERIES
JEANYNE B. SLETTOM, GENERAL EDITOR

ISBN 978-1-940447-28-5
Printed in the United States of America

CONTENTS

kerygma

koinonia

SERIES PREFACE: THEOLOGICAL EXPLORATIONS

This series aims to explore the implications of Whiteheadian philosophy and theology for religious belief and practice. It also proposes that process religious thinkers, working from within many different traditions — Buddhist, Confucian, Christian, Hindu, Indigenous, Jewish, Muslim, and others — have unique insights pertinent to the critical issues of our day.

In 1976, we published a book, *Process Theology: An Introductory Exposition,* in which we aimed to "show the creative potentiality of a process perspective in theology." In addition to its explanation of process concepts and their application to Christian doctrine, the book noted the contribution of Whiteheadian thought toward "intercultural and interreligious understanding" and took an early stance on the ecological threat, claiming that process theology was prepared to "make a distinctive contribution" to this challenge.

Since the publication of that book, we have seen many others explore these and other themes in articles, books, and conferences. At the same time, the threat to planetary health and the need for "intercultural and interreligious understanding" has only accelerated. This series is an effort to support theologians and religious philosophers in their ongoing exposition of possible Whiteheadian solutions.

John B. Cobb, Jr.
David Ray Griffin

OTHER BOOKS IN THIS SERIES

God of Empowering Love, David P. Polk
God Exists but Gawd Does Not, David Ray Griffin

Preface and

Acknowledgements

THIS WORK FUNCTIONS AS A CONCRESCENCE or "growing together" of many different influences, both practical and academic, in my life. One might question whether this is an ecclesiology at all. As it dismantles orthodox constructions of church, one may wonder whether perhaps it is an anti-ecclesiology? It certainly does not conform to traditional debates on the nature and work of the church, and it rejects traditional approaches to *kerygma, koinonia*, and *diakonia* for a much more radical trajectory. From the outset, a tension is apparent: I love the church, though I hate the phrase "the church." As you will see while reading this book, I believe that it is impossible to write a universal ecclesiology. This is not a project about the nature and work of the church universal. This is a particular project, in a particular location, with particular problems that it seeks to address. That said, it is not a work of sectarianism or isolationism, either.

In another way, this project could very well be considered a radical missiology as it explores the mission and calling to which church-life responds. It thinks about the witness of Christians as a way of living, acting, and interacting with the world around us. A

i

church that develops out of this paradigm could just as readily be called a mission center, and from a sociological perspective it might feel more like a social movement. But it would be a movement rooted in spirituality and a sense of the divine moving within and between us.

Even as we each come into the world from a specific frame of reference, we are accountable to each other in what we do, say, and affirm. While this project comes out of a very specific context, weaving together many different thinkers, experiences, and insights, it does not remain as an isolated monad. Rather, like the very process of becoming that it seeks to ecclesially unfold, it is offered back into a world of infinitely diverse and singular perspectives. Because of this approach, it is entirely fitting and appropriate that the reader should know a bit more about the location from which I enter into this work.

. My personal background has been shaped by church communities, and I have many clear memories of those experiences, from "Time for Children" lessons at the Presbyterian Church of my grandparents to Easter 1993 when I was baptized for a second time (that I was baptized as an infant was unbeknownst to me as my mom thought it should be my decision). I have been an ordained minister for over nine years, have served as an associate pastor for three years, have been a student ministry intern in three different congregational settings (not including my time as a chaplain at an HIV/AIDS housing center, a chaplain at a homeless shelter, and a summer intern for the Disciples Peace Fellowship and Disciples Home Missions in Yakama, WA and San Antonio, TX). Most recently, I have served as the executive director of the faith-rooted social justice nonprofit Progressive Christians Uniting in Los Angeles.

Surviving cancer in college clearly accentuated my radicalizing trajectory both politically and theologically. Questions of divine power and providence and an implicit process theology of divine persuasive power that works with the wreckage of life were born within me, as well as a commitment to using the one life I had to further respond to my calling to faith-rooted social justice ministries to the greatest extent possible. If my ecclesial project at times feels impatient about the state of church communities and their weak witness, it is doubly true for how I hold myself accountable.

My home congregation of First Christian Church of Paducah, KY was an early context for thinking about how our faith is public as well as how it is discussed (or avoided) internally. The Rev. Dann Masden was an early mentor who encouraged my questions and never once told me to not raise them in church, even if larger church-wide discussions rarely materialized. Anecdotes, observations, and reflections come from this congregation, as well as from my time participating at Pilgrim United Church of Christ in Carlsbad, CA; All Peoples Christian Church in Los Angeles, CA; (a)Spire Ministry in Pasadena, CA; Webster Groves Christian Church in Webster Groves, MO; Compton Heights Christian Church in Saint Louis, MO; and visits to dozens of other Disciples, United Church of Christ, and mainline congregations over the past fifteen years. Between the writing of the earlier dissertation and this current book, additional reflections while serving at Progressive Christians Uniting sharpened insights that previously remained only implicit.

There are many apparent tensions inherent within this project. It is skeptical of current institutional configurations of church but respects the need for institutional organizations. There are strong undercurrents of liberationist and postcolonial theology, but the arguments are often directed at relatively privileged persons within the United States. The book is theoretical, but written with the express intent of making practical changes to the way of Christian faithfulness. Some might see it as a classic calling back to the original Jesus Movement (and in this way repeat its thoroughly Protestant roots); however, my goal is not to imitate the past, but to push church into a radically different context of planetary globalization and interdependence. The argument is post-Christian in its use of philosophical and political sources and the trajectory of some of its conclusions, but the book is written out of an intense love and commitment to the way of Jesus lived out with others. If successful, the book will help to transform such tensions from oppositions into mutually enriching contrasts, increasing the potential for a more dynamic and just flourishing of life in our world.

This project is not a description of a church as it exists, but it hopefully functions as a "real potential" that can be actualized. To be clear: I do not offer a blueprint or list of universal steps that emerging instantiations of churching should replicate. Instead, readers will find general guideposts along the way. Those hoping to find suggestions on how to tweak existing congregations will be disappointed. But those with the eyes to see will find that the Spirit is already working persistently, and churching is happening all around us.

Who can benefit from this book? It may be too theoretical for the average congregant, and some academics will dislike its constructive quality. This work is meant to be particularly useful for process and liberationist thinkers and theologians, who often see their concerns in conflict and methodologically in opposition. Those who are serving outside of a congregation but feel deeply that their work is part of the gospel (especially those former pastors and trainers who sought to transform existing congregations only to run into a brick wall of apathy or reticence) will find this work a helpful if theory-heavy ally, as may progressive clergy still fighting the good fight within their congregations. Seminarians who see the writing on the wall with existing congregations and are looking to live out alternative forms of being church should also find this helpful. Finally, I also hope that people who are skeptical of church institutions but are nevertheless drawn to Jesus's way would find this book an encouragement to reclaim that path alongside others.

I write particularly for those who like myself desire to hold together as inseparable both spirituality and social commitments. They are not merely two things that are held in tension or as a paradox. Rather, they are inextricably bound together. Yet they are not identical. This basic premise, that things are interwoven without becoming the same thing or subsumed within an overarching superstructure, undergirds the way that this work is written. One finds many voices in close proximity together in each chapter, sometimes of people who would not be interested in each other's projects. Yet somehow, there is the sense that these thinkers need each other, that what they are saying is connected so thoroughly, even though they offer different insights. This project seeks the maximization of different experiences and perspectives for potential incorporation into an intense and harmonious whole, which is then offered for others to feel and respond to, either positively or negatively.

The same could be said for the general contents of the chapters: one finds theology, political thought, and process philosophy as the threefold elements I hold together amidst my wrestling. Ever since I was an undergraduate double major in Religion and Government, people have often commented how these are such strange or contradictory fields to study together. Yet the relationship of religion and politics is deeply embedded within me, something that for years I have sought a way to weave together: this project is by far the most extensive weaving of the two.

Likewise, it is very easy to think about process thought without so much as a nod to what it means to exist as church, or what (if any) ecclesial or political implications are within process thinking. All three are held together, but this is not done in the abstract. Every instance of interrelationship is always a specific, particular coming together. There is no universal interrelationship even if there is the transcendental condition of interrelating happening. It always happens from a location, from a perspective: this project comes out of my Christian background, as I demand my tradition to be held accountable to planetary problems for a planetary gospel.

It reflects my struggle with what it means to live as church, or as I will describe later as *churching*. Various readers will almost surely disagree with some of my conclusions, and this is to be expected. You have your own experiences and frames of knowledge that are different than my own. It could not be otherwise. I have sought to learn from as many people and perspectives as I can coherently hold within myself, but for anything to become concrete, there is always a principle of limitation that cuts off or ignores something. For some of you, these forsaken elements may be the key to the entire ecclesial puzzle. Churching will look different, perhaps radically so, in different contexts. Any unity comes out through the interrelationship of the given diversity, and not the other way around.

I intend to be as clear as I can with my motivations and priorities, but I know that miscommunication so easily occurs. Nevertheless, we are never isolated monads, windowless and closed off from all but the world within. Communication *happens*, growth *happens*, and we learn and become so much more because of these encounters. This task is by no means a finished product, especially if ecclesiology is always in a process of becoming. May that process continue, as it seeks *to respond to its relevant environment*, whatever it may be.

I must thank my friends and colleagues in the Claremont School of Theology community and the Center for Process Studies for the many conversations and (hopefully!) mutual support we have offered one another. Who cares if one can construct a relational system if one is not eager to live relationally? Otherwise, it is so much straw! Special thanks must go out to Philip Clayton, Monica Coleman, and Helene Slessarev-Jamir who served on my dissertation committee and whose mentorship helped me craft a project that could be reworked into this current manuscript. I'm likewise grateful for the opportunity at Progressive Christians Uniting to theologically reflect on applying my thoughts to the work we are called to and for the rich discussions with staff and board members there.

I am grateful to the two people who more than anyone drove me on the path towards my theologian-activist-minister approach to religion: my professors Rick Axtell of Centre College and Michael Kinnamon formerly of Eden Theological Seminary. When I think of the kind of scholar I want to be, and the way I want to hold together the theoretical and the practical, I think of them. I hope to emulate them to the best of my ability.

To my parents, Michael and Brenda, I thank you for giving me the space to explore my faith formation in ways that were compelling and enriching. They encouraged me to think for myself and be willing to ask faith questions that I had been afraid were out of bounds. As any of my Missouri-Synod Lutheran, Southern Baptist, Church of Christ, or Mormon childhood friends can see from the result, asking questions and challenging presumptions is indeed a slippery slope to what may look like for some people as little more than atheism alongside a garnish of theological language!

Just as the first will be last, I close with gratitude to my wife, Candace. It is only because of her that I have been able to devote the time and energy to this book. She has graciously commented on this book-in-the-making from its earliest stages until the close. She encouraged me when I questioned whether it was worth the effort to continue. We have made it to the other side, each of us different from how we were, yet more dynamically together. Thank you.

CHAPTER ONE

Introduction

My challenge can be put very simply. I am proposing that
the church take as its mission working with God for the
salvation of the world. ~John B. Cobb, Jr., "A Challenge to
the Church"

WE LIVE IN AN ERA THAT REQUIRES US TO RADICALIZE what
"church" means. This call immediately creates problems for
many people. They feel uneasy and associate the word "radical"
with groups they have little in common with. Our popular media
do not help by almost exclusively using radical as a negative to
be feared, such as radical Tea Party members, radical religious
extremists, etc. Americans generally use the term "radical" as a
way to dismiss a group we don't like. We imagine angry, violent,
intolerant people who refuse to learn from others and try to impose
their will by force.

However, I believe that we need to be radical, but by that I
mean we need to get down to the roots of problems. In that way,
radical ideas or actions go beyond small adjustments to otherwise
just systems. If a problem or injustice in our world is rooted in deep

1

cultural, political, or religious assumptions, then looking at its roots becomes critical.

Historically, the word radical has also been a way to describe church communities that have emphasized church as a distinct way of living, particularly those belonging to the Radical Reformation. These include the Church of the Brethren, Mennonites, Quakers, and those sympathetic to this approach. Additionally, there are newer groups focusing on "radical discipleship" as a key component of what it means to follow Jesus.[1] This book reflects such an attempt at getting at the root of multiple problems, and in so doing it reconstructs what church can become as it addresses the most pressing problems for our world today. After all, the way you define a problem greatly affects the solution you propose. What may at first seem to be critical issues can actually be distractions from more pressing concerns. This is especially true when thinking ecclesially.

GLOBALIZING EMPIRE

The root problems this work of ecclesiology attempts to address are not primarily doctrinal, nor are they solely focused on a church's self-enclosed internal life. It is to this world, this planet and its innumerable relationships, both liberating as well as destructive, that an ecclesiology should respond. However, I do not pretend that the experience of this world comes from no place; rather, it is rooted in the location of the United States of America and its complex relationships to the dynamics of globalizing Empire.

From Jesus's day until ours, Christians have lived amidst empires of various forms. Yet despite the diversity of empires, their purpose has consistently been to dominate and oppress others. We live in an Empire today. In our time, Empire's goal is the maximization of economic growth where all other values are subordinated to that objective, and in the process it applies market criteria to all aspects of life. In our world today, there are many religions, but above them all, one "religion" dominates: the worship of economism, with the use of state-sponsored violence to enforce the propagation of this god internally and globally. The process ecotheologian John Cobb notes that "economism . . . is the subordination of all other values to economic growth."[2] Today, notions of value are skewed in the direction of the economization of all value. In contrast to this perspective, wealth should not be understood as the supreme value.[3]

Lamentably, while people pursue many objects that are different from economic acquisition, these pursuits are rarely in direct conflict with it. As the Brazilian theologian Jung Mo Sung recognizes, "The pursuit of wealth has become the most important objective for the lives of the majority of people, particularly those integrated in the market."[4] It acts as a source of transcendent value or an overarching framework for religious communities in the United States. Internal church life has too often become a place for individuals to consume and fulfill the desire to feel okay about themselves.

As the Roman Empire welcomed the many different gods of subjugated peoples into its system so long as they did not question Caesar as Lord and Savior, so American Empire welcomes many religious communities (Protestant churches, Jewish synagogues, Muslim mosques, Buddhist temples, etc.) so long as they do not challenge the hegemonic values of America's macroreligion. By Empire, I mean two things: 1) the economic system of extracting value within globalized capitalism, and 2) the spirit of domination and oppression in our world, generally described through the interrelated systems of racism, classism, neo-liberal capitalist globalization, colonialism, military hegemony, (hetero)sexism, and ecological appropriation.[5] In general when referring to Empire, this latter spirit that oppresses and devalues the world is meant, except when speaking explicitly about theories that interpret globalized capitalism in the early 21st century.

To the extent faith communities pledge allegiance to this higher power, they remain complicit in the domination and oppression of peoples occurring both locally and globally. It is not simply that we live in an imperial world, for it also affects the way we think about theological issues. As the theologian Catherine Keller has

provocatively indicated, "Christian theology suffers from an imperial condition."[6] It is the call of churching to *counter* this reality with
an alternative witness, even as we know we remain complicit in the
dynamics of domination and oppression, for there is no pure place
from which to oppose Empire's reach.

This imperial condition is the relevant context, and I propose that
counter-imperial churching needs to resist this idol and organize in
order to more faithfully confront it. This may seem like a tall—if not
impossible—order, but as Keller claims, "It is *because* the church is
implicated in empire that we can decode and transcode the idolatries
of empire."[7] Economic systems function as faiths, and so they need
to be challenged on theological grounds. It is possible for church to
become a counter-witness to the idolatries of neo-liberal economic
theory and free-market capitalism. Churches should seek to enact
and witness to an alternative conceptualization of how people can
live and interact with each other in more healing and just ways. To
the extent that existing faith communions will not or cannot address
this situation adequately, *then new faith communities need to emerge
as radical witnesses and partners for social transformation.*

The most basic question to consider, the one that is most relevant
for today, is to ask whether churches are furthering Empire or
subverting it. At a minimum, by ignoring this question we conform
ourselves to the prevailing assumptions of our dominant culture
while mislabeling the broadest context we find ourselves in. Tragically,
sidestepping the key problems is not an uncommon practice for either
churches or systematic theologians. Liberation theologies have made
this critique abundantly clear in recent decades. Much of American
liberal theology and liberal churches have acknowledged that there
are problems that need to be resolved, but they see the church's calling
as making changes in the aberrations of what is otherwise a relatively
just society.[8] However, a growing number of people recognize that
simple reform is not enough. The problems are worse than most
liberal churches imagine. These churches do not have the power to
impose changes, but this is when resistance is most needed.[9] For John

Cobb, there are several key problems where reform will no longer suffice and resistance becomes a clear task for progressive (and for me, radical) Christians: consumerism, poisonous inequality, American imperialism, scientism (and its dualisms), and global warming.[10]

Challenging Empire focuses not only on the political-economic side of oppression, but also on ecological devastation. Since economics and ecological health are mutually implicated, by focusing on one, we are simultaneously addressing the other. Process theologians have constructed effective ecotheologies and spoken passionately about ecology, but they have failed to address what this means politically. As a way to correct their mistake, this ecclesiology will spend much more attention on political thought. Subjects some liberal Christians wish to keep separate are inextricably interconnected and often in ways they might not expect.

The theologian Mark Lewis Taylor incisively notes that the vast majority of Christian congregations in the United States have at least a *de facto* complicity in, or acquiescence to, colonizing Empire, if not an outright celebration of it. Taylor laments that "any postcolonial theology will have a tough time finding an ecclesial or religious group as its social mediator in the U.S. today."[11] Cobb imagines a future where faith communities become this group by making visible the vision our world needs and convincing people that this vision is being implemented. If that might be the case, people would be more likely to dedicate their lives to this effort since "joining a congregation significantly involved in saving the world would seem important."[12] This project aspires to a way of practicing church that creates the condition where passive complicity to colonizing idols can be effectively resisted in contextually relevant ways.

The daily existence and self-understanding of mainline Protestant denominations of the United States are only tangentially related to these problems, and few pay attention to those outside their country. It is not for a lack of intent in the denominations, such as the Christian Church (Disciples of Christ) and the United Church of Christ's joint Global Ministries program, which sends missionaries to partner with others around the world via invitation and share those relationships with local congregations. However, in practice these function as top-down efforts at raising awareness; congregations may feel that this work is admirable but is not essential to who they are. Thus, American Christians too readily ignore planetary concerns beyond what the corporate media deem newsworthy, and they miss hearing the voices of Christians and institutions from other parts of the world who have a different perspective on what *matters*.

Because of this lack of conscious interaction, for example, "the picture of American liberal Protestantism that has emerged from viewing its role in relation to American imperialism and capitalist exploitation in Latin America is profoundly unfamiliar to the American liberal church."[13] Profound statements of faith, such as the Kairos Palestine 2009 document (which reflects the struggle of Christians in the Occupied Territories), are too easily dismissed. Could it not be that a serious engagement with these experiences provides the hinge on which to orient American faith life?[14] Process-liberationist scholar George Pixley describes the situation aptly: "*The major divide among Christians today is . . . between those who oppose the profound injustice at the core of the contemporary world and those who ignore or support it.*"[15]

Although ignored by American Christians, the Accra Confession of 2004 by the World Alliance of Reformed Churches (WARC) makes a strong theological critique of neo-liberal economics as an imperial project that destroys people and the planet.[16] Using the imagery of Romans 8:22, WARC sees "a dramatic convergence between the suffering of the people and the damage done to the rest of creation."[17] Challenging the logics of Empire, sacrifice, value, free-market capitalism, and the power networks that maintain them through violence, WARC questions what for many American Christians is simply unquestionable.[18] These are the fulcrum issues, either by ignoring or resisting them, that reveal the priorities of church communities and set the conditions for counter-imperial churching. According to the Accra Confession, "global economic justice is essential to the integrity of our faith in God and our discipleship as Christians."[19] This document clearly articulates the context and the problems for Christianity on this earth, yet they are so easily made invisible to most mainline Protestants by merely residing in the United States.[20] For too many American Christians, the problems they *do* see are all too parochial.

MAINLINE MALAISE

In the midst of this globalizing context, the institutional mainline (or as some call them, oldline) denominations are in a period of rapid transition and institutional decline. Obsession with these changes has become the inappropriate fulcrum of church renewal efforts. It certainly is true that membership numbers have decreased every year for decades. For example, in 1968, the year the Christian Church (Disciples of Christ) was officially organized as a denomination, there were slightly over 1.6 million members.[21] As of 2014, that number had dropped to just over 497 *thousand*, a decrease of sixty-nine percent.[22] As far as actual participating members of the Disciples of Christ, the numbers are fully one-third lower at less than 307 thousand, with an average weekly worship attendance of 177 thousand.[23] The United Church of Christ (UCC) does not look much better, as it has averaged losses of over 30,000 members every year for the most recent decade in which statistics are available.[24] Paralleling the numerical decline of the Disciples of Christ, the UCC has lost over fifty percent of its membership since its founding in 1957. This data alone has resulted in great concern among denominational leaders and those who track such statistics.[25]

Mainline Protestant congregations make many assumptions that will be subject to substantial critique. For example, the Disciples of Christ emphasize unity and being one in Christ as central to their identities. In their Statement of Identity, they claim, "We are Disciples of Christ, a movement for wholeness in a fragmented world. As part of the one body of Christ we welcome all to the Lord's Table as God has welcomed us."[26] They posit a macrotranscendent unity that inappropriately overwhelms their plurality: theologically, this is described as Christ as the church's head; politically, it means being a good American. Other oldline denominations follow this pattern. As in liberal political theory, plurality becomes a problem that must be overcome. In their quest for unity, mainline congregations have the bad habit of trying to avoid conflict and controversy. This does not help them address planetary exploitation. When these middle-class churches say they are non-political, their rhetoric belies a politics that defends their privileges: they do not fear conflict itself but rather they fear conflicts that might take away privileges of class, race, sexual orientation, gender identity, global position, and military dominance.

Many mainline Protestants have little practice constructively examining their own complicity in the oppression of others. One of two things frequently happens. They ignore other perspectives or see them as threatening with nothing positive to offer. Just as damaging, these encounters sometimes act as earth-shattering moments but are then simply reappropriated or consumed for our narrow benefit.[27] Without practice and discernment, the commodification of another's experiences can be equally devastating as open hostility or apathy. We visit simply to be entertained, to take in, or to consume the other. But we are *not* the other. We never can be. Likewise, privilege can blind one to inequities of power. Philosophically speaking, privilege misreads the loss of intensity that comes from the preservation of power as gain because it is the reassertion of dominant identity. To stabilize one's identity above all change, to endure in the midst of chaos and be the norm that defines what is chaos, is the privilege of extracting oneself from the planetary eco-process.[28] It reads loss as gain and stagnation as security.

The loss of members among Methodists, Presbyterians, or Episcopalians leaves the statistically obsessed shaking in fear at the collapse of "the Church." However, this net loss of members does not take into account the substantial growth in immigrant churches over the past twenty years. It might be better to say that the *white* mainline church is dying, at least in the form in which it has existed in recent generations. These churches so often seek their own preservation, replicating the logic of maintenance over mission.[29] Again, new communities will likely need to emerge to address the gospel in our time and practice authentic churching.

For many members, the decline in status, numbers, and influence are experienced pessimistically and with lament. Having visited many local congregations, I understand their pessimism. Many, if not most, of these congregations take a reactive stance to the challenges of their society. They look inward and worry about "trying to get more young families into the pews" or paying the bills in the absence of an urgent sense of call. For those who take a more progressive stance, mainline Protestant Christianity critiques the way culturally dominant churches have been too exclusive, against open-minded values, and boring. Therefore, they try to make church more welcoming and relevant for younger people.

For example, the meeting style of generations past is no longer as compelling for Generation X or Millennials such as myself. Long task-oriented agendas and reports do not match their spiritual longings for connection. Robert's Rules of Order is a great method for making decisions if the goal is to finish within an hour but is a poor method for relational discernment. It is important to acknowledge that church does not need to be about passively listening to sermons, status, politeness, agreeableness, robes, and hymns.[30] While this is good, it is insufficient to the Generation X or Millennial context. Reforming these practices does not yet adequately address the critical planetary challenges mentioned above. Specific practices should not be the primary focus of an ecclesial project, but rather an important but secondary effect of shifting ecclesial priorities.

Certain social structures through which the church was previously expressed are falling away, and new communities are emerging to take their place. Since the 1960s, American religious institutions have been in a deinstitutionalizing phase. The way that the mainline church was institutionalized represents an institutional imperialism of internalized racism, the preservation of privilege, and the inability to communicate constructively through conflict. Today, these structures themselves create obstacles to practicing radical discipleship in our world. Churches cannot be faithful to the divine call upon them through the same methods that serve imperial domination and oppression. Churches that keep traditional structures while engaging in radical actions and commitments must inevitably work against their structures' assumptions. A better alternative would be to replace these structures. There may be institutional manifestations of church worth saving, but it is because they help coordinate the tasks of churching, not because they are already institutionalized. Some have called this an opportunity to claim our deinstitutionalization in American culture; I would call it becoming a spiritual social movement. The loss of institutional stature is not a tragedy, for we should not have had it in the first place. Mennonite theologian John Howard Yoder has provocatively called the desire to direct one's dominant culture the Constantinianism of the church.[31]

From a process thought perspective, one will find in this project a dynamic between selectively affirming past actualizations while pressing on to novel configurations. This is certainly true for my relationship with mainline Protestantism. There are several elements of liberal Protestantism that I find important and want to affirm. For instance, I want to retain a commitment to a critical faith, where we are free to ask questions and reformulate what has come before. The past decisions and conclusions of previous communities are not boundaries within which we must stay but are rather markers of where others have gone before. Past affirmations and confessions were important to a particular group in a particular time, but they may be transgressed; they are helpful guideposts but are not uncrossable boundary markers.

Unlike those who find nothing valuable from the past, I affirm certain past successes. Holy Communion has rightfully been central to Disciples from the very beginning at the Cane Ridge revival until today, where it remains a weekly part of worship life, but how wide we set the table as well as its concrete practice will look different.

Since 2001, the Disciples of Christ have affirmed that we seek to be an anti-racist/pro-reconciliation church.[32] This was a positive step, and dismantling racism should remain as a high priority.[33] For all their limitations, most mainline denominations have increasingly sought out partners across the planet using a cooperative style and mutual learning, at least in intent. They have encouraged experimentation for what makes for a thriving community and meaningful practices.

Denominations often say the right things at the national level. As John Cobb describes the United Church of Christ (UCC), it is the one mainline denomination that has "completed the process of repentance with which for fifty years our more progressive denominations have been preoccupied," such as racism, sexism, heterosexism, militarism, etc.[34] Since it has worked through its homophobia, Cobb believes the UCC can focus on the most critical issues facing the planet like ecological cataclysm. At its national levels, the UCC has promoted and approved numerous resolutions and statements concerning issues of social justice and solidarity. However, the majority of local congregations do not take these statements seriously, and many, if not most, members downplay their own internal complicity. Inappropriately, Cobb questionably asserts that "the process of repentance is largely complete" for the UCC, even though he simultaneously admits that there remains a basic "failure to reject and oppose economism and all its consequences."[35] If this is the key idolatry confronting our planet along with American-centric loyalties, the process of repentance remains incomplete, to put it mildly.

Denominational statements, resolutions, and declarations will rarely move people's hearts or inspire repentance or *metanoia*. At best, they can act as witnesses for what has already happened for some people and be offered as an invitation for others as an evangelical testimony to do likewise. We will find that what matters far more are encounter and practice. See, judge, act, and you will be changed, or at least be more likely to change, especially when reflecting theologically about one's experience. The majority of oldline congregations fail to offer real opportunities to have a different experience of those who are "other." They fail to claim a good news that challenges their lives and the structures they participate in, and they fail to prioritize resistance to cultural, social, and political evil as what church is and does. All the while, this proclamation and work is grounded in its specific planetary location. What we need are new faith communities that can have these tasks at the center of their life together. This project will describe how this reorientation is possible.

What we believe about ourselves, our relationships with others, what church is or should be, and its role in society can have a dramatic influence on what we do and how we make meaning from what we are doing. This book will take very seriously the variables of this equation. In some ways, much of my theoretical analysis can be understood as an argument for people to act first and then reflect theologically. With this, I seek to construct a vision of churching that can incarnate those practices and worldview that best enable this process to be fruitful.

ANECDOTES

The following anecdotes come from both colleagues and my personal experience of congregations. They describe a number of problems I find in existing Protestant communities. In some, people misidentify the key problems that church needs to answer in favor of some lesser parochial goal. Some examples reflect symptoms of an internal fixation, unhealthy relationships with others, fear of conflict, cultural racism, American exceptionalism, or describe additional problems. Reconstructing church will eventually help answer many of these challenges, and positive vignettes will occur throughout the following chapters.

> IN A SANCTUARY *there are many things: stained glass windows, pews, a communion table, a pulpit, a lectern, a choir loft, a baptistery . . . and two flags—one of the Christian Church and the other of the United States of America. One day, I move*

the flags out of sight. Nothing is mentioned of their removal in worship; they simply vanish. Within a few days, complaints have reached the ears of the church secretary: "Why are they gone? Don't you know we have veterans in our church? That flag is one of the ways we honor them and they feel connected with God." Its absence becomes a barrier to their worship.

IT IS ANOTHER DAY FOR WORSHIP, *and people call out the prayer concerns that are on their hearts. Someone has cancer, another is in the hospital, and someone else is looking for work. Then, a voice asks to pray for the troops and remember them for all their sacrifices and preserving our freedom as Americans. I add, "Prayers also for those in Iraq and Afghanistan fighting those they see as occupiers, for those so desperate they become suicide bombers, for members of Al-Qaeda, and for all families who grieve the death of loved ones. May all our weapons jam, for deserters and the disobedient, for the resisters and the court-martialed, for peace." Yet the last prayer is said only in my head . . . unspoken. Church is not the time or the place for such prayers. Someone might get offended.*

A HIGH SCHOOL YOUTH GROUP *goes off to a weeklong mission trip. It is summertime, and they have decided to go to a poor community and stay at the mission center there. None of them have been there before. The leaders found the option online and it looked to them like an eye-opening experience for their youth group. Asked what they hope to get out of the trip on their first night, some say, "We're here to work. Put us to work. We want to help out." At the end of the week, I ask them what they have learned. Several answer, "I just feel blessed and grateful for what I have. I realize how not everyone is as fortunate as I am." The adult leaders are asked whether they would consider coming back. "Perhaps, but we like to keep things varied up in order to keep people interested so that they will go on these trips. But this was a great trip: it was lots of fun."*

THE CHURCH MEMBERS ARE COMMITTED. *They have met and planned. They are organized to carry out the work before them. The time has come to put words into actions: the parking lot will be repaved. Many have complained about its wear and tear. Tree roots break through in places. There are never enough spots in the lot built many years ago. Now more people than ever commute in from across the area. People ask, "How can they be a welcoming church and invite new people into discipleship if there is no place for them to park?" They agree to not only repave but to expand the lot.*

IT HAS BEEN ANOTHER HARD WEEK, but a long-time church member looks forward to Sunday morning. Work is difficult, and she knows that worship gives her the strength to get up and go back to her job on Mondays. Worship refuels her; here she knows she is somebody, and that is a blessing. But she cannot remember ever hearing anything in worship that connects her work-life with the love of God for her. She wonders if there indeed is an unspoken relationship between them, other than to endure in her struggles. Is there more to church than recharging depleted batteries?

SHE IS ENERGIZED to have her first call as a pastor. She serves in a small town in a rural area. She looks forward to bringing the gifts she's learned. Yet, after one year, she is worn out. She feels isolated. She misses seminary where she worked collaboratively with her colleagues. Here she does a little bit of everything. She loves preaching and worship, but finds Christian education and children's ministries a chore. Just because she is a young woman, why does everyone assume she has gifts for children's ministry? She wishes she could focus more on her primary passions and sense of call.

A MIDDLE-CLASS white American mainline Protestant man is walking down the street. His family and friends consider him a decent and caring person. However, he is not used to encountering members of another race in the neighborhood in which he dwells or the church he attends. He sees a group of dark-skinned teenagers walking down the street in his direction, and certain feelings crop up. There is a vague sense of discomfort and awkwardness. His defenses perk up. He feels a slight tinge of shame at getting defensive in the first place. He does not know these teens, and he has no conscious animosity to them. As far as he's intellectually concerned, there is nothing suspicious about them. Nevertheless, there is a response, a cultural scar inside him, in spite of himself. From his church community, he has learned the value of being nice to others. He has heard generic reminders on the importance of being welcoming, yet his local church is silent on structural racism. As the teenagers pass by without incident, I push my feelings aside and forget about them for the time being.

A SUBURBAN CHURCH sends money and volunteers to Haiti every other year. However, it does not work with the congregation of the same denomination five miles down the road, even though it is in a poor neighborhood. It's different—that is not a safe part of town.

These anecdotes represent just some of the many concrete ways that church communities live inadequately in their contexts and fail to prepare their congregants for a life of radical discipleship; it is indeed far removed from their daily routine. Positive examples of faithful practice, as well as additional challenges, will be interspersed throughout this book.

THE WAY TOWARDS CHURCHING

Conceptual and theoretical resources in certain bodies of literature point towards pathways of articulating what counter-imperial churching for a planetary gospel should look like. This time of institutional transition can be a tipping point in which church shifts into a more healing and liberating way of living. This is the perfect time to reconstruct church into something new, what I call *churching*, the activity or process of living out the way of Jesus with others.[36] Which resources should we use, and why are they better than other options?[37]

One of the primary resources of this project is the process philosophy of Alfred North Whitehead and interpretations coming from that school of thought. Of all the philosophical options, why is process the right tool to address transforming church? After all, there are good reasons to be suspicious of its use. Some thinkers have been tempted to objectify Whitehead's own thought as a new universal, but process thought should not become a foundation. They forget that he too came from a particular perspective and social location. He does not have all the right answers nor does he address every topic with which I am concerned. In some areas, his explicit answers clash with my commitments. No matter how profound his insights, Whitehead is still a Victorian British gentleman of the early 20th century, which shapes his social imagination in colonizing ways. His comments on cultures beyond Europe are often utterly cringe-worthy.[38] Furthermore, in his documented conversations where colonial activities come under discussion, he never once criticizes the imperial logic supporting these activities.[39] To the detriment of other process thinkers, most do not link Whitehead with his socio-political context.[40]

Whitehead's uncritical colonialist perspective cripples much of his sociological and political analysis. He is thoroughly Eurocentric and overly optimistic of the United States being the future source of progressive civilization. For this reason alone, it is clear that he cannot be the sole source of a politically radical, counter-imperial ecclesiology. Yet this fact does not mean that he is superfluous, only limited. Ironically, Whitehead himself gives insight to this paradox, saying, "There will be some fundamental assumptions which adherents of all the variant systems within the epoch unconsciously presuppose. Such assumptions appear so obvious that people do not know what they are assuming because no other way of putting things has ever occurred to them."[41] Put more straightforwardly, "Each generation criticizes the unconscious assumptions made by its parents."[42] Cognizant of how Whitehead's social location shaped his global perspective, we will use different sources in political theory but relate them to resonating aspects of his thought that have enduring relevance.

In light of his social location, how can Whitehead become useful for a counter-imperial theology of churching? Fortunately, while one's location influences and constrains the possibilities of one's vision, it does not determine it. You can utilize a thinker in ways that may be the opposite of their own personal conclusions. A recent example is the reemergence of "the decision" from Carl Schmitt's political theology.[43] While Schmitt was an advocate of theologically abhorrent National Socialism in Germany and used his theory to support its political values, others have interpreted his thought towards forms of radical democratic participation. It is not difficult to misinterpret process thought's relationship to critiques of inequitable power relationships in part because they are not central to Whitehead's analysis. What was central for him was a metaphysics in light of science and in dialogue with past European philosophies. Almost in spite of himself, a critical analysis of power dynamics resides implicitly in Whitehead's cosmology: those of us who care about them must draw them out. While Whitehead was a British imperialist, we will find it quite manageable to construct the contours of a radically counter-imperial ethos from his thought.

While I am not developing a new ethics, I intend to apply Whitehead's thought to a new understanding of church that is thoroughly subversive and spiritual. Of course, he is not primarily a constructive thinker of ecclesiology nor of political thought. Excluding historical analyses of either, his comments concerning both are infrequent. Nevertheless, I find that I am repeatedly drawn to his work, the depth of his insight, and the scope of his vision. I do not believe that this is merely an historical accident of temperament but indicates an ongoing validity and power to his work. That said, I am not particularly interested in simply explicating Whitehead's work but in putting it to *use* to help churching address core problems.

The relationship of applied process thought and the church has been misconstrued in practice. Most churches have not engaged with process theology, but those that do often end up making it an attribute of church or just another available resource. An example of this comes from the organization "Process and Faith," whose main focus has historically been to offer resources for pastors leading churches.

It provides prayers, lectionary commentaries, or other materials that pastors can use to preserve the institution as it is. Is belief in God unreasonable or are you struggling to make sense of your faith in light of tragedies? The program indicates that process theology offers plausible accounts to such questions.

In this function, "Process and Faith" is institutionally conservative. It responds to the anxieties of those comfortable enough to sit back and ask these questions. Without critical insight, simply adding process thought to strengthen whatever project a congregation is already doing may undermine the gospel witness. If white South African churches added process elements to their liturgies in the 1980s, without questioning apartheid, most process people would instinctively not see this as an improvement.[44] From a more generous reading, many of the questions people have about suffering and tragedy arise irrespective of social class. The problem is not that people are asking questions: the problem is that the questions are removed from actual life or contain within them socially decent assumptions that preclude more intense possibilities.[45]

This book is not the first attempt to create a process ecclesiology (though I believe it makes a number of key improvements!). Starting in the early 1970s, there have been multiple ecclesial works that diversely incorporate process thought. Some tend to what we could call a minimalist approach. Here there is very little in terms of process concepts beyond the idea of change and "divine creativity." Moreover, they do not really impact the life of the church, which remains one in service to benevolent paternalistic mission, gradual progress, and social decency.[46] On the other end of the spectrum is a maximalist approach: what the church does may remain traditional but the tools of process thought thoroughly reinterpret church life. Early examples follow a systematic structure by beginning with God, then Christ, the Church, and finally ending with the sacraments and pastorate (and sometimes eschatology).

These early ecclesiologies tend to come from Christians from a high church background, namely the Roman Catholic and Anglican traditions.[47] For example, Norman Pittenger sees the church as a social process throughout his career, with a strong eschatological element of moving to the future of God's Kingdom in line with Jürgen Moltmann, and where the four classic marks provide "the meaning of the word 'Church' itself."[48] Marjorie Suchocki's ecclesiology largely follows this later model and will play a major interpretive role in Chapter 5. All of them fail to the extent that they make transforming church the telos of their project rather than seeing the transformation of the world as the center and secondarily explaining how church itself can be transformed in the process.

While I will be emphasizing the necessity of churching's public witness, K. Brynolf Lyon has insightfully suggested that congregations are ambiguous organizations filled with an "unconscious, intersubjective matrix of complex relational patterns."[49] Congregational life is more than faith's public side: it is also how complex personal subjects internalize faith, as our personal expectations affect how we experience groups.[50] Mainline Protestants like to assume that they are rational agents controlling themselves, but this assumes a false sense of autonomous individualism. I will explore this anthropological challenge in Chapter 3, especially with regards to Catherine Keller, and institutional intersubjectivity will be highlighted as a major contribution of Suchocki in Chapter 5.

At issue is whether process thought should be used to prop up a faltering institutional church or to help motivate the creation of something new. The former makes process an instrumental tool that is evaluated positively to the extent that it is "useful" for existing churches. For example, the 2006 dissertation "The Church in Process" by Daniel Ott has an uncritically traditional feel of protecting existing institutions. Ott attempts to present a universal ecclesial nature in light of issues of continuity, change, and pluralism.[51] Crippling his project, he abstracts the church from its planetary and political context, which makes much of his argument irrelevant for the problems we face. He affirms that part of the good news is that the church offers creative transformation to the world[52] and seeks to overthrow hierarchies in favor of love and justice,[53] but what are these contextual hierarchies? Ott is shockingly silent.

What do I mean by the tasks of churching? The German radical theologian Dorothee Sölle notes that there is a three-fold task of church in the New Testament: "kerygma, diakonia and koinonia, i.e. proclamation, service and community."[54] Sölle's paradigm will be fundamental to this project. It clarifies how what may look to some as anti-ecclesial (challenging traditional marks and structures of church) can just as readily be seen as an authentic ecclesiology. I will not closely follow Sölle in the content of these three tasks, though Chapter 6 will show similarities in our final constructions. For now, it is sufficient to say that this three-fold task of churching functions more in a liberationist line of ecclesiological thought, though the verbalization of a noun (from church to churching) has strong roots in process assumptions. This three-fold task closely parallels the model that early Black liberation theology offered, where the task of the church is proclaiming divine liberation (*kerygma*), participating in the liberation struggle (*diakonia*), and being a manifestation of the reality of the good news (*koinonia*).[55]

Admittedly, I am not the first process thinker to frame church through these tasks. There are a few others who have done so, namely Clark Williamson, Ronald Allen, and Bernard Lee. They identify four critical tasks: they combine preaching and worship in kerygma, teaching and learning in *didache*, companionship as koinonia, and service to the needs of the least as diakonia.[56] Alternatively, I blend in didache with the other three tasks; I am certainly not against teaching![57] In fact, all churching has a teaching function. In his solo book, Williamson uses process theology and challenges cultural Christianity, wisely reminding that the church needs to be an alternative to American culture. Otherwise, one should not be surprised when "so many 'good Americans' find no need for the 'middle man' between themselves and American culture."[58]

In a short article stressing the need for intentional communities and challenging the individualist ethos of the United States, Lee adds the task of *leitourgia* in ritual life, through prayer, songs, scripture, and celebration, to the core three of kerygma, koinonia, and diakonia.[59] There is no absolute reason to restrict the tasks of church to merely these three. For example, some even add in *martyria*,[60] so the list of ecclesial tasks could theoretically be expanded to at least six. One of the key differences between Williamson/Allen and myself is they focus more on what existing churches need to do differently than on forming new kinds of communities.[61] Likewise, we each have different understandings of diakonia, where they reflect a paternalistic colonialism by describing it as acts of service to the needy. Beyond these significant differences, there remain strong resonances with how they approach koinonia, especially in understanding the universe as a vast koinonia and prioritizing cross-cultural experiences.[62]

[handwritten margin note: Colonial service or servant hood]

Unlike those tempted to essentialize ecclesiology, I am using these three tasks more as a helpful heuristic than as a rigid categorization. I will use these tasks to relate process philosophy, liberation theology, and political theory together, and to explain how their interaction addresses the planetary context of domination and oppression as their key frame of reference. The tasks of kerygma, koinonia, and diakonia roughly mirror Chapters 2, 3, and 4 of the book. Even so, their full import and interdependence will be expressed only in the last two chapters. This project unsettles traditional ecclesial thinking in potentially shocking ways, but it does so out of a commitment to follow the way of Jesus.[63]

Broadly speaking, kerygma is affirming planetary value, koinonia is practicing differentiated solidarity, and diakonia is resisting Empire. When the kerygma-proclamation is for increasing the potential for value-production in the world and its inhabitants, it more clearly indicates that churching orients itself more for this life than for an afterlife. A koinonia-fellowship of interrelatedness and mutual interest helps explain how relationships we have traditionally defined as "external" to the church are often even more important than the ones that are "internal" to the institution. A diakonia-service of resisting Empire recognizes the power differentials at play in any attempt to construct a more just world and focuses on both enhancing quality of life and seeking liberation from oppression. There can be no pure division of kerygma, koinonia, and diakonia, just as each of these components inevitably implicates one another. For example, a particular proclamation of good news must address some specific bad news being experienced. What/who is being exploited and how, and what does affirming their interconnected value mean concerning what they need and how we can support one another? To answer these questions is to discern the planetary gospel.

It is unproductive to refight the doctrinal debates the 16th, 18th, or 20th centuries. These debates should not define our understanding of the church. Most have emphasized marking a clear boundary of who is in and who is out, whether through soteriological concerns or by saying the Church is where the Word is preached and the sacraments are rightly administered. What one believes, whether as a liberal, orthodox, or radical, should not be the starting point of what it means to be church, however conceived. Beliefs and worldviews matter but only insofar as they shape and are a reflection of our actions. Instead of first believing in order to belong to church and finally expressing one's faith through actions, we need to rearrange the order. As the process theologian Philip Clayton has pithily said, the priority is "*belong, behave, believe.*"[64] As liberation methodologies suggest, first comes the encounter with injustice and the "great revulsion"[65] against it, *then* reflecting theologically on the experience and where the divine is at work, and then being inspired to engage in new actions that promote wellbeing and/or resist evil. Theological reflection and doctrinal formation are a secondary activity after living our faith.[66] Dialectically, "solidarity should feed reflection, and reflection should deepen and improve solidarity."[67]

This counter-imperial ecclesiology has a close affinity with other liberation theologies and communities. There are many forms of liberation theologies, from Black and womanist, queer and feminist, ecological and Latin American, to indigenous and Two-Thirds world theologies. Each speaks from its particular location, set of experiences, resonate images, and revelatory encounters. At their best, they engage in mutual critique and are transformed through the insights of each other. Where does this leave predominantly white, middle-class Christians situated within the dominant American culture? As part of this common matrix, we only hurt ourselves when we cut ourselves off from the revelatory sacred experiences, as well as the oppressive, demonic experiences, of others. As part of the multitude, it is in our mutual interest to practice solidarity, even as we do not shirk from recognizing our particular unjust privileges and divesting both ourselves and our institutions (or engaging in the *kenosis*) of them.

[handwritten margin note: white role?]

Process thought needs political theory alongside it for its social critiques to find ground. At its most basic level, political theory is the reflection and evaluation of how societies are to organize themselves and what relationships people do or should have with each other and their surroundings. Political theory can function, like process thought, at high levels of generalization and abstraction. The forms of political theory and applied process thought I will be using combine this groundedness and abstraction. Those even casually familiar with Whitehead's work have come across his famous image of the airplane that takes off from some specific location or body of knowledge, makes generalizations in the clouds, and then returns to land in a new location, examining and evaluating its conclusions in light of this new situatedness.[68] Without a grounded perspectivalism, all that is left is drifting in elevated abstraction, taking some supposedly universal position and imposing it on others.

Churching involves a persistent pattern of subversion and alternative making.[69] In the Jesus Movement, this was presented through parables that inverted people's frames of reference and images of the *basileia tou theou* or Divine Commonwealth as a real possibility. Today, what this looks like ecclesially are indecent practices that subvert the normativity of Empire and seek a world with real potentialities, i.e., enhanced capabilities, of what the planet and its singularities and planetary bodies can become.

This project does not rely primarily on postcolonial theory, even though it engages with postcolonial theologians shaped by process thought. In particular, it interacts with those who demonstrate a deep-seated and complementary recognition of patterns of relationality, differentiation, and movement. Helpfully, as a group they are clearer in their notions of inequitable power structures than are many process theologians. They will function as dialogue partners. Theologians shaped by a process-tinged postcolonialism who will make appearances in this project include Marcella Althaus-Reid, Marion Grau, Wonhee Anne Joh, Jea Sophia Oh, Kwok Pui-lan, Joerg Rieger, and Mayra Rivera.[70] I do not claim to be a postcolonial theologian, but I work with them as a counter-imperial theologian using a poststructuralist process worldview and taking materiality and global power imbalances seriously for our interrelated mutual benefit.

How can so many different voices be held together in this project without a resounding clash and subsequent thud? It would be so easy to place these thinkers and projects—process, politics, theology, church, postcolonialism, and liberation—into oppositional terms. They do not even produce a binary, but more like a cacophony of voices arguing with each other, the reader, and the author. Yet, I am aspiring to hold these many perspectives in a creative contrast that adds some real value to the world and authentically responds to the challenges that its innumerable creatures face. By selectively prehending positively and negatively many different disciplines and voices, I hope to create something novel and timely. This book does not attempt to paper over the differences among them but to *affirm the value* of their relationship as a diverse *solidarity* in the face of destructive *Empire*. In so doing, we come to what I hope is an original yet faithful way to practice churching.

When seeking to follow the way of Jesus, there is at least one thing (among many others!) that distinguishes such radical discipleship from more conventional approaches. In particular, it assumes that whatever gospel we share, it will be good news in *this life*. Far too much attention is often placed on speculations and assertions about some form of an afterlife. While I affirm some endurance of ourselves beyond this life, to the extent that such speculations direct us away from this world, I believe they are a distraction.

This world, this life, these relationships that surround us make us who we are. They are not religiously irrelevant. In Exodus 33:18–23, Moses asks to see God's face. Instead of the front of God, Moses sees God from the back. I like to think that the world itself is the divine backside. As Jesus's life reveals, the Divine shows up all the time in the everyday (a fancy way to say this is "God incarnates"). The Divine shows up in the world, is known and experienced through the world, as the very back, if not face, of God.

In fact, I am convinced that the most faithful way to follow Jesus today is by devoting ourselves to this world, to this web of planetary relations we call Life. For when we do so, we show that this earthy existence *matters*.

The suffering of the planet, of people trying to be free, of assassi-nations and police brutality—these injustices crucify the planetary sacred over and over again, reducing possibilities for the world and its creative transformation. These events are *theological* issues, not merely sociopolitical ones. Being church, or churching as following the way of Jesus, compels responses to what is most significant to this context. If, like Cobb, we want to save the world from ecological devastation, we must challenge the economic systems of Empire. More importantly, we have to challenge the *values* that justify such devastation, particularly the logic of sacrificing others for some ideal. As resistance for the sake of resistance is not enough, churching will offer an alternative vision to aim towards and proclaim a different value-system through applied process thought that undergirds resistance even as it does not become another dogmatic foundation. By living out and proclaiming an alternative value system for the world, a radical ecclesiology addresses the real crises we face together and offers hope that another world is possible.

CHAPTER OUTLINE

Each subsequent chapter addresses one or more of the problems raised thus far. We face a misguided ideology that believes the world is only a series of isolated and autonomous units, but Chapter 2 will show that everything is interrelated in a moving and mutually immanent process of becoming. Following the Enlightenment, liberal Protestantism tends to bifurcate facts and values. Facts are for the realm of the secular disciplines and are objectively measurable, while values are the subjective, often religious, experiences of people. This is the sad legacy of the Enlightenment's anthropocentrism and dualism.[71] In contrast to the dominant instrumentalization of all value in terms of economic productivity in the idolatry of Empire, process thought provides a distinct axiology where everything that exists is a value process for itself, the other, and the whole world in terms of intensity and harmony.[72] A radical process ecclesiology will kerygmatically proclaim this in its planetary witness, teaching, and invitation for people to live out an alternative to the dominant (de) valuing systems.

Chapter 3 will argue that humans exist within a social ontology that is both complexly and mysteriously a part of the larger cosmos. When thinking about humanity, there is the tendency towards emphasizing either separable or soluble selves: the former is referred to economically as *Homo economicus*.[73] The ecofeminist and process theologian Catherine Keller brilliantly articulates these dynamics from the lens of sexism in her inaugural book, *From a Broken Web*. Her analysis of a social ontology will be explored in the first half of Chapter 3. Where interest is generally thought of either as self-regard or benevolent other-regard, the second half of Chapter 3 articulates the critically important notion of mutual interest and compares my notion of *differentiated solidarity* with Joerg Rieger and Kwok Pui-lan's *deep solidarity*. The final section looks at the implications for the spiritual practice of encounter and draws out the connections with postcolonial and liberationist missiologies.

While offering many insights to politics, Western political liberalism ignores the most important questions of its own material violence as well as its own economic and ecological exploitation. In contrast to these limitations, Chapter 4 will explore a deeper understanding of Empire and resistance to it, the role of capabilities in pursuing quality of life issues besides any final liberation, an alternative understanding of justice as a social process, and the necessary place of political theology. These ideas, along with a power analysis, can help us better understand what churching must resist. Concerns about capabilities, marginality, solidarity, and agonistic politics will help reinterpret the practice and service of churching. There can be no neutral position concerning politics and church. Claims of neutrality are themselves a political perspective and have political implications. This construction will replace political notions of unity, privateness, univocity, and neutrality. Specifically, it will deconstruct the way political liberalism functions in much of liberal mainline Protestant churches. Church practices and values that mimic Rawlsian moves will also be critiqued as I construct a radical diakonia.

By articulating several political theories, Chapter 4 shows the limitations of liberal thought for counter-imperial churching. We need to accurately analyze the problems that churching struggles against, and I will examine theorists who further the analysis begun in this chapter. Second, we need to know what we will be struggling for politically. This will involve liberation but not to the exclusion of quality of life concerns. It will have a planetary dimension, which dynamically holds together local and distant considerations as ways to manifest that struggle. Third, we need to be clear to what extent political theory can helpfully express a way of organizing church either as a completely deinstitutionalized way of life, or with some institutional structures of representation necessary. Chapter 5 will more directly address this matter.

Chapter 5 will highlight the missional, process-relational, and subversive elements of the ecclesiologies of Jürgen Moltmann, Marjorie Hewitt Suchocki, and Marcella Althaus-Reid in contrast with decent and respectable discourses. Instead of the church existing for its own perpetuation, churching will be oriented towards a novel future in light of the activity of Jesus. Instead of seeking to repeat past traditions and successes, churching will anticipate the potentials for itself and the world for creative transformation. While it affirms the need for institutional structures, counter-imperial churching dissolves past exemplifications towards new structuring patterns of coordination. Instead of being heteronormative in sexuality and global politics, this radical discipleship becomes queer in the eyes of the dominant world system and immanent in planetary struggles. Instead of fitting uncritically into the Constantinian creedal marks of one, holy, catholic, and apostolic, churching will affirm how these traditional marks are interrelated to the counter-marks of being many, secular, particular, and novel.

Chapter 6 is the final constructive chapter that will synthesize and summarize the previous chapters' claims. Rather than submitting to Nicaea or the magisterial Reformation in determining what constitutes the practice of churching, it looks towards a liberating New Testament model: kerygma, koinonia, and diakonia. It develops the analysis of the preceding chapters and offers concrete examples of how churching can appropriately respond to its planetary context through its proclamation, fellowship, and service. Churching includes a decentralization of clerical roles with a reaffirmation of the priesthood of all "practioners." This includes the practice of deep listening and reflecting on our shared stories across experiences and communities. Intentional communities will be lifted up, while still defending a role for novel institutional structures. Churching seeks a way of practicing one's faith with others that is infused by a passion to maximize the possibilities of the planet's polycentric actualizations. There are many alternative yet complementary ways to configure this project. It is an ecclesiology of the multitude; it is radical discipleship; it is living as subversive church; it is indecent churching; it is counter-imperial churching for a planetary gospel.

Kerygma

CHAPTER TWO

Proclaiming the
Planetary Gospel

A Process Cosmology and Theory of Value

Have a care, here is something that matters! ~Alfred North
Whitehead, *Modes of Thought*

E VERYONE INEVITABLY HAS A WORKING METAPHYSICS. It may be
implicit, but it is there. My affirmation of process philosophy
is a way to be honest with the metaphysical assumptions that
profoundly shape my idea of churching. Even so, process philosophy
has certain problematic tendencies. In its most scholastically
rigorous forms, its debates can appear similar to asking, "How
many angels can dance on the head of a pin?" A process equivalent
would be "do eternal objects ingress solely through hybrid physical
feelings or are actual occasions the partial self-creators of atemporal
objects?"[1] Not infrequently, process thought has the task of trying
to prove that it is the "right" metaphysics.[2] At its worst, it can
remain an esoteric high-order word game of dogmatic fidelity to
Alfred North Whitehead's magnum opus *Process and Reality*. As
the ecofeminist theologian Catherine Keller has said, participating
in such arguments can exhaust what lured some people to process

thought in the first place.[3] Nevertheless, at its best, process thought is doggedly empirical, returning again and again to *this* world — *this* matter — *these* experiences.

To be an applied process thinker, one does not need the bulk of one's work to be fixated on Whitehead's words. As process theologian John Cobb has said, being a Whiteheadian does not mean that you are primarily focused on metaphysics. One's primary field may be law, psychology, environmental ethics, or cultural studies, to name but a few. Yet on the issues that divide philosophies, one finds oneself aligning with Whitehead, just as someone else might side with the philosophers Immanuel Kant or G. W. F. Hegel.[4] In this way, I am a Whiteheadian even though I engage with a variety of thinkers, many of whom do not themselves interact with him, and I am primarily concerned with the challenges the world faces and how counter-imperial churching can most appropriately respond. Additionally, I sometimes side with Whitehead's late thought on one theme while being drawn to his earlier work on another. Thus, to be Whiteheadian is not to simply follow Whitehead, or even to assume a univocity within his thought, but rather to emphasize certain themes or directions in his work. This remains true even if some process scholars would view them as "counter-readings" to a supposed Whiteheadian orthodoxy.

The purpose of this chapter is ultimately about affirming a planetary gospel for the process of churching. To arrive there, we must first understand *how* things are interconnected. It does so by presenting the basics of a process cosmology, emphasizing the process of concrescence and the category of mutual immanence.[5] In so doing, I will also address notions of potential, creativity, aims, intensity and harmony, and God, setting the stage for much that comes later in this book. The second half of the chapter describes how this metaphysic issues forth a novel theory of value. (Those who are less interested in a technical background of process thought may jump ahead to that section called, "A Theory of Value Worth Proclaiming.") While I discuss process philosophy's implications for all of planetary life, my dominant emphasis in subsequent chapters will be on the roles and responsibilities of humans who are churching. Unlike those who proclaim a once-and-for-all unique revelation of God through Jesus Christ, this book's *kerygma* or proclamation at its most abstract is the notion that all entities are related value-intensities; this constitutes the good news, elsewhere described as the planetary gospel. Later in this book, we will find why it is impossible to be satisfied with an abstract gospel, but before we do so, we need to first review the contours of a process cosmology.

THE PROCESS OF CONCRESCENCE

Unlike earlier substantialist philosophies from thinkers like René Descartes and Immanuel Kant, which posit a fundamental division between subjects and objects, essences and attributes, Alfred North Whitehead offers an innovative nondualistic philosophy. Actual occasions, or events, do not have relationships in the way that a subject has a predicate; rather, events are their relationships to other events, which are themselves relationships. Thus, everything is a relationship of relationships. This changes everything, because it understands all of reality as profoundly interrelated and dynamic.

All actual occasions are a process of unification and differentiation called a concrescence, which is a Whiteheadian neologism that means "growing together" or "many things acquiring complete complex unity."[6] This is necessary, because if occasions were only a gathering of many different elements, then the trajectory of the world would relentlessly drive towards a totalizing unification of oneness. To prevent this, occasions also have a multiplying side. Whitehead describes this dynamic through his pithy and now-famous statement: "The many become one, and are increased by one."[7] An entity becomes one concrete fact, but there is an ongoing pluralization of becoming facts that prevents any final unity in the temporal world.

The philosopher Philip Rose has noted that there are actually two processes at work: a macroscopic process and a microscopic process.

Other ways to name this distinction is public becoming and private becoming, or the external process and the internal process.[8] Within each of these pairs, the former focuses on the relationship between multiple occasions, while the later focuses on the self-creativity of individual actual occasions. Neither takes precedence over the other, for "both processes are mutually supporting . . . as distinguishable elements within the totality of process."[9] Following Rose, I will first describe the macroscopic process of efficient causation, followed by the microscopic process of self-construction. These dual processes enable us to understand how all things are both connected and creative.

The macroscopic process describes the efficient causation between actual occasions, which explains how what "already is" sets the conditions for what is "not yet." In effect, the first and last stages of concrescence are the same but from different perspectives. The decision acts as a determinative quality for future becoming occasions, which they receive as a datum. As Whitehead explains, "The 'datum' is the 'decision received,' and the 'decision' is the 'decision transmitted.'"[10] The end of one occasion is identical to the beginning of the next occasion. This efficient relationship sets limits as an objective constraint or "brute fact" to which subsequent occasions must respond.[11]

In this macroscopic process of antecedents, contemporaries, and consequents, the future does not have the same relationship with the present as it does with the past. Causal efficacy is unidirectional, meaning occasions internalize their past but externalize their future; the present can't change the past or be controlled by its own future.[12] Contemporary events only internalize their contemporaries indirectly as a form of expectation. To avoid their mutual determinism, the relationship between two "presents" means they are not fully immanent in each other. As Whitehead explains, "The vast causal independence of contemporary occasions is the preservative of the elbow-room within the Universe."[13] Contemporary events are only indirectly related insofar as they prehend a common past and anticipate a common future.[14] Beyond that, however, they are causally independent.

Unlike the macroscopic process between occasions, the microscopic process of becoming looks at the internal development of an occasion. Internally, an occasion is its own final cause. Said in another way, it's the boss. Whitehead describes this process in a variety of ways throughout his career. Most simply, he calls it the cycle of "data, process, issue."[15] Alternatively, the process includes past influences, self-creation, and being an influence for others. Occasions physically feel their past world, conceptually choose from ways to integrate these feelings into a novel whole as an intense and harmonious pattern, and then finish and become objects for others. In their internal process, they have a three-fold cycle in their becoming. This cycle has a logical order but does not happen sequentially. From the "inside" of an occasion, one can imagine a sequence, but from the "outside" of an occasion, the cycle happens all at once.

According to Rose, the first internal phase is a response to a past occasion's satisfaction as the initial datum.[16] In so doing, this first phase is the prehension of the actual world within the occasion. This is one of Whitehead's most original ideas, for it is a key way in which he avoids falling into an essentializing dualism. But what is a prehension? According to Whitehead, it is an "*apprehension* which may or may not be cognitive [emphasis in original]."[17] While prehensions may also be called feelings, it would be wrong to say that actual entities *have* feelings. Rather, actual entities do not have feelings as if they are subjects that have some external agency beyond feelings; they are constituted by their feelings and the *way* they feel them.[18] If we keep that in mind, we can use the word feelings.

There are three aspects to a feeling: the subject feeling, the datum felt, and the subjective way (the how) the subject feels the datum.[19] In addition to positive feelings where data is taken in, there are negative feelings where data are excluded from the becoming occasion. An occasion physically prehends or feels the entire actual world that has gone before it, though most past actual entities have a trivial relationship to it. However, these negative prehensions neverthe-less contribute their subjective form, or the way in which they are excluded.[20] As Whitehead says, "A feeling bears on itself the scars of its birth."[21] The way an occasion feels its inherited data is its sub-jective form, which is the second stage of the microscopic process.[22] There are in fact mental feelings as well, but let us skip them for a moment. There is nothing wrong with this because the internal pro-cess does not happen in time. It is perfectly possible, as others have done, to describe the sequence in alternative arrangements.[23]

The third and final stage of an occasion is its completion as a satisfaction. This is where it "becomes fully self-constituted or synthesized."[24] It is fully just what it will be for itself and others as a subject-superject. This is also referred to as the perishing of the occasion where it "attains a final, determinate unity."[25] Once it has actualized, it becomes an active object for others. It demands a response, either positively or negatively, as a superject to be felt one way or another in the world.

We now return to the second half of prehension: the mental side. The mental side draws us into a discussion of potentials, the divine, and aims, which allow for new things to happen. If the whole actual world is felt in the act of physical prehension, what remains to be mentally prehended? Whitehead's answer leads us to one of the most misunderstood terms in all of his philosophy, often resulting in the charge that he is nothing more than a Platonist in disguise: eter-nal objects or, as Whitehead later calls them, potentials. However, unlike Platonic ideals, potentials are not the most real things but are abstracted from the world process while facilitating macroscopic continuity. Eternal objects or potentials are indeterminate, for only with actual entities can such determinacy be established.[26]

These pure potentials are not actual, but according to his Ontological Principle, all real things are grounded in actual entities. The question arises: How then can becoming actual occasions pre-hend these potentials? Whitehead answers with the notion of God as the actual entity that holds these potentials. In addition to pure potentials that have not yet ever happened, there are real potentials that are available for actualization. These real potentials have been shaped by the entities that have actualized them. For example, a proposition is a real potential for becoming, which may or may not be actual yet; it functions as a lure of what could be.[27] Real potentials generally (but not always) come from the relevant past of a concrescing occasion.[28]

The one exception to the structure of actual occasions is God, who is not an actual occasion but rather an actual entity. Whitehead asserts that God should not be an exception in his philosophy but the chief exemplification, but how can he consistently make this claim? Implicit in his answer is the notion that God should not be compared to an actual occasion but rather to the World.[29] God and the World interact dynamically through a "reversal of poles" in a symmetrical fashion. While actual occasions begin with the physical pole and are followed by their mental pole, the actual entity of God begins with the mental pole and is followed by the physical pole. These are technically called the primordial and consequent natures, respectively. Another way to say it is that the world starts by feeling what is and then feels what could be, while God starts with what could be and offers these possibilities to what is.

More recent models of the divine in process theism have suggested, not unlike the theologians of the future such as Jürgen Moltmann and Wolfhart Pannenberg, that God (as the collection of all possibilities) comes to the world as its eschatological future, drawing the world to become itself.[30] "In Whitehead the potentials that are actualized in an occasion may never have been actualized before," writes Cobb, and "to think of them as belonging to the future or as coming to the occasion as from the future is not much of a stretch."[31] In this way they are pure potentials, rather than real (or as Whitehead sometimes calls them, impure) potentials. Through them, radical novelty becomes possible in the world. At the same time, what the world does affects the divine, including the new potentials that will be offered to the world, for there is a transition from pure potentials to real potentials in the divine primordial nature or Divine Eros.[32]

Every occasion has a subjective aim, which is how it decides how it will create itself. Additionally, there is the initial aim, which sets limits to how the past can be creatively incorporated into a novel fact. Without this limitation it would be impossible for an entity to actualize. Traditionally, process theologians have claimed that God gives each occasion a single ideal from which it may freely actualize or derivate. The main problem with this idea is that any creativity an occasion expresses becomes a function of the Hebrew notion of "missing the mark" and implicitly results in equating creativity with sin. A more recent option says that God offers more than one equally good way for an occasion to actualize itself, though this improvement still limits creativity to fitting into a pre-determined arrangement.

Instead, I am working with a third option that sees the initial aim as itself indeterminate; thus the Divine Eros (i.e., God) offers indeterminate ideals. This allows for the greatest affirmation of the occasion's creativity. Here, the divine lures the occasion into its interstices and the crystallization of the web in which it finds itself. An occasion is called to creatively become its most intense and harmonious self, which will be novel and unpredictable. As an image of my own creation, I think of this as a space, place, or range where any decision within this range would be equally intense and harmonious for the occasion's setting without being an objectifiable ideal. It is the empty space, the indeterminate space of decision. The initial aim is an empty space or range of decision, but there also remain lesser potentials for actualization available in a graded scale. One advantage here is that Whitehead never says that the initial aim is determinate. Many have misinterpreted the end of *Process and Reality* on how God gives particular aims for particular entities. However, elsewhere Whitehead says that "each temporal entity . . . derives from God its basic conceptual aim, relevant to its actual world, yet with indeterminations awaiting its own decisions."[33] I am reading this as suggesting that the initial aim is an indeterminate range waiting specificity of subjective aim, i.e., *how* the occasion will integrate its multiple feelings.

Another, and perhaps more practical, way to consider the nature of aims is to see the initial aim as a gift of both creativity and subjectivity.[34] It is the beginning of the occasion, where it is given to itself before it becomes itself. This subjectivity comes from divine self-difference. It is what allows the occasion to feel, cut, include, and decide. Counter-intuitively, this subjectivity comes before the occasion has actualized, yet from the future. As the gift of creativity, it is an invitation to do something unexpected, unpredictable, and novel: to realize something and make a difference. Here the divine exclaims, "This is the range where you can be your most beautiful and intense self: now surprise me!" The divine does not decide but points towards how the occasion can best be itself. There is not a universal standard that an occasion hits or misses: there is only the relativity of intensity and harmony of value to be achieved from this location and context or another. There is risk, for there remain relatively better and worse options to actualize. An occasion may become its lesser possibility, but that is the risk of the creative process, of seeking differences over self-sameness, novelty over simple repetition, and an open future of creative becoming.

For the most part, the world is shaped by causal efficacy, where novelty is at a minimum and the transference of data leads to the endurance of forms of entities.[35] This is the case for what we call inorganic matter, from electrons and rocks on up to stars. They endure for vast quantities of time. Only with the increase of novelty, or the mental pole of entities, do complexity, novel difference, and life emerge. Meaningful creativity requires genuine novelty that avoids perpetual causal repetition. However, there is no severe division between entities that primarily replicate the past and those that exhibit novel concrescences. Every entity exhibits these tendencies to a greater or lesser extent. Whitehead clearly expresses this when he says, "[T]he energetic activity considered in physics is the emotional intensity entertained in life."[36] While there is a great deal of difference, it is a quantitative difference instead of a qualitative one; there is no fundamental split between the physical and the mental. Process philosophy expresses existence as on an interrelated continuum.

MUTUAL IMMANENCE AS DIVINE MATRIX

For better or worse, readers will not find God-language pervasive throughout this book. This may seem odd for an ecclesial project. However, the Divine Presence is not absent from the creative process of life and churching. In part, this is because the Divine is immanent within all planetary becoming, though my position is distinct from pantheism, which says that God and the World are identical. Said another way, the Divine, the creative process or Creativity, and the World are inseparable while distinct. In effect, when talking about one — and we will be looking very much at the world and its problems when forming counter-imperial churching for a planetary gospel — we are always talking about the related others as well. This section delves into that interrelationship called mutual immanence within and between the World, Creativity, and God.

Mutual immanence is the most general metaphysical condition in Whitehead's philosophy, for it is "the general common function exhibited by any group of actual occasions."[37] It is not merely an inert state of relationship but points to movement. It is relationship and becoming, connection and creativity. In this way it holds together the previously described macroscopic and microscopic processes. Whitehead considers this an unavoidable aspect of experience: "The togetherness of things involves some doctrine of mutual immanence. In some sense or other, this community of the actualities of the world means that each happening is a factor in the nature of every other happening."[38] Mutual immanence only appears as a distinct term relatively late in Whitehead's thought, starting in 1933 with *Adventures of Ideas*. It reframes his earlier discussions on creativity, which he considered to be ultimate in *Process and Reality*.[39] His discussion of creativity emphasizes the temporal quality of process, where the future is not simply a repetition of the past. Likewise, mutual immanence is the spatialization of the creative process, the condition for relationships and differencing to occur, "the medium of intercommunication," empty except for its instantiations.[40]

This is not to imply that Whitehead's earlier writings on creativity do not hold both the macroscopic and microscopic processes together. There are two sides to creativity: there is creativity as an active self-creativity of an entity's constitution, and there is transitory creativity that functionally results in the causal production of other events.[41] In this latter function, creativity parallels the extensive continuum. Marjorie Suchocki describes it thusly: "[T]hat which is concrescent creativity from the perspective of one entity is transitional creativity from the perspective of another: prehension is transitional creativity, subjectively appropriated."[42] The difference is that the extensive continuum is primarily a spatialized way to think about creativity beyond any erroneous implications of atomic isolation, which Whitehead is keen to avoid. It allows for the receptivity of entities to one another, uniting all in a common universe of real communication.[43] Thus, as pure receptivity, creativity is not self-present to itself but is kenotically formlessness and movement, being nothing for itself and so "provid[ing] everything as communication with everything else as [a] moving whole."[44] Creativity is a desubstantialized activity that is actual only in its instantiations. There is no separate "thing" called creativity apart from the relationship within and between actual entities. Negatively, every entity is empty of substance, but positively, every entity is cumulatively interdependent with every other entity. This is expressed through the notion of creativity, which is the ontological yet empty ground of all events' connectivity.

Mutual immanence functions as the most transcendental condition within process: it is itself completely empty but is expressed in every instantiation of coming together. Additionally, it avoids the logic of the One because there is never a solitary unity that *then* enters into relationships. It is the descriptive condition of all potential becomings. However, just as there can never be a single solitary entity that then pluralizes into a multiplicity of relationships, there cannot be a single term that encompasses this phenomenon. Thus, its mirror term — mutual transcendence — is implied in this construction.[45] No entity or concept provides a totalizing perspective or absolute unification.

Every entity is the center of its own world, transcending its relevant world, but it is only one of an infinite network of alternative centers in a relationship of mutual immanence. There is not a unified consistency to the world but only this plane of intercommunication. As French philosopher Gilles Deleuze correctly reads him, "For Whitehead . . . bifurcations, divergences, incompossibilities, and discord belong to the same motley world that . . . [are] made or undone according to prehensive units and variable configurations or changing captures."[46] Mutual immanence does not require consistency or a particular order among its entities. Actual occasions are mutually immanent to each other, but that does not necessarily mean they have a common relevance. Without any relevance to one another, they are a nexus which "does not presuppose any special type of order, nor does [a nexus] presuppose any order at all pervading its members" besides mutual immanence.[47] Thus, the mutual immanence of actual occasions can be a type of chaos. For Whitehead, mutual immanence does not guarantee any specific order to actual occasions but is rather the basis that there can be order at all.

Therefore, Whitehead needs a principle of limitation for order to arise, since mutual immanence alone cannot fulfill this function. "Harmony is limitation," says Whitehead, because, "unlimited possibility and abstract creativity can procure nothing."[48] As a relationship among entities can simply be that of a chaotic nexus, the notion of God is his way of enabling patterns to emerge that are not mutually negating. Elements of God's function were explained in the previous section concerning potentials. However, how does the Divine relate to the world's mutual immanence?

To talk about mutual immanence is not to ignore the divine for the world: they are inseparable though not identical. Theologically, one way to talk about the relationship of mutual immanence and the divine is through the divine matrix. It is the "space" or place out of which occasions become. It is not identical with God, but is the ground of God and all actual occasions, or the mutual immanence of communication and intercreativity.[49] The divine matrix takes place within the world, within God, and between God and the world. In the world, it is the fact of communication and self-creativity between and within occasions, i.e., the macroscopic and microscopic processes, respectively. Without creativity, there could be a web of interconnected relationships, but these would be a static, immobile fact. Without relationships forged through intercommunication, there could be creativity as self-formation, but there would be no new data that would be available for entities to feel in their own self-constitution. Wherever there is creativity and communication occurring, there is the divine matrix.

Talking about God as dipolar emphasizes the relationship of God and world, while talking about the divine matrix emphasizes the relationship of God and creativity. However, these two can be held together, for the world is made up of all actual occasions, and an actual occasion is an instance of creativity and communication. Creativity is not a substance but an activity. Thus, the concepts of dipolarity and divine matrix can bleed into each other without becoming identical. Whitehead sees this dipolar God as the primordial instantiation of creativity.[50] Wherever one can observe creativity and communication, one finds the divine matrix, either as the nature of God or as the self-emptying of God as non-different creativity in the world for the world's becoming.

The philosophical theologian Roland Faber has previously taken this approach in looking at the non-difference of God and creativity. Using Whitehead's brief mention of the superjective nature[51] and the implications of a reversal of poles between the world and God, Faber reads God's superjective nature as the theopoetic difference of

God and creativity where God differentiates creativity from Godself for the sake of the world.[52] From God's side, the superjective nature is the divine nature, self-creativity, but from the world's side it is the *khora* where God's kenosis means that there is pure communication empty of God.[53] It is the reconciliation of conceptuality and actuality and the communication of the two sides of God together, i.e., the divine matrix within God. The primordial nature is the Eros luring and desiring the world to make differences or Sophia/Logos from a Christian perspective. It is complete yet creative, not static but dynamic, the infinite aesthetic intensity and the absolute future that offers possibilities to the world.[54] The consequent nature makes the multiplicity of the world into a contrast, and saves/redeems the world.[55] Along with Catherine Keller's tehomic imagery,[56] the divine matrix also expresses the spirit as the communication of entities to each other.

Thus, the ultimate reality of process thought is mutual immanence where God, creativity, and the world are mutually immanent to each other; they are co-arising.[57] In God, the world and creativity are non-different, while in the world, God and creativity are non-different, and in creativity, God and the world are non-different.[58] The ultimate is the cumulative interpenetration of the one, the many, and creativity. This relationship, which is presupposed in any particular actual configuration, is one of mutual immanence (and sets the condition for creaturely mutual interest, to be discussed in Chapter 3).

Even as I have been discussing the divine and its functions, I do not wish to further dwell on the speculative side of the internal character of the Divine. It is necessarily mysterious to the extent that any actual entity in its private self-creative moment is mysterious. What it is for others, however, is public and available. Through aims that connect the divine and the world, mutual immanence, and the two aspects of creativity (as self-creative and transitional) for value intensification, one encounters the non-difference of the divine. Yet it is always the backside of the divine — never the face.[59]

This is not a problem to lament, for I want to subordinate an analysis of the divine nature(s) to a concern for the world and its most pressing problems as it relates to a planetary gospel. How the divine is internally affected by the world is less important in this project than how the divine functions in the becoming of the world process. That is not to say that the world's becoming is the only thing that matters but only that internal speculation should be relativized for a more empirical exploration of the divine's insistence on difference and differentially related values for actualization. For Whitehead, God has a clear role to play in the process of valuation, for God's purpose is to help the world attain value while providing aesthetic consistency to it.[60] In effect, the function of the divine is by being "that factor in the universe whereby there is importance, value, and ideal beyond the actual."[61] It is to the production of value in the process of becoming to which we now turn.

A THEORY OF VALUE WORTH PROCLAIMING

It has been often noted that process thought offers an ethics in the form of an aesthetics. As Whitehead himself declares, "All order is therefore aesthetic order, and the moral order is merely certain aspects of aesthetic order."[62] At first, this can feel off-putting to those of us committed to building a more just world. Process-feminist theologian Marjorie Suchocki includes "justice" as part of the primordial vision of God,[63] and likewise the process-womanist theologian Monica Coleman describes God's vision of the common good as including "justice, equality, discipleship, quality of life, acceptance, and inclusion."[64] For those of us who cringe at inequities of power and seek to increase real capabilities for life fulfillment, the idea that these are simply a matter of aesthetics may feel intolerable. We feel the need to shout, "God is on the side of the excluded, not on the side of aesthetic satisfaction!"

What does it mean to suggest that process thought offers an aesthetic worldview? I mean that it describes the world as a network of values, composed of intensity and harmony, or as Whitehead names them in the primordial vision, Beauty.[65] The process philosopher Brian Henning helps us better understand ethics in light of aesthetics. For Henning, "like the creative process of the universe itself, morality must always aim at achieving the most harmonious, inclusive, and complex whole possible."[66] This is often referred to in terms of seeking beauty. Admittedly, there is great risk in saying that "the telos of the universe . . . is aimed at the achievement of beauty."[67]

How does this not become a bourgeois ethic, where those with sufficient leisure capacity seek aesthetic stimulation? Henning is at pains to distinguish a process conception of beauty and aesthetics: "Just as creativity is the universe's drive toward a complex unity that does not devour individuality, beauty is the achievement of a whole that enhances the value of each part while not being destructive of them."[68] He finds that there is an "obligation of beauty," where one should "always act . . . so as to bring about the greatest possible universe of beauty, value, and importance that in each situation is possible."[69] In this way, Henning complements my telos of maximizing the potential for future becoming.

It is my contention that counter-imperial churching should seek maximization of the potential for intensity and harmony, which requires that we seek the maximization of different experiences and perspectives for entities' potential incorporation. This alludes to Chapter 4 and my understanding of *diakonia*, which includes resisting the dissolution of multiple perspectives, rejecting their assimilation into dominant perspectives, demanding space for multiple views (even beyond the one proposed here), and resisting attempts to diminish them. In fact, this is one of process thought's primary ways of understanding evil: as the destruction or diminishment of what *is* from what *could be*. It is like a person who is degraded to a hog; a hog is not evil, but a person living like a hog and with its limited horizon of concern is evil.[70] In this way, evil is self-defeating as it draws on the production of value through degradation. Left to its own devices, it would eventually destroy all value and lead to a bare nothingness.[71]

Why are the concepts of intensity and harmony the right ones for the problems we face, and how do they assist us in thinking about what a counter-imperial ecclesiology proclaims? Intensity and harmony are expressions of the process of becoming and how value is formed through that process. There are two sides to every event: how much feeling or data it holds in its constitution, and how the data are integrated together. The former is intensity, and the latter is harmony. Intensity names two things: "the force or emotional impact of the qualitatively complex and aesthetically organized array of feelings in an entity . . . [and] the ontological status of an entity in temporal processes of becoming transcendent of its own."[72] When elements lack any coordination but are mere diversities, the result is the triviality of experience. They are felt as separate and unrelated. When elements are not recognized as distinct but are felt as the same or identical, the result is vagueness of experience.[73] With appropriate narrowness so that an experience can be definite, and with appropriate width of scope so that it can be complex, an experience-entity is intense and harmonious. For Whitehead, "harmony requires the due coordination of chaos, vagueness, narrowness, and width" and "intensity is the reward of narrowness."[74] Aes/ethically, "morality is always the aim at that union of harmony, intensity, and vividness which involves the perfection of importance for that occasion."[75]

One of Whitehead's themes is the overcoming of oppositions through a contrast. In everyday language, the idea of a "contrast" centers on the difference between two things and how they are opposites or unlike each other. The emphasis is on the difference between them, but this is not what Whitehead means by a contrast. While he focuses on various technical aspects of contrast in his philosophy, one of his primary themes is on the intensification or increased complexity of felt experience through contrasts. The relevance of a contrast is in the paradoxical mutual relevance of previously incompatible terms:

> The intensity arises by reason of the ordered complex-
> ity of the contrasts which the society stages for these

components . . . The mere complexity of givenness which procures incompatibilities has been superseded by the complexity of order which procures contrasts.[76]

The significance of a contrast is in its harmonization of seemingly irreconcilable opposites. A contrast therefore does not focus on the oppositional quality of two or more elements—it highlights their novel relational relevance. For example, the notions of peace and justice are often placed into an oppositional pairing. However, when made into a contrast, they form the idea of a just peace, where equitable relationships are expressed through mutual dignity and nonviolence.

Events that can integrate seemingly divergent elements into a related whole are understood as a contrast. In effect, intensity and harmony go together. The contrast of many elements together in a related event leads to a more intense value-experience. Harmonization happens as an activity of concrescence. Yet, even though it is an activity, it does not produce a hierarchical relationship because it is an open harmonization. Whitehead brilliantly summarizes his view of value and actuality, saying:

> Everything has some value for itself, for others, and for the whole. This characterizes the meaning of actuality. By reason of this character, constituting reality, the conception of morals arises. We have no right to deface the value experience which is the very essence of the universe. Existence, in its own nature, is the upholding of value intensity. Also no unit can separate itself from the others, and from the whole. And yet each unit exists in its own right. It upholds value intensity with the universe. Everything that in any sense exists has two sides, namely, its individual self and its signification in the universe.[77]

By this, Whitehead demonstrates the inseparability of all actualities, whether past or present, with the creation of values for themselves and for others (thus implying a relationship of mutual interest). This is radical good news; it is the generalized heart of the gospel any particular situation of churching will proclaim.

In their exploration of a theology of life, biologist Charles Birch and theologian John Cobb endeavor together to explain how entities can have intrinsic value rather than merely instrumental value. Birch and Cobb think it is critical to acknowledge intrinsic value, which they believe should be "measured by richness of feeling and capacity for richness of feeling."[78] In effect, all things have value for themselves, because they all have a measure of agency and subjectivity, however slight.[79] For electrons and particles, conceptual novelty is almost nonexistent to the point that they are almost exclusively physical replications of past prehensions, i.e., causal efficacy predominates. Nevertheless, Birch and Cobb dispute emergent models that claim that "life emerges from the lifeless. Mind emerges from the mindless."[80] Their Whiteheadian epistemology helps them justify this claim by arguing that we can only know the nonhuman from what we know from our own direct experience of being human.[81]

In promoting value, Birch and Cobb's stated primary concern is "the realisation of existing potentialities."[82] However, I believe this is the wrong conclusion. Rather, it should be the maximization of real potential for actualization. This alternative affirms the self-creative moment of what will be done with potential. In fact, even they are eager to affirm this point when describing subjectivity and self-creation as the ground for richness of experience. Birch and Cobb could easily move in this direction, as they say, "Justice entails that people will participate in decisions about their own destiny."[83] After all, value can only arise from free decisions.[84]

The future potential becoming of humans or other entities is radically shaped by the intersections that novel events make out of their relevant world. To maximize the diversity of events is to increase potential intensity through the harmonization of richer contrasts. While Birch and Cobb use slightly different language, they likewise argue that "to maximise the richness of experience is to maximise the quality of human life with minimum impact on non-human life,"[85] which results in seeking both "quantity of rich experience and variety of types of experience."[86] This is grounded in the unavoidable interrelatedness of planetary becoming, because values or "richness of experience is richness of relations and depends upon the richness of what is experienced."[87]

In Brian Henning's complementary reading of process philosophy, there are no facts in isolation of values, and no values in isolation of facts; there are only fact-values.[88] No entity is ever static: it is a value process of intensity and harmonization. To be a value for oneself inherently means that one is also a value for others. Whitehead's panexperientialism implies "a sea change in the conception of value: if everything is a subject of experience, there can be no mere facts."[89] Panexperientialism is not a term that Whitehead himself uses but rather comes from process theologian David Ray Griffin.[90] Even so, it remains an apt way to describe Whitehead's perspective, including his notion of the reformed subjectivist principle. By this, he claims that there are no actual objects that are not also subjects: "apart from the experiences of subjects there is nothing, nothing, nothing, bare nothingness."[91] It is emphatically *not* the same as panpsychism, or the idea that all things, from rocks to atoms, are conscious. These are often aggregates of entities, which as a collectivity have minimal conceptual novelty.

Henning wisely argues for an expanded notion of intrinsic value. He wants to prevent a process ethics of value from collapsing into an "axiological subjectivism" whereby intrinsic value is only understood in terms of concrescing occasions where, once satisfied, past occasions retain only instrumental value for present occasions.[92] Marjorie Suchocki, Judith Jones, and others[93] fit into what Henning calls the "ecstatic interpretation" of Whitehead, wherein satisfied entities do not become merely passive matter for the instrumental use of other concrescing entities. Rather, they maintain a form of activity as superjects for others' creation. Concrescence does not result in a static product but rather a contrasted intensity, which was the very aim of the process to begin with![94] As Whitehead himself affirms, "Thus its own constitution involves that its own activity in *self*-formation passes into its activity of *other*-formation."[95] The macroscopic process prevents any axiological subjectivism of solely instrumental value.

Henning distinguishes between several different varieties of intrinsic value, determining that for Whitehead, one implication is that entities are valuable outside the consideration of whether others value them positively or not. However, intrinsic value has been regularly misunderstood by examining entities as autonomous individualities. Entities cannot be atomistic insofar as meaning they are separated from all others. This is where previous depictions of actual entities' intrinsic value have made a major mistake. As seen in the previous section, actual entities/occasions should not be understood in light of any essentialized separation but as interconnected through a processual matrix of creative becoming. It is critically important for Henning that intrinsic self-value does not result in solipsism, for self-value requires other values as actually present via "objective functioning." Value intensity for oneself is also value intensity for the universe, and so functioning objectively or publicly does not negate an entity's enduring intrinsic value status. Moreover, it is not merely a question as to whether an entity has intrinsic value in isolation but whether it feels and affirms others' intrinsic value, too.[96]

With a stable environment, sufficiently complex value entities produce what we call life, which has great intrinsic value. However, it is a problem to understand life itself merely as the stabilization of certain enduring characteristics. According to Whitehead, it is rather "a bid for freedom."[97] As the postmodern ecotheologian Luke Higgins understands Whitehead, life's intensity is related to the amount of complexity and chaos it can hold within itself coherently. Therefore, the presence of static characteristics is more akin to an inorganic rather than an organic society. Life, in contrast, involves dynamically integrated contrasts of feelings so that new fact-values can be expressed. Higgins observes that both Whitehead and Deleuze-Guattari affirm that intensity comes from bringing new things into interrelationship as never before. What distinguishes an "entirely living nexus" is the ability to dwell in the middle and avoid

reifying such shifting flows and relationships.[98] Life happens—value
is produced—in that empty middle space of complex, relational
decisions.[99]

One implication for churching is that there is not a pre-ordained
plan, even in this moment, which Christians must actualize. There
is a variety or selection of indeterminate actions that may actualize the greatest intensity and harmony in any particular selection.
Therefore, a spirituality of "sitting" or "listening" to the deep, empty
spaces within our own becoming is one way to respond to the divine
moving within us. However, these actualizations of responses and
values need a principle of limitation and cannot be completely
abstract.

THE PLANETARY GOSPEL

> *PRAYER CONCERNS are mentioned in worship. People listen and
> pray in silence. Suddenly, Spirit, a service and companion dog,
> barks aloud a prayer. The congregation (including me) laughs
> and says spontaneously in unison, "Amen!" Not every prayer
> or proclamation involves human words. . . . Sherbert the cat
> slinks into the sanctuary and hops onto a pew next to a congre-
> gant. They sit together, sending and receiving affirmations to
> one another through purrs and strokes on the back. . . . infants
> are brought forward to receive a blessing one day, and on
> another there is a blessing of animals, each beloved, each part
> of the community of faith in their own distinct way. Churching
> is in no way reserved for the merely human.*

The resulting generalized *kerygma* for churching is the proclamation of the value and importance of all entities (both for themselves and each other). One can love oneself and one's neighbor as
oneself because each is valuable, both intrinsically and instrumen-
tally. There are no barren facts. As Whitehead puts it, "our sense
of the value of the details for the totality . . . is the intuition of
holiness, the intuition of the sacred, which is the foundation of

all religion."[100] Skeptics should hesitate before washing their hands of this project as an anti-ecclesiology, for this is thoroughly good news, especially as it can counter Empire's proclamation of what is ultimately valuable.[101]

This kerygma celebrates that all entities are valuable for themselves, for others, and for the whole world, and thus it demands a multiplicity of diverse value-entities. However, this does not demand just any difference but demands the intensification of value. One could say the destruction of intensity into triviality is a novel difference, but that would reduce value-intensities for themselves and for each other. This obviously has profound ecological implications, as well. To reduce the variety, the multiplicity of creatures, is to reduce the potential for new "combinations" or synthesizations, i.e., it is to reduce intensity and harmony of potential life, and it is in complex, novel living where greater value is produced.

With a process theory of value, Charles Birch and John Cobb reject aspects within theology and the Western intellectual tradition that understand animals as merely having instrumental worth. Consistent with their support of panexperientialism, by which they affirm "unconscious or non-conscious experience"[102] and starting with human experience, they conclude that "if our value is not only our usefulness to others but also our immediate enjoyment of our existence, this is true for other creatures as well."[103] In this light, they express how a process theory of value understands there to be continuity within all of creation. However, this does not mean that everything has equal value, for not everything has equally intense experience, such as rocks in comparison with humans. Therefore, "plants, like the cells which compose them, can appropriately be treated primarily as means [but] extremely important means which we abuse at our peril!"[104] They are willing to see levels of value rooted in richness of experience without arguing for a pure instrumentalism.

As insightful as Birch and Cobb's position is, their placement of humans at the apex of value is inappropriately hierarchical and anthropocentric. For example, some plants may actually have a center of experience like animals. Evidence has shown that plants will communicate with each other when one is attacked by a pest in order for the others to preemptively release either a chemical that repels the pest or a scent that attracts the pest's own predator. This seems to indicate some level of central coordination on behalf of the whole plant.[105] Thus, it seems that while they are using Whitehead's categories of levels of experience from atomic particles, molecules, single cells, plants, animals, and up to humans, Birch and Cobb have overly objectified these categories. I would affirm their own self-critique that "judgments of value among species will have a subjective element, and similarity to human beings is likely to play a distorting role at times."[106] All activities are part of a valuing process. Birch and Cobb imply that this is a hierarchical set, but it is truer to say that there are many hierarchies of value rather than only one. Without simpler creatures, such as phytoplankton, more complex ones cannot persist, so there can even be "lowerarchies" of value, too![107]

One implication of regarding values through a prioritization of maximal diversity of potential becoming is that it opens space for novel living entities (which we classify into different species) and their complex experiences. This variety is good not only because it increases intensities of experience but also for its differentiated levels of experience. While a human may have the most intense experience, its consciousness is also a simplification by exclusion of elements of its environment that "lower" entities may feel more directly. Thus, the multiplicity of species themselves is good, and the loss of any group not only diminishes the intensity of life now but also reduces the future potential becoming of novel living entities (following Luke Higgins), as there is less for future concrescences to work with. While the emergence and extinction of novel species is simply the unavoidable process of the world, their casual elimination is a genuine cause for grief. Whatever their sources of origin, further intensities are most likely when the maximum diversity of potentials are available for their concrescence. Homogenizing or reducing potentiality decreases such future becomings' intensity of contrast and must be avoided.

Process thinkers have done an exceptional job in demonstrating how process thought can help reconceive the value of the "non-human" world. They have been successful to such an extent that for the philosophically inclined, process thought has become a key resource in reflecting on environmental ethics and animal rights, and in issues varying from climate change to animal experimentation. These contributions are important and it is not my intention to diminish them. Thus, Roland Faber notes that when rethinking value, "the political consequence, then, is not the preservation of humanity and the struggle for its survival *per se*, but the *diversification of its environment in order to allow for the most creative openness for novelty that does not exclude humanity but does not center around humanity, either* [emphasis in original]."[108] By proclaiming the importance of the maximization of future potential becoming of intensity and harmony, churching should not make this argument only on behalf of humans, but for *the whole life network*. We do not affirm the network of life merely for its own sake nor for our own, but for their related mutual benefit and flourishing. Without this sense of mutual interest, our proclamation becomes either paternalistic or narcissistic.

When discussing processual understandings of value, it is to the "natural" world that theorists generally direct themselves and less towards interhuman relations. Part of the reason for this is that most theories of value have focused on the rights and values of the human world, and so process thinkers have sought to go beyond such anthropocentric orientations. Nevertheless, where does this leave the still crucial role of human relations, particularly when it comes to issues of inequitable power relationships? While some people have addressed this in part, such as the ecofeminist theologian Marjorie Suchocki in *The Fall to Violence* concerning sin, this has been an area of less concentration. Chapter 3 will pick up this theme in detail.

Any ecclesiological construction will necessarily tend to focus on humans and their relationships with one another and their larger environment, given that the church has traditionally (and erroneously) been understood as constituted solely by humans. My primary focus in the upcoming chapters is geared towards the relationships of humans, but a processual notion of intrinsic value also recognizes the distinct and nonanthropocentric value of the biosphere and life forms that make up ecosystems. To proclaim that all entities have intrinsic value, or better yet, *are* intrinsic values, which are mutually implicated in each other such that the wellbeing of one affects the wellbeing of all and vice versa, means in large part that our spheres of concern are meant to expand to the point of reaching out to the entire planetary system.[109] We are called to proclaim good news that is for all of planetary life, of which we are an inextricable part! It shapes how we should live and interact together with others, and it drives us to serve in particular ways in the midst of values and practices that work to undermine this proclamation.

When some people hear planetary, we think instantly of the planet Earth. We may think of trees, animals, and far-off distant places. These are the planetary, but so is the ground beneath your feet. It is the apartment complex you live in and the neighbors that dwell within. It is the utterly human of social existence, and it is the depths of the sea. It is matter itself and its lived, experienced relationships. Caring for the planetary, and proclaiming a gospel for it, is simultaneously the most contextually specific one can be, and the most connected between the various communities, powers, and relationships of one's own horizon of divine concern.

In the past decade, postcolonial theologians have noted postcolonial theorist Gayatri Spivak's insightful distinction between the global and the planetary.[110] Spivak suggests that we need to "imagine ourselves as planetary subjects rather than global agents, planetary creatures rather than global entities."[111] The globe is what can be abstracted and objectified, with lines and grids mapping it out. You can hold a globe and try to control it, but the planet is the whole of matter and life that is interdependent upon one another. By affirming the planetary as opposed to the global, I am emphasizing the material conditions and concrete interdependencies of life rather than simply the abstraction of relationship. As Alfred North Whitehead so cogently recognized,

> [philosophy's] business is to explain the emergence of the more abstract things from the more concrete things. It is a complete mistake to ask how concrete particular fact can be built up out of universals. The answer is, 'In no way.' The true philosophic question is, how can concrete fact exhibit entities abstract from itself and yet participated in by its own nature?[112]

A planetary gospel, rather than a colonizing global gospel, follows this same logic. It starts with the actual living conditions and problems of a context. Larger patterns and interconnections can and will emerge from there, but one must not jump prematurely to any universals. Starting with universals that are applied to various contexts is the opposite of what is been suggested. While we have arrived at a generalized answer to a gospel of value, much more will be said in Chapters 3–5 on how this relates to power dynamics and our particular social location, for without them, a theory of value, much less a living planetary gospel, is utterly barren.

CHAPTER THREE

KOiNONia

Practicing Differentiated Solidarity

Via Social Ontology, Mutual
Interest, and Encounter

Injustice anywhere is a threat to justice everywhere. We are caught in an inescapable network of mutuality, tied in a single garment of destiny. Whatever affects one directly, affects all indirectly. ~Martin Luther King, Jr., "Letter from Birmingham Jail"

CHURCHING AVOIDS ANTHROPOCENTRIC FOUNDATIONS, yet it is necessary to further elaborate this paradigm with regards to humans in particular. As they are the primary (though not necessarily exclusive) constituents of churching, this chapter devotes a special concern towards their interrelationships. I begin by reviewing ecoprocess theologian Catherine Keller's work in order to reinterpret human becoming in terms of a socially complex ontology. This framing of human interrelationship is followed by my emphasis on the importance of mutual interest as a key insight that helps motivate radical discipleship. I will then examine the centrality of liberating encounters through an analysis of some postcolonial missiologies. In so doing, this chapter will also clarify what I believe should be a complementary relationship between process and liberation theologies.

The result will be that "differentiated solidarity" will become the key element in this ecclesiology's emerging understanding of *koinonia*, rather than traditional Christianity's definition as being the believing community's mutual support of one another.

CATHERINE KELLER'S SOCIAL SELF-BECOMING

Catherine Keller is probably the most creative process theologian of her generation, weaving together mysticism, process theology, ecofeminist insights and concern for creation, and poststructuralist philosophy. She offers invaluable insights in line with my understanding on what it means to be human. This form of complex relational interdependency will be crucial to demonstrate later arguments concerning mutual interest. Understanding *how* humans relate to each other will eventually help us in articulating how it actually benefits each of us to practice differentiated solidarity with those on the margins of our society. In fact, it will become a sacred practice of churching.

Keller's thought on the self, with which I am broadly in agreement, can be seen as going through two distinct stages, or "folds," as she could call them. The first stage uses a process-feminist lens and focuses on the internal relatedness that constitutes each human, while the second stage delves more into poststructuralism and apophatic mysticism. The former is more "kataphatic" with its positive analysis of a social ontology, while the latter is more an un-saying of that dynamic process. These stages are consistent with each other but are different expressions or sides of her (trans)feminist perspective.

In *From a Broken Web*, her first book and primary work on the construction of the self, Keller, using feminist theory, boldly questions the idea of the inherent separateness of humans. Traditionally, this idea assumes that humans are clearly and obviously divisible from the world and remain the same over time. Her thesis is that separation and sexism have worked together to form a coherent patriarchal worldview in our culture. This worldview says any agent must be understood by what it is not.[1] By revealing this alliance, she creatively intends to deconstruct the patriarchal self this worldview has formed.

Keller insightfully identifies two primary tendencies in understanding the self, both of which are dependent on each other and mutually destructive: the separative self and the soluble self. While the former asserts total autonomy, the latter's primary function is to support that illusion. In this construction, a man's selfhood is acquired at the cost of a woman's selfhood. Men do not inherently have a separative self while women have a soluble self, but these are descriptions of how they have been patriarchically constructed. The soluble self is subjectively internalized from the dominating position of men into one of emotional dissolution.[2]

There are two basic ways contemporary women have responded to this dichotomy. They have either been complicit by exemplifying the complementary feminine or have been co-opted by taking on the masculine autonomous self as their own. Keller observes that this latter co-optation has been required for women to be brought into roles traditionally reserved for men. In the moment of supposed feminist liberation, the self was again enslaved to another form of patriarchal power definitions. Therefore, both complicity and co-optation are unhealthy and inauthentic human alternatives.[3] Keller proposes a model that incorporates positive aspects of both and in the process radically transforms them.

Keller believes the ideal is a form of differentiation in relationship that simultaneously affirms complex human connection but avoids notions of dependency.[4] Differentiation does not imply separation or an essential otherness but is inherently a relational activity where entities embrace their freedom to create themselves out of the relevant relationships of their world.[5] One *feels* the difference with others and so is related to them. In revising an understanding of immanence, she asserts that in experiencing others, those others enter into one's self-constitution and make a difference in oneself. These influences don't just shape us from the outside but help constitute who we are on the inside.[6]

While looking at a variety of stories and psychological perspectives on the self and its patriarchal construction, Keller determines that the philosophy of Alfred North Whitehead offers significant possibilities for moving past a separate/soluble self dichotomy. As Keller aptly reads Whitehead, what connects actual occasions with each other is that they feel each other. It is not that self-sufficient things reach beyond themselves with feelings to connect with other self-sufficient entities. The way they feel makes them what they are. We do not have experiences; we are experiences. We are these "throbs of experience," unifying within ourselves a vast world of felt difference. Instead of a Cartesian substantial self, separate from everything else, she understands the self as one of composition, where substances dissolve in place of becoming-events.[7] This mimics the process of concrescence and formation of value-entities as described in Chapter 2 but applies it to human becoming.

Keller helps guide us beyond even Whitehead's own intent in challenging the fallacious patriarchal notion of the self. Because it is a fallacy, its foundations are always giving way. Therefore, the male ego construction is inherently defensive, because this assumed permanent, autonomous self is constantly being permeated by the surrounding world and so is in perpetual need of reinforcement for its preservation. Women have a slight advantage in recognizing their true selves, not because of anything intrinsically superior about them, but because of their contextual situation. For Keller, women have been less prone to deny their own inherent dynamic connectivity (which is the reality for all people) because of patriarchy's organization: only in this way is being female more relational. Men seek to control women for their perceived relationality, because deep down men recognize the instability of their attempts to maintain an isolated, enduring selfhood. However, if humans are inherently relational, no one group needs to be forced into service as the glue holding us together.[8] An oppressive dependency is not necessary once human nature is seen for what it is.

In dominant Western culture, the ideal self is supposed to be temporally stable and constant as well as spatially separate. Keller contrasts this definition with the idea that a self is an actual occasion that feels its world, makes a decision of how to relate to that world, and then offers itself back to that world. One might falsely interpret her as saying that an individual person is a moment of coming together and passing away, but this is not her intention. Keller posits a differentiation between a self and a person. Her reconstruction of the self and the person allows both for radical becoming and continuity through time. A person as we perceive them is not the same self through time but multiple selves that have a personal continuity. The unity of a person comes through a connected chain of occasions, with all things, including one's soul, flowing through the present occasion as one's self. Thus, a person is their own self, but yet is not an isolated self. To help clarify this difficult concept, she notes that there are two aspects to consider: the multitude of actual entities that are woven together into oneself in any moment, and the stream of moments that connect like pearls on a string as one's continuous personality.[9] Each moment is a distinct self that has intrinsic value, but none are perpetually isolated enduring entities.

Keller's process-feminist ontology of the self suggests four dyads from which relational selves are complexly composed: being one/being many, being public/being private, being body/being soul, and being here/being now.[10] The oneness of the self is tied up with its manyness, for its integrated complexity is what holds it together.[11] A person's many selves are both public and private as a dipolar continuum of creative extension and singularity. Our personhood is synonymous with our soul, though at the same time, we are not separate from our bodies. We do not merely have sensory perception but rather we feel the world with our whole bodies, which we also feel, even if these feelings are more often than not pre-reflective. Lastly, a self is a particular place and time, but it is connected with everything else and so is a potential for the becoming of everything else. Thus the feminist self is one that makes up both space and time via self-spacing.[12]

We cannot limit the understanding of our relational selves with a critique of patriarchy and sexism alone, and luckily Keller does not stop either. In the second "fold" of her career, Keller creatively incorporates the themes of poststructuralism and apophatic mysticism, moving her to a more transfeminist stance. Her understanding of what it means to be human endures, even as she has used novel sources like queer theorist Judith Butler and the mystical thought of Nicholas of Cusa. To Keller's excitement, Butler's more recent work has affirmed that the "I cannot muster the 'we' except by finding the way in which I am tied to 'you,' by trying to translate but finding that my own language must break up and yield if I am to know you."[13] Except for the poststructuralist terminology, Keller retains the basic insight from her earlier work: "We creatures fold in and out of each other moment by moment, as Whitehead's idea of 'prehension'—transcribed by Deleuze as 'the fold'—would elaborate."[14] The advantage poststructuralist thought brings is that its deconstructive stance helps feminism transcend its own closures and essentialisms.[15]

It becomes untenable to maintain the binary of gender as a construction while sex remains an essential given. This binary has run its course to exhaustion, which is why Keller finds Butler's imagery to be so helpful. Keller sees Butler moving away from pure constructivism and toward a more nuanced stance of "poststructuralist relationalism." To name gender and sex as constructions does not make them nothing, for they are constructions of their felt worlds. Keller's later position shows that just because all concepts of human nature or nature in general are socially constructed does not mean that we can dismiss the material cosmos as mere construction.[16]

Likewise, Keller and I find a mystical ally in Nicholas of Cusa's thought: "[A]ll are in all and each is in each."[17] In de-centering the universe, everything becomes its own center even as it remains just one of an infinite number of centers. Beating quantum physics by centuries, Cusa says, "The world machine will have, one might say, its center everywhere and its circumference nowhere."[18] The results are surprisingly consistent with Keller's early work.[19] Following this mystical line of thinking, Keller believes "that the apophasis of gender—not its cancellation . . . opens feminism itself to its own multiple unfoldings" to the point that "the many become the manifold."[20]

Looking at four folds in feminist theology, Keller shows the complication that is the self. The first fold recognizes and affirms woman and gender difference. Recognizing such distinctions becomes a clear locus for human wellbeing. It negates "complementary hierarchies" and sees them for what they are: constructed. The color fold complicates earlier feminist accounts of subjectivity, as it demands accounts of non-Eurocentric white women's experience. The third fold as queer fold negates and transgresses earlier biological sex foundations on behalf of expanding former closures of human thriving.[21] One important implication I read from this is that transgender wellbeing and liberation become demands of theological priority, especially for transgender women of color, who experience great violence directed against them alongside transmisogyny. The result is that "our racey gender difference is further differentiated by sexuality, but of a sort that deconstructs the binary of straight/gay right along with that of male/female."[22]

The fourth and final fold is the manifold, a multiplicity that transitions us away from any final stasis and towards unknown horizons. The multiple is different from the plural, for while the former folds voices into itself to create something new (like this ecclesial project!), the plural is only a list of many self-enclosed entities. A mere plurality misses the quality of interrelationships in which we unknowingly participate as "ontological thickets" or "rhizomes." Here Keller's mystic turn comes to the fore, emphasizing how we cannot begin to understand all the influences and connections that enter into us. Yet the concept of those manifold influences can be "a dignified account of our own unaccountability." This ultimate unknowability of the self prevents any "exhaustive account" of all that has shaped and formed her, for it is the entire network of (inter) planetary relations.[23] In a very real sense, one's own self remains a very real mystery. Nevertheless, it remains a real, *material*, mystery, for a mere poststructuralist "formulaic *anti*-essentialism may silence

(handwritten margin notes:) (1) gender (2) color (3) sexual (4) multiple

all sense of connection to our bodies, our communities, and our earth."[24] I fully agree with her conclusion that one must avoid any type of romantic essentialism, even as poststructuralist-relational thinking requires us to take our embodiment seriously.

The complexifying trajectory I am endorsing overlaps nicely with certain postcolonial sensibilities, which, through the experience of exclusion and seeking pure origins, recognize that we are complex selves that do not neatly fit into any one single identity. This is where the notion of hybridity comes from, such as with people from indigenous and colonized backgrounds encountering a blending of cultures and worldviews. As theologians such as Wonhee Anne Joh have noted, this term is best used descriptively rather than as simply a normative good, because hybridity does not happen in a power vacuum but often under terms of domination. Joh notes three approaches to hybridity and aligns herself most fully with the last and strongest option: one, it emerges out of oppression and assimilation; two, it deconstructs established, oppressive binary thinking and undermines its power; and three, it is a way to describe the inherent complexity and mutual agencies of all locations while still challenging unjust structures.[25] The ecotheologian Jea Sophia Oh agrees with Joh, suggesting that hybridity occurs not only from oppressive power or by undermining binaries but is "the multidimensional direction of power . . . suggesting the mutual agencies of all sides."[26] It is another way to describe the complex agential power of the becoming-self.

The work of Brazilian neo-liberationist theologian Jung Mo Sung offers yet another surprisingly complementary understanding of the human person to the one I am affirming. One key idea of modernity was replacing God as the subject of history with humans as the subjects constructing history as their object. For Sung, history is not merely an object, and he affirms the phenomenon of the world's self-organization as "autopoiesis," with emerging patterns of complex relationality. In critiquing the Enlightenment notion of the historical subject, which has skewed most forms of liberation theology, Sung suggests that liberation theology needs to dialogue with quantum physics.[27] Such complex self-creation is true for humans and the market, though this latter universal (though not single!) subjectivity is not free from error.

Sung eventually affirms a processive understanding of the human via the liberationist theologian Franz Hinkelammert: a human being is neither simply a subject (as the Enlightenment would describe it) nor an isolated substance, but it is a becoming potentiality in process where it becomes a subject. For him, it is too much to say that the subject can be reduced to the web from which it emerges, for it also transcends that web, which I understand as the self-creative empty space that makes something out of its prehensions. Sung shows his support for my interpretation by emphasizing that no system or web of relationships can exhaustive a human's "potentiality and subjectivity." Amazingly, even though humans are his focus, he extends this self-creativity beyond them, which is a rare move for liberation thinkers, but one that is consistent with my position.[28] To see both process and liberationist thinkers reinforcing similar insights gives us hope that it is indeed possible to create a more intense contrast of interwoven ideas for churching!

MUTUAL INTEREST AND DIFFERENTIATED SOLIDARITY

If humans are as complexly and connectively existing as Keller and cohorts indicate, this will directly impact how we understand the concept of interest. Whereas most discussions of interest work out of the assumption of separate and autonomous selves, interrelated selves will imply an interrelated understanding of interest. This matters greatly to the extent that solidarity with communities experiencing oppression does not result from an attitude of paternalistic benevolence. Rather, relatively more privileged persons and communities should practice such acts out of the stance that their own healing is a partial motivation. As process philosopher Brian Henning has so helpfully explained, "[S]elf-value is always intertwined with the value of others and with the value of the whole."[29] In a way, this section is a response to this chapter's opening quote from Martin Luther King, Jr. as well as an insight from the apostle Paul. Paul writes to the Corinthians concerning the body of Christ: "If one member suffers, all suffer together with it; if one member is honored, all rejoice together with it."[30] I am endeavoring to make the case *how* these insights are true beyond being mere assertions or beautiful poetic metaphors. Without a deeper understanding of interest, there remain diminished opportunities for cross-cultural and experiential networks of solidarity for creative transformation. To make this case, this section combines process and liberation/postcolonial theological considerations.

An interrelated understanding of mutual interest means that one's wellbeing is tied up in the wellbeing of others, even if this relationship is not immediately clear or obvious to oneself. Given Keller's folds of unknowing, this should not surprise us. This tendency happens often in situations of privilege, where it is in one's narrow self-interest to not understand the situation, even though to understand and respond would be in one's greater interest for wellbeing and justice. Consider the example of white mainline Protestants and their obliviousness, their *unknowingness*, to their racial situation. As the founder of Black liberation theology, James Cone, notes in *The Theology of Black Liberation*, they commit acts of oppression from which they need to be liberated, but they do not know the character of the liberation they need.[31] Even if one can accurately say that everybody is oppressed, not everyone is oppressed in the same way, and the ones who primarily benefit will not without assistance be able to articulate the way in which they are oppressed. Only those excluded, those experiencing oppression, will be able to do that.[32] The latter transcend the oppressive act even as it seeks to objectify them.

Persons experiencing the illusionary benefit of unjust privileges are in power positions that enable them to *pretend* that they are whole, separate selves. They are convinced that they are simply themselves, normatively complete as white, as American, as male, as straight, as able-bodied, as capitalist, as Christian, etc. Yet the experience

only oppressive *acts* and *experiences*

of disbelonging, of dislocation through the other, can reveal our own ambiguous unknowings of ourselves as complexities.[33] Simply put, people are not as whole as we often think we are, and privilege allows us to avoid confronting this reality. It hides our interest in transformation by making changes appear as a loss we should fear.

One difference between Cone's classic liberationist approach and my argument is that ontologically there is no oppressor and no oppressed in my construction; there are only oppressive acts and experiences of oppression. While it is possible that certain persons may integrate into their constitution such a network of oppressive acts or experiences of oppression that for all practical purposes it would be appropriate to refer to them as an "oppressor" or "the oppressed" without too much of a gloss, a problem nevertheless remains. There is always a reserve, a complexity in the constitution of persons such that one can say they still remain valuable or retain a modicum of subjective agency that can help them transcend their current dominant functioning.

interesting I'm certainly getting there

I have already indicated that mutual interest implies seeking justice, but how can this be appropriate for a processive framing? Monica Coleman notes that Alfred North Whitehead's writings lack any explicit discussion of systemic justice. However, Coleman points out that there is a space for this in his late work, where Whitehead says that a system may "fail in another sense, by inhibiting more Beauty than it creates. Thus the system, though in a sense beautiful, is on the whole evil in that environment."[34] This leads her to conclude that certain systems are evil in that they inhibit more beauty than they create and cause environments to experience a relative loss.[35] Just as a system understood in isolation may have its own limited achievement of beauty, its contribution to its larger environment may function as a decisive loss. Coleman refers to the institution of American slavery as limiting a potential greater "beauty of the freedom and flourishing of African Americans, and the wider society was also constrained because of its acceptance of racism."[36] She thus adds the notion of justice as part of a Whiteheadian aesthetics, which points in the direction of an engagement with notions of mutual interest.[37] From a more limited perspective, not being able to act in certain ways may feel like a tragic limitation of freedom, but from a larger frame of reference it can help set the conditions for a more equitable flourishing of life.

By using the term "mutual interest," I do not merely mean what other philosophers such as Adam Smith, founder of classical capitalist economic theory, have called an "enlightened self-interest." Enlightened self-interest is the idea that instead of having a narrow, individualistic notion of actions that benefit oneself, one recognizes that another's good is part of one's own good. An example of crass enlightened self-interest would be a small business owner who wants the working-poor to be paid a higher wage so that they are able to purchase more of his store items. While this is an improvement over narrow self-interest, we can do still better. For Whitehead, "To be an actual entity is to have a self-interest. This self-interest is a feeling of self-valuation; it is an emotional tone."[38] Interconnected value unavoidably means interconnected interest. Late in his career, Whitehead notes that "at the basis of existence is the sense of 'worth' . . . It is the sense of existence for its own sake, of existence which is its own justification, of existence with its own character."[39] Mutual interest is possible because of the way value is produced and interrelated amidst the condition of mutual immanence as expressed in Chapter 2.

As Marjorie Suchocki has insightfully noted, "The responsibility to self and other is not exactly 'enlightened self-interest,' since it could just as easily be called 'enlightened other-interest.' We are interwoven."[40] If both terms are used together, they become synonymous with my notion of "mutual interest." Roland Faber makes a similar point when he holds self-creativity and self-transcendence together in a dipolar structure: rather than the dualism between egoism and altruism, the poles are connected in moments of creative transformation.[41] The language of "enlightened self-interest" can act helpfully as a middle axiom to the extent that it makes discussions of mutual interest more accessible to those who are not open to process-friendly conceptualities.[42] Religious communities should not speak only in the language that they find persuasive but need to be able to articulate their commitments in such a way that others may "go and do likewise" out of complementary motivations.

Theologian Joerg Rieger and postcolonial theologian Kwok Pui-lan advocate for an understanding of mutual interest that they call "deep solidarity." Rieger and Kwok understand deep solidarity primarily in economic terms, where the middle-class realize that they actually have more in common with the working-class and poor than they do with what has recently been called the one-percent. In their eyes, deep solidarity happens when, "Without glossing over the differences, we begin to see their fate as our fate. We are also the 99 percent."[43] They maintain that there is an internal diversity to this unity such that deep solidarity doesn't happen with those who we feel are identical with us even as we face similar problems.[44] In fighting separation brought out by the one-percent, many say we are all the same. While an improvement over rejecting "the other," it does not see them as unique and valuable on their own terms.[45] In this configuration, Rieger and Kwok want people to recognize that their salvation partially depends on others' salvation and that one's needs and the needs of others are mutually implicated in a reciprocal dynamism.

While Rieger and Kwok use the term deep solidarity, I have chosen a term that includes yet also transcends their economic model. We need to practice "differentiated solidarity," a term coined by the feminist political theorist Iris Marion Young, though I am utilizing this phrase beyond the scope of her original intentions.[46] When placed side-by-side, these two words function as a paradoxical tension, or, more exactly, they exist as a contrast. They interact together in much the same manner as Catherine Keller's affirmations of "poststructuralist relationalism" and "differential relations."[47] One modest difference away from Keller and towards Rieger is that by using the term "solidarity," I hope to better emphasize the power dynamics at work in all relational configurations that she sometimes deemphasizes. By solidarity, one instinctively thinks of a solid, a unity, or a form of togetherness that cannot easily be broken. This is how solidarity is generally understood, as a standing together, often in the face of oppression. Yet the word "differentiated" implies the opposite: distinction, singularity, and otherness. These terms mutually transform one another, for differentiated solidarity is the sense or activity of participating with, standing alongside, and encountering those who are not identical with yourself, all the while recognizing that you are partially constituted by these others. We need each other, and we are in each other, but we are *not* the same.

Differentiated solidarity does not pretend that we are all identical, or even desire exactly the same things. Those living with privileges cannot simply declare their profound solidarity with the oppressed and join in a common struggle as if everyone is in it together and from the same location. Such perspectives ironically ignore their own social location! Nevertheless, differentiated solidarity is grounded in an understanding of social ontology and a profound sense of mutual interest. Beyond Rieger and Kwok's more restrictive use of deep solidarity to primarily focus on the class solidarity of the 99%, my use of differentiated solidarity extends beyond that context to wherever one sees and is moved by oppressive actions (which quite often include class dynamics). Our fellowship is to be one of solidarity, but you likely have certain unjust privileges within this togetherness. Get rid of them, or even better: *use* them to undermine the endurance of these privileges.

It often goes unnoticed that there are actually two types of privilege. There are privileges that place some over others by giving them access to resources or preference in speed or quality. This may include belonging to a race or class that is considered normative while others are seen as derivative. These are the types of privileges that come at the direct expense of others and are never just. They exist solely to place some above and to subjugate others. The long-term goal here is towards the elimination of their power advantage or systemic deconstruction (of their power relationship, not the individuals themselves experiencing them). However, there is a second type of privilege that is frequently absent from discussions. These are what might be called "positive privileges" such as growing up in an affirming community with opportunities for education and leisure. To the extent that their perpetuation is not conditional on their being maintained through the oppression of others, they are not "bad" per se. They are things that we actually want more people to be able to enjoy, as they are nonexhaustive and improve the collective quality of life. Nevertheless, these positive privileges frequently result in what is called "being sheltered," where members of that community lack exposure to the suffering of others and can become alienated from their siblings. One should, to the extent possible, become conscious of both forms of privilege.

The term solidarity can also be used to mean simply social ontology, as with Marjorie Suchocki, who writes, "Through the organic solidarity of the [human] race, we are affected by the sins of others, and our own sins likewise have an effect upon all others."[48] Suchocki recognizes relationships' power dynamics in this comment. However, I am using differentiated solidarity not as a descriptive but as a positive term that sees these power relationships but expresses them in such a way that highlights maximum intensity and harmony, particularly for undoing oppressive practices.

This experience generally requires some sort of proximity or encounter, which will be addressed in the next section. However, this experience of mutual interest through physical proximity is not always mandatory. Whitehead himself discusses this possibility through his notion of "Peace," which transcends the particularity of one's existence and sees oneself as part of the larger cosmos. You let go of your particular utility of intensity and harmony, seeing part of yourself as connected, yet not identical, with the whole. As Whitehead puts it, peace "is a broadening of feeling due to the emergence of some deep metaphysical insight," a surpassing of personality that becomes "a trust in the efficacy of Beauty."[49] Moreover, Peace "results in a wider sweep of conscious interest. It enlarges the field of attention."[50] This is mutual love beyond one's own private results and for humanity (and the planet) as a whole. At their best, religious institutions "explicitly express the doctrine that the perfection of life resides in aims beyond the individual person in question."[51] Again, this speaks to enlightened other-interest. Yet you must remember that both you and others are not separate and stable entities. In my reading, this is the central presumption of mutual interest and a mystical form of differentiated solidarity, which may help motivate novel encounters for the purpose of greater mutual flourishing and value-intensification.

Seeking mutual interest for oneself and others is very similar to how the evangelical process theologian Thomas Oord defines love. According to him, love knowingly acts to increase wellbeing in response to feeling each other and the Divine. Overall wellbeing indicates that love is not merely other-regarding, but implicates oneself, as well. This is in spite of the fact that Oord critiques what he calls the "mutuality tradition." His concern is that it sentimentally implies that relationships are inherently loving, when in fact many are abusive and destructive. There may be a place for self-sacrifice, even though this is not the standard requirement for love, for it may at times benefit both ourselves and others.[52] Whether as *eros* or *agape*, love seeks to promote overall wellbeing as the affirmation and enhancing of values for others and ourselves. Even though this will often be a differentiated love towards those more proximate to us, such expressions may impact others positively as well through our unknown interrelationships.[53]

It is important to mention one other area of intersection between process and liberationist thinking. Process aims for the maximization of intensity and harmony, and it is my contention that this maximization is functionally equivalent to a preferential option for those experiencing oppression. Indeed, it is with the excluded and oppressed where their potential intensity and harmony, i.e., their real opportunities for transformation, are diminished. However, liberation is not *us* achieving results for *them* any more than an entity can actualize the potential on behalf of another entity. In spite of this limitation, it involves us using our power to set conditions for their decision since their subjectivity is constrained by an oppressive and an overly limiting environment.

Let us briefly return to Charles Birch and John Cobb, for they also implicitly support such a preferential option. Since Birch and Cobb remove an absolute notion of equal intrinsic value for humans, because humans have different experiences, they claim that "one should promote richness of experience wherever possible. There is a gap between what is potential and what is actual in each person."[54] Human flourishing is accomplished by developing potentialities within diverse cultures and by seeking to lure those cultures into affirming such personal transformation.[55] Birch and Cobb do not intend to support a colonialist triumphalism that says that the context that dominant Westerners have known is the supreme actualization. Rather, they offer a transcontextual critique concerning the vast majority of cultures:

> [They have made a portion of their] members inferior in their capacity to grow and have thus justified denying them the means to do so. The result has been an actual inferiority of experiences on the part of slaves, peasants, women, ethnic minorities and other classes. This actual inferiority has been appealed to as justifying the practices which created it.[56]

Their solution is that to the extent that people have been denied their potentiality, there will be the need for preferential access to opportunities for growth.[57]

Birch and Cobb suggest that each person needs to "have the maximum opportunity to develop to the full his or her talents and to promote the richest possible experience for all."[58] By this, I am interpreting their phrase "richest possible experience for all" to be equivalent to the maximization of intensity and harmony. As far as mutual interest is concerned, Birch and Cobb agree that we are to "share each other's fate." We primarily are called to be responsible for our particular interests and improve the lives of those close to us, but this responsibility extends even to future generations, paralleling Oord's thought. Thus, we are called to respect those circles of relationships that we feel most immediately, but ultimately this extends to all of life.[59]

Though Cobb and Birch do not explicitly connect these commitments with a preferential option for the poor (broadly construed) as do many liberation theologians, they make numerous implicit allusions to this prioritization. One way we can rethink this is that our primary concern for proximate family and friends should be seen in light of the larger web of relations. Thus, what may seem to be at odds with proximate wellbeing may actually contribute to the greater overall wellbeing, particularly when it is tuned towards the excluded and marginalized, i.e., those who have not had the opportunity to fully develop their potential because certain possibilities have been unjustly stripped away from them.

Though Birch and Cobb do not claim it, it is my contention that seeking the interest of the "other," specifically the oppressed other, may be what is most healing for those closest to us *even if they do not themselves believe it.* This is yet another way to understand the planetary gospel, which addresses our situated problems and concerns, but relates them far beyond our potentially narrow horizons of positive feeling. Since Birch and Cobb affirm that there are inevitable limits to economic growth because of the Earth's limits, one conclusion is that the materially wealthy should not be materially better off until those forced to go without are able to meet their needs.[60] They rightly recognize that individuals opting out from dominant patterns of the desire-oriented consumption that Jung Mo Sung also critiques will not change the planetary situation, but it does contribute to forming a culture that is more open to novel possibilities of transformation.[61]

It is not hard to imagine that some people might wrongly interpret this argument as saying that the sacrifice of some is part of the necessary losses for creative becoming. After all, life is at once both a process of becoming and perishing. In such a reading, sacrificial victims would contribute to the creative becoming of others for the purpose of greater intensity and harmony. This typically occurs in the justification of existing societal pattern, and, to our great shame, it is regularly found within white Christianity. In Western culture, those less competent in market law are often sacrificed because of their weak economic productivity on behalf of supposed progress.[62] However, Sung excludes this option from a Christian process perspective, for, as he puts it, the center of our faith is the resurrection of Jesus, which is essentially "the confession of the innocence of a victim of a sacrificial system.[63] Rejecting the logic of sacrifice prevents the maximization of intensity and harmony from becoming a brutal theory of social Darwinism: I cannot feed off another's potential to fulfill my own narrow satisfaction without diminishing overall beauty and degrading our interpenetrating interests.

ENCOUNTERING THE OTHER

WALMART WORKERS GATHER TOGETHER *in response to the mistreatment and firing of their coworkers. Interreligious religious leaders are present for the day's activities, too: speeches, marches, blessings, and civil disobedience occur. Some are there to protect their families and have their dignity recognized, others because they want neighborhood employers to reflect their faith values. They are together in the struggle, but they come from different perspectives and experiences. Arrested and handcuffed, enclosed together in vehicles, they share the stories and experiences that motivate them: this is real fellowship. . . . A church in St. Louis visits an Ecuadoran church every other year to do mission work and learn from the community about the struggles they face. They have done this multiple times and real relationships have emerged. In between these southbound visits, every other year a mission group from the Ecuadoran church leads a mission trip to the American community. Financed by the wealthy*

*northerners, they are able to do mission in the USA and learn
about the struggles and challenges the American church faces.
Americans and Ecuadorans alike encounter one another.*

By recognizing our inherent interrelationships through a process
social ontology, we can avoid the risk that too many people have
fallen into when seeking dialogue with "the other": there is no space
for romantic nativism. The "other" does not become the epistemological true source from which revelation proceeds. Rather, any encounter is a touch-point in which transformation becomes possible. In
fact, the other is inherently a relative term. From another person's
perspective and social location, my community will be *their* other
whom they can encounter. Avoiding the collapse of any person or
community into an ontological other is critical to understanding the
place of mutual interest. At the same time, we are not merely interrelated but are also different from each other. If we were identical,
the experiences of others would be redundant or superfluous. Instead,
being non-identical, we need each other. One needs the other because
the other remains as other, i.e., is non-identical. Their experiences
and perspective are non-redundant. As indicated in Chapter 2, they
increase planetary value, and, because of our inherent interrelationship, they increase the potentials available for future self-becoming.

However, it is important to admit that the *ideas* of an interconnected social ontology and mutual interest will not automatically
change human priorities, much less the world. Such claims would
fall under a dead-end idealism that laments, "If *only* people would
see things differently!" Such utopian wishing ignores the material
conditions out of which our relationships emerge. Simply explaining how we hurt ourselves when the powerful among us ignore or
oppress others is insufficient and naïve. Sin as the logics of structural
oppression run too deep; power relations and their privileges remain.
As philosophical theologian Roland Faber notes, "The repetition of
the sinful past enlarges or enhances the demonic within the nexus,
thereby introducing *structural oppression* and making resistance
more difficult."[64] One may intellectually recognize the advantage of

a practice different from what one embodies but then immediately turn around and ignore it out of narrowly interested considerations. Experience demonstrates that people do not consistently respond to arguments alone.

Readers may rightly ask: how can relatively privileged people, who may be oblivious to their privilege, recognize that they are not only participating in the exploitation of others but also destroying themselves? As noted earlier from James Cone's thought, you may be oppressed, but you will not know how you are damaging your own life. Many mainline Protestants, pastors, and theologians sense that they are enmeshed in oppressive patterns; it is not that they do not care but that these patterns fall out of consciousness all too easily. Many compassionate people have the privilege to revert to ignorance or walk away when struggles become inconvenient. It feels less costly to disassociate, with the result that they damage their souls.

More typically, mainliners all too often see the deconstruction-destruction of their privilege as a tragic loss rather than as a gain. The ability to celebrate this deconstruction, to make it central as part of our mutual interest, can only be done by intentionally entering into solidarity with people who have different experiences of power relationships. This effort does not strive for a rigid or unified sameness but rather affirms divergent singularities that are nevertheless relationally connected: this is yet another way to describe differentiated solidarity. By encountering others, experiencing aspects of their struggles, and recognizing such relationships as the incarnation of *koinonia* fellowship, churching communities enlarge their horizon of concern and become more fully the radical disciples that divine activity is calling them to be.

While it is critically important, even essential, to seek encounters with those who are different from us as we construct counter-imperial churching, there are several important warnings to consider. We may affirm the intrinsic value of people who have different life experiences and cultural affiliations from us. We may seek to develop forms of relationship that are non-exploitative and of mutual interest. But there are risks. What about relationships of differentiated power that have been historically oppressive or colonizing? What does this encounter between distinct groups look like in real life to reduce oppression? For the final section of this chapter, the theologians Marion Grau and Joerg Rieger will be particularly important conversation partners, especially in terms of their missiological analyses.

Unlike those who uncritically view mission as saving others from hell or rescuing them from injustice, Marion Grau rethinks mission for a postcolonial world, for we are never the only relevant actors. In doing so, she offers us a number of considerations to keep in mind when thinking about on-the-ground missional encounters. Entering a novel setting with good intentions does not mean that one will be experienced this way. This is particularly pertinent for those people who assume their innocence historically or naïvely. Grau wisely offers cautionary advice:

> When we step on sacred ground, insult a person, take liberties that offend, refuse to pitch in, or do too much, talk too much or too little, are too careless, barge into events or spaces not open to us, think we should have access everywhere, think people should trust us right off the bat, while we ourselves may reserve not to trust them, and so forth, we are stepping on hidden landmines.[65]

Grau discusses this through an international lens, but it is equally true within a culturally diverse country like the United States. First-time white volunteers should not expect to be instantly and warmly received at a gathering of Black activists working against police violence. Demanding instant and unearned camaraderie is not solidarity but the reassertion of privilege. Nuances will be lost in translation in intercultural communication, and there is the constant risk of projecting our context onto theirs.[66] In some settings, it is important to avoid too tight a grip when shaking hands. While a firm grip can be a sign of strong character to a white American farmer, it is often interpreted as aggressive to many American Indian peoples living on reservations. The same logic follows regarding how much one should look a stranger in the eye: you may think you are exhibiting character but be experienced as coming off as aggressive.[67] Mutual relationship is a possibility, but it is necessary that those with colonizing power need to not feel superior nor try to save the colonized; rather, they must become open to receiving from others.[68] It is a practice of the Divine Spirit.

Grau offers further practical advice on encountering the other and how it might allow for mutual growth. It is easy to state that one wants to create mutual relationships, but this is undermined to the point of becoming almost impossible when power dynamics are ignored. Rather than jumping in blindly and feigning ignorance (either willfully or through naïveté), she offers the following crucial suggestion, shared here in full:

> When encountering cultural, religious, and power differences with painful histories, you might want to consider (1) the history of the community and encounters with past and present others that shape it; (2) how these encounters were informed by certain persons, circumstances, groups, and events; (3) the profound ambivalence in many of our encounters with the Sacred and with each other; (4) what we can learn from history and mission studies for constructive theology.[69]

This ambivalence and risk-taking reveals our own complicity in oppressive actions when encountering the other. However, it should not cause us to shirk from these opportunities and replace them with mere charity work. We can neither succumb to despair at the supposed infinite power of colonizing regimes nor view encounter as the consumption of exotic cultures for our own self-gratification.[70] The resulting cultural exchange is a move beyond "simplistic dualisms" and towards becoming a "polydox mutual mission" of "mutually transforming toward greater justice."[71] The other is never simply other to us: they are a relational other (perhaps even a differentiated non-other?).

For such mutual encounters to bear fruit, the theologian Joerg Rieger is rightly convinced that projects of benevolent outreach must be abandoned. Particularly for churches, this has to do with their understanding of mission not as mere outreach nor only building "relationships" but also "inreach." Missional encounter must also be a way to deconstruct the unjust internalized relationships of dominance that persist within us. With the one-sidedness of missional encounter, Rieger points out that missionaries see themselves as doing the primary work. They may feel that they have grown or received something in the encounter, but the emphasis remains on them serving needy others, made possible through their group's historical accumulation of power and wealth.[72]

An alternative to this colonizing approach looks at how such encounters shape our self-understanding. Rieger cuts right to the core: "What if the question is not first of all, What can we do? but, What is going on? and, How might *we* be part of the problem?"[73] Most crucially, such benevolent charitable acts of service function in such a way as to perpetuate inequitable power relationships. Helping others without addressing power dynamics works alongside the idolatrous attempt to shape them in our image. With such cultural triumphalism, not only do we not change: we reify our demonic image.[74] At their best, critical encounters assist us in our mutual transformation.

Relationship itself is not inherently liberating, for relationships of dependency, or where one attempts to function exclusively as subject, and the other as object, preclude the potential for creative transformation. As Alfred North Whitehead noted, "The relationship is not a universal. It is a concrete fact with the same concreteness as the relata."[75] What matters is a commitment to dismantle inequitable power relationships, which can best be realized through novel encounters. Without such encounters, how can people know their location and specific relationships with others? We are required to explore our own complexity, for "unless we understand who we are and become aware of these differentials of power, we are simply not in a position to learn from the other and to share authority in any meaningful way."[76] It is through encounters that we are able to see new possibilities for how we can be different. Otherwise, we too easily maintain the illusion of wholeness.

It is important to remember that encounters are not exclusively enacted through the interpersonal face-to-face act. Reading stories and analyses from the perspective of the other are also useful. These have the benefit of respecting others who are experiencing oppression and may find it spiritually and emotionally draining to *explain again* the rudimentary elements of power and oppression. Learning before encountering face-to-face respects the other's time and wellbeing. Communities experiencing oppression often find they need a few representatives to speak to groups on their behalf to protect themselves from a flurry of micro-aggressions from those who may wish to be allies but are not yet in solidarity. This need also provides a useful function for members of dominant groups as they educate their own communities so that encounters can be mutually productive. There is no substitute for actual encounters for transformation to occur, but we know these necessary encounters will almost *inevitably* re-wound members of already hurting communities. Encounter is a delicate dance.

Seeking the wellbeing of others is not simply done out of the goodness of one's heart, but also leads to new understandings of how each of us is wrapped within these patterns of power. This is particularly pertinent for predominantly white, mainline Protestant communities. As an example of a backhanded compliment, Rieger points out that "[w]hile the mainline churches on the whole are past the stage at which they actively promoted colonialism, the problem is that we are not aware of how much of what they do feeds into the invisible structures of neocolonialism."[77] No wonder so many volunteer or mission groups often find that "recipient" communities are less than enthusiastic about their presence!

Rieger believes that emphasizing the transcendence of God helps relativize every human endeavor. I appreciate this argument, especially if we understand transcendence in terms of God's reciprocal transcendence of the world, which comes through the gift of novel initial aims for the world's self-creation in unexpected ways. In doing so, we would find a similar move made by the postcolonial theologian Mayra Rivera. Rivera argues for a relational transcendence where we touch the "irreducibly Other" but do not capture it, where "God can be perceived as the extreme instance of interhuman difference."[78] In fact, at its best, *transcendence designates a relation with a reality irreducibly different from my own reality, without this difference destroying this relation and without the relation destroying this difference.*"[79] Such a relational transcendence expresses our ongoing need for a *koinonia* of difference. This aligns with what process feminist theologian Marjorie Suchocki calls "horizontal transcendence," where the divine can be encountered in the face of the other by expanding beyond the self.[80] The gospel of Matthew famously echoes this claim, saying "Truly I tell you, just as you did it to one of the least of these who are members of my family, you did it to me."[81]

The call for maximization of intensity and harmony is simultaneously a call demanding difference over sameness, multiplicity over unity, and relationality rather than identity. This can best be experienced through a process of encountering the other. Once again, we find an ally with the neo-liberationist theologian Jung Mo Sung. Sung likewise sees the requirement of encounter offering the possibility of seeing the wellbeing of the "other" as part of one's mutual interest. Sung claims that the enduring value of liberation theology is not its conclusions but its basic commitment and starting point, its ground, which is in the face of those suffering and the desire to respond. Before the cycle of action, commitment, and theologizing, there exists "the 'zero' moment . . . [of] the spiritual experience of encountering the person of Jesus in the face of the poor."[82] Sung gives a concrete example of such encounter:

> The first contacts between Nenuca's group [of missionaries] and the street people are difficult and marked by suspicion on the part of the street people. But with the friendship that starts to grow, little by little, insofar as they let each other get closer physically and emotionally, this suspiciousness is

Matt 25:31 (handwritten margin note)

transformed into the perception of the 'something different' that not only causes the street people to feel better but also causes the group of volunteers to feel better.[83]

He notes the disappointment of activists who wanted to not just be a face of divine graciousness but to really liberate the poor. However, their disappointment again reflects an inappropriate conception of historical subjectivity rooted in modern Enlightenment assumptions.

The liberationist methodology I am advocating follows a process of encounter-action-reflection. The first step "is the *praxis* of liberation that grows out of ethical indignation in the face of situations in which human beings are reduced to a subhuman condition."[84] This can be expanded to also mean outrage when other groups are oppressed or the environment desecrated.[85] Through these encounters, one internalizes the commitment to the suffering other. It is only afterwards that theological reflection comes to the fore in light of these experiences. Reading these experiences as revealing our socially complex ontology leads to transformed commitments. Yet encounter alone is no guarantee of transformation: one might simply pull away[86] or anesthetize oneself.[87] As Sung beautifully articulates it, "The wisdom that needs to be taught and understood throughout the world is that which teaches us that one cannot be happy and truly love oneself if one is unable to open oneself to the suffering of other persons; if one is unable to have a solidarious sensibility."[88] In this statement, social ontology, mutual interest, and encounter reveal their internal complicity with one another.

A width of experiences of difference can lead to transformed self-understandings. The Korean ecofeminist theologian Jea Sophia Oh uses the term "listening" instead of "encounter." The result is that "through the process of listening, one transcends him/herself to become the molecule's level to empty (allow) a space for embracing the other immanently within her."[89] This is why many Americans who have spent time in another country or become fluent in a language beyond English so often see the world differently from those satisfied with a narrower set of experiences. They have partially transcended their constricted location, incorporating an aspect of the other's perspective into their own vision. However, with globalization, aspects of encountering the other through language differences have diminished as English has become the dominant language of international trade and exchange. Around the world, if people want to advance financially or participate in global relations, fluency in English has become almost a mandatory requirement.[90]

Returning to process terminology, this is a problem in its aesthetic affects. Different languages are different ways of experiencing and perceiving the world. For example, there are villages in Papua New Guinea where it is not uncommon for people to speak at least half a dozen languages. One of the results of such multilingualism has been a delay of dementia and Alzheimer's disease; the brain is kept more nimble.[91] Over the past fifty years, language variety has diminished as certain linguistic traditions have been lost across generations. This reduction of variety is a reduction of the potential for new contrasts. Potential intensities are lost as more of life becomes homogenized across the planet; this reduces opportunities for creative transformation.

Sung identifies the need for spiritualities of solidarity to counteract the many injustices the world is facing, which would lead to the First World repenting of its consumer patterns and "limitless accumulation of goods."[92] When we integrate liberationist concerns with a poststructuralist process perspective, we are able to make the following assertion: Rectifying power differentials (with power understood as a relationship rather than as something possessed) and celebrating/demanding a multiplicity of perspectives and locations is *equivalent* to seeking the maximization of potential intensity and harmony for a situation and its relationships. For in experiencing another, when it is critically reflected upon, we find that our own healing process is inextricably tied with the wellbeing of the other. At its heart, it builds a counter-imperial ethos and is central to the formation of a koinonia of churching, which will be further unfolded in Chapter 6. Whereas churching's koinonia is an activity of radical boundary crossing and dominant power subversion, it likewise describes our local mutual indwellings.[93]

I experience much unjust privilege, but it is in my interest to dismantle these privileges. We are interconnected with one another, but without critically encountering others with different experiences, the spiritual calling and motivation to be transformed remains abstract. *The living gospel is never abstract.* This is not just my problem but also the problem of any Christian living with privilege in an unjust, interconnected world. Foregoing an isolationist fellowship of purity, since we live in an interrelated web of mutually implicating relationships, our fellowship crosses the artificial boundaries that are meant to isolate us from one another. We *need* each other for a fuller flourishing of life to reign. When we practice this form of solidarity, which simultaneously recognizes and celebrates our differences, we are that much closer to maximizing intensity and harmony as part of a liberatory planetary fellowship!

diakonia

Political Influences in the Struggle for (and Struggles of) a Radical Ecclesiology

In proposing and advancing the possibility of living beyond Empire, resistance recovers the public that Empire threatens to destroy, reinstalls the sense of freedom and hope, and stirs up the forces of the messianic. ~Néstor Míguez, Joerg Rieger, and Jung Mo Sung, *Beyond the Spirit of Empire*

IN THE PREVIOUS TWO CHAPTERS, we examined some of the major process themes that contribute towards churching, including entities as value-intensities and mutual interest through differentiated solidarity. The former points towards churching's *kerygma* (proclamation), while the latter addresses its sense of *koinonia* (fellowship). This chapter emphasizes the *diakonia* of counter-imperial churching, while layering new insights on the previous themes. Chapter 1 touched on several of the problems that churching aims to address. At the time, they functioned more as broad strokes, raising more questions than they answered. Specifically, what is political liberalism? How do practices of the mainline churches reflect it? Why is this a problem? What is the character of globalizing Empire, what are its sacred idols, and how can it be subverted? What do we mean by oppression, and how important are quality of life concerns?

87

To answer these questions, we will need political theories as radical and subversive as the uses of process and liberationist thought have been up to this point in this book. We will find that some theories, like political liberalism, are simply not up to the task. Alternatives like theories of Empire, aspects of the capabilities approach, and postmodern feminist political theory will get us much closer to where we need to go. I will close this chapter by shifting towards a political theology that deconstructs the boundary between the "political" and the "religious" and undermines the notion of the separation of "church and state," thus urging religious engagement in seemingly political matters. In developing an understanding of diakonia beyond traditional notions of charitable service to the needy, this chapter intends to accomplish three tasks: one, to describe what spiritual-political powers counter-imperial churching will be struggling against; two, to show what such radical discipleship will be struggling for; and three, to clarify how political theories should affect the structural organization of churching groups.

JOHN RAWLS'S INADEQUATE LIBERALISM

The political philosopher John Rawls is most famous for his articulation of political justice in his 1971 book, *A Theory of Justice*. However, I am less concerned with his specific theory of justice than with his understanding of what makes for a politically liberal society. This section will critique some of the weaknesses of Rawls's political liberalism, namely his anxiety over conflict and desire for unity. These and other weaknesses are largely reflected in the political assumptions of American mainline Protestant denominations. In effect, mainline Protestant churches express a form of religious liberalism in line with political liberalism. To draw out these parallel frameworks, it is necessary to review Rawls's political liberalism, particularly his understanding of comprehensive doctrines, reasonable pluralism, an overlapping consensus, and background culture before offering a critique using the political theology of Paul Kahn.

Rawls's book *Political Liberalism* is an attempt to answer criticisms that his earlier work received. To do this, his method is to relegate his idea of "justice as fairness,"[1] which was formerly his central insight, to the status of one among many potential comprehensive doctrines. By comprehensive doctrines, he means beliefs or worldviews that explain the world or what humans are to do in that world in a holistic way. They answer questions like "What does it mean to be human?" or "What is the good life?" These doctrines may be grounded in religious or philosophical theories of "the person" that try to answer other questions. These doctrines often are pursuing particular conceptions of the good, which may radically diverge from one another. People regularly address these questions with different comprehensive (or partially comprehensive) doctrines.

Rawls recognizes that there will never be unanimity among comprehensive doctrines, at least insofar as people are able to decide among doctrines for themselves. Since we cannot talk our way to a consensus on ultimate truths, he unrealistically suggests that we bracket this effort out of political considerations. Each person or group is supposedly able to have their own particular conception of justice to the extent that this does not impinge on other individuals or groups being able to have their own conception of justice, or the good, and so on.[2]

Rawls fears the expression of comprehensive doctrines because he believes they result in instability and conflict. The religious wars of Europe fought between Catholics and Protestants are paradigmatic of conflict's dangers for him. Understandably, he wants to avoid future wars that follow this pattern. Neither group could recognize the legitimacy of the other, and so there was great violence and political instability for generations. Rawls seeks a way for societies to endure through time and thus be stable.[3] Empirically, societies have rarely had a consensus regarding comprehensive doctrines, so he endeavors to make these differences irrelevant for the purposes of political justice. He puts the question as such: "How is it possible for those affirming a religious doctrine that is based on religious authority . . . also to hold a reasonable political conception that supports a just democratic regime?"[4]

While there can be diversity in the comprehensive doctrines people affirm, not every single doctrine can be incorporated into Rawls's ideal of political justice. They need to fall within what he calls a reasonable pluralism. This reasonable pluralism consists of groups that maintain their comprehensive doctrines but will not require others to affirm something that violates their own particular doctrines. Instead, they should seek to exercise fair cooperation.[5] Since there will never be unanimity among citizens regarding one comprehensive doctrine, Rawls concludes we need a reasonable pluralism.

Reasonableness denotes the mutual concepts of reciprocity and playing fair. By reciprocity and fair play, Rawls means that when someone proposes "terms of fair cooperation, those proposing them must also think it at least reasonable for others to accept them, as free and equal citizens, and not as dominated or manipulated, or under the pressure of an inferior political or social position."[6] So long as different conceptions are willing to support this notion of society for political purposes, Rawls is willing to grant that there is more than one legitimate type of political liberalism. They must all universally adhere to "the criterion of reciprocity, viewed as applied between free and equal citizens, themselves seen as reasonable and rational."[7] Beyond that criterion, there is freedom.

When the many doctrines of a reasonable pluralism are placed side-by-side, they should reveal what Rawls calls an overlapping consensus. An overlapping consensus "does not provide a specific religious, metaphysical, or epistemological doctrine beyond what is implied by the political conception itself."[8] It exists when people who hold a number of distinct reasonable comprehensive doctrines are able to agree on a political conception. They do not agree for the same reasons, since each will justify their adherence to the political conception from their own framework, which may include understanding their comprehensive doctrine as being more ultimate.

In contrast to a *modus vivendi*, where people go along with a democratic system of governance because they lack the power to overturn it, Rawls wants them to be able to enthusiastically endorse the political values and ideals of their culture. He considers whether those of faith can support constitutional structures that may threaten their comprehensive doctrines.[9] Rawls believes that reasonable comprehensive doctrines should be able to affirm a reasonable pluralism for its own sake. This means that these doctrines will need to eventually reflect some form of political liberalism. He acknowledges that the ideal he is proposing requires people to accept the possibility of listening to those whom they oppose. Rawls also requires people to propose only structures they believe are fair for others to accept without feeling oppressed, i.e., they should reflect the value of reciprocity. Shared political reasoning does not mean that it is universal in some ultimate sense even as the overlap among groups is as wide as possible.

Values that an overlapping consensus cannot contain are narrowly restricted to the background culture, which includes churches. Rawls places unnecessarily rigid limits on what can be argued in the public sphere, even as he attempts to make private space for the particular political reflections of individuals and associations.[10] Essentially, so long as one is thinking to oneself, or arguing out these ideals in one's particular community like a church or university as part of the background culture, then the rules of debate are much more free. Such debates are not held to the same standard that would define them to be part of a reasonable pluralism. Ultimate reasons and motivations can be legitimately discussed in this background context. Rawls wants to give plenty of space to the background culture when people are in general agreement regarding political justice. However, in the public arena, only noncomprehensive political values should be presented in most circumstances. If you or your community think this agreement is a mistake, you will be marked as unreasonable.[11]

Rawls recognizes that there are problems of extension to his understanding of political liberalism, and they remain unsolved problems. One of the most crucial areas that he does not challenge is the sacred functions of the American nation that subvert his politically liberal intent. Political theology has for decades studied how political ideas like sovereignty are really secularized theological ideas.[12] The clearest elements of American civil religion include "the Pledge of Allegiance, the iconography of the flag, or the memorialization of citizen sacrifice."[13] The American flag functions as a sacred object, which is implicitly affirmed every time someone laments its desecration, for only something that is sacred can be desecrated. The state declares its exclusive legitimacy over the power to kill and to ask for the sacrifice of life. This is what it means to die for one's country, which is commonly understood as sacrificing oneself for others' sake; one's blood renews the redemptive power of the nation for which one gives one's life.

Political theologian Paul Kahn rightly challenges Rawls's theory for never taking seriously this state violence and the larger values to which it justifies itself. Rawls's liberalism sees violence as merely accidental and not central to democratic political life, rather than what Kahn correctly understands it to be: "Political violence has been and remains a form of sacrifice."[14] Sacrifice exists alongside law, and, depending on the situation, one or the other can be the focal response, which Kahn ties to debates about the role of torture.[15] He understands that the function of the rule of law needs to be reconceptualized, because "for Americans, the rule of law is not that which eliminates the need for the violent defense of the nation, but that for the sake of which violence is deployed."[16] It falsely incarnates the sacred to which one willingly dies on its behalf. Here the theological concept of redemptive suffering and the national sacred join. The state is secular neither in the way Rawls claims nor in the way it defines itself.[17] In acquiescing to the narrow paradigm of liberalism, mainline Protestants fail to challenge the theological content of both their nation and larger socio-economic structures.

One of the major shortcomings of Rawls's discussion is that he tries to separate religion from the political by assuming that the focus of religion is primarily belief or assent to particular doctrines. Much of his discussion places religion firmly in the framework of the role of comprehensive doctrines in public reason. What if religion is also the way people live, like practices and rituals that draw them beyond their particular communities and connect them with those who would not identify as part of that same religious tradition? Religious practice can be a way of relating with others and how one lives one's life, especially as it concerns interacting with those who might be considered by some to be "enemies." Religion may be comprehensive, but not as Rawls intends. Rather than offering articulated comprehensive doctrines, it may offer a comprehensive way to live in the world, including challenging political idolatries. When religion is understood in this way, the religion-political boundary that Rawls is so intent to maintain begins to fade. One sees that there are very political religious practices, and there are very religious political practices.

Nevertheless, we must ask how does political liberalism relate to mainline Protestant churches? In some ways, this should be apparent. For over a century, mainline Protestant churches were close to the halls of American political power.[18] Well over half of our presidents have come out of these traditions, even though they make up less than ten percent of the American population today. These denominations were able to have significant political access in part because they absorbed many of the properties of political liberalism and disproportionately represented the American economic and political elite throughout much of the 19th and early 20th centuries. However, now that mainline Protestantism is declining as a cultural force, politicians easily ignore it. Thoroughly enculturated, mainline churches retain the old form without the old benefits!

The problem is not simply that a Rawlsian political liberalism demands that groups such as mainline Protestants diminish their comprehensive doctrines in the wider community. Remember: for Rawls, churches do not need to use public reason when they are internally focused but only when they are externally oriented on *we are embarrased by our theology*

Yes

fundamental political matters. Nevertheless, mainline Protestants have internalized this disposition to such an extent that they see their own particular theological claims as embarrassing, with the result that they avoid advocating for them not only in the larger public but *even in their own communities.* It is left to each individual to have their own comprehensive doctrines, which they keep to themselves and which too easily dissolve into unthinking. Dissenting from the hegemonic consensus is marginalized in the United States. To challenge it is counter-cultural, so many church members become anxious by this prospect. Rawls wanted religious groups to endorse the values and political ideals of their society. This ideal has worked lamentably well in mainline Protestant congregations, but the result is the individualization of church life.

Many congregations look like a Rawlsian society. To the extent that an issue is controversial, meaning that it will lack an overlapping consensus, congregations are reluctant to engage with such issues.[19] The overlapping social consensus forbids one to challenge the sacredness of America, á la the Rev. Jeremiah Wright, without facing marginality. This consensus, which is part of the stabilizing political culture Rawls affirms, remains prevalent *even in what he would call the background culture of churches themselves!* Topics of a controversial nature, whether explicitly political or of a different character, are more often than not relegated to individual opinion without providing a larger relational framework in mainline faith communities. Rawls's theory provides no assistance in challenging an understanding of the autonomous nature of human beings, since a critique of it would be a politically unessential comprehensive doctrine.[20] The liberty of individuals and the freedom of the market go hand-in-hand in political liberal democracy; Rawls's theory cannot help us resist these values beyond mitigating excessively unequal distributions of wealth.[21]

Church members frequently identify with their nation's sacred images as well as their faith tradition, often expressed in the presence of both an American and Christian flag in sanctuaries. Many ministers know all too well the level of controversy generated with suggestions that the former be removed.[22] "God and Country" are seen as complementary elements to life, which is consistent with Kahn's analysis of the political sacred. There is no tension or division in background and public sphere here; there is only a sameness that conforms local groups into affirming the idolatrous image of the American sacred, even if they critique specific policies around the edges. Nevertheless, it is not merely to national or patriotic loyalty that people devote themselves, for this is in fact geared towards a larger project, that of Empire. It is to this that our next thinkers devote their primary attention.

MICHAEL HARDT AND ANTONIO NEGRI'S THEORY OF EMPIRE AND THE MULTITUDE

I have chosen to talk about Empire as the general condition of domination and oppression that churching needs to address. From Christianity's beginnings in ancient Palestine up to today, it has had to deal one way or another with empires. Historically, most empires were centered around a single people, city, or nation, such as Rome. While their use of the term "Empire" is not fully identical with my own, the political theorists Michael Hardt and Antonio Negri go a long way to deepening the analysis of what contemporary Empire looks like.

Hardt and Negri persuasively describe contemporary Empire as a transglobal productive network instead of one that is centered in sovereign states. Their work revolves around showing how there has been a paradigm shift via sovereignty from nation-centric imperialism to a new logic of rule called Empire.[23] The logic of imperialism focuses on particular nation-states controlling and extracting value from subordinate countries for their own use. Through their notion of Empire, Hardt and Negri argue that this has become a more decentralized process. No longer can one simply say that the West is benefitting and the global south hurting from economic exploitation, for now one sees the first world in the third and the third world in the first.[24] Empire is open, expanding, and includes the entire world potentially, where even the most marginalized group is at the bottom rung of the system rather than outside it altogether.[25] This global network uses perpetual violence and militarism to maintain the system of production and extraction.

The United States' use of perpetual violence, made especially manifest after the attacks of 9/11 and the Iraq War, reveal the U.S. as Empire's chief enforcer. Hardt and Negri claim that Empire makes war into a permanent exception for preserving the global order as just and inevitable.[26] Police forces become militarized; perpetual police action is used to control the barbarian-terrorists, and public protest is delegitimized as threats to Empire.[27] Dominant countries use the global system to try others for war crimes and never to try their own citizens; while torture by others is evil, for liberal democracies it is a tragic necessity. This also means that Hardt and Negri take the role of governments more seriously in books after *Empire*. Before, they focused on governments more as administrators who serve the global order. Later, they rightly say that the global economic order cannot function on its own; it is only through government policies and trade agreements that Empire exists at all. The Davos summit in Switzerland is a clear example of where governments help construct Empire even as none of them directly controls it.[28]

Hardt and Negri contrast the bad news of Empire today with their notion of the multitude. The multitude replaces the function of the proletariat in Marxist discourse. While the latter was generally conceived of as industrial workers, the former includes potentially everyone on the planet. This is made possible through a reinterpretation of the idea of production. For them, the multitude is engaged in the social production of life itself, which is called the biopolitical, and which overlaps with their notion of immaterial production, where what is produced are relationships and services.[29] In contrast, Empire is more like a vampire that extracts the surplus from this production for its own perpetuation as biopower.[30] By

multitude as everyone not just working poor

showing that the multitude is involved in production, Hardt and Negri explain how the multitude and even the unemployed are actual agents of the production of value. As labor increasingly becomes immaterial both at the high and low ends of the scale, it shows that everyone is laboring in the form of producing life and relationships and can thus be an agent of change. Specifically, the multitude can become a force of counter-globalization that avoids Empire's controlling functions.

Hardt and Negri describe two forms of multitude: 1) there is the multitude as it actually exists and engages in the production of all social life and relationships, and 2) there is the political project of the becoming multitude that remains a real potential not yet actualized. When emphasizing the novelty of Empire, I read their early position as implying that the existence of the multitude is enough to create a "spontaneous" communism of pure immanence.[31] There is the problematic hint of inevitability to this process, though other readers can interpret this comment as saying that if this communism occurs, it has sufficient internal mechanisms within it to not need any form of representation to sustain itself. Nevertheless, in later works Hardt and Negri emphasize much more clearly that the existence of the multitude simply makes revolution *possible* rather than inevitable.[32] There can be a global counter-globalization movement of many singularities communicating on a common matrix (the divine matrix of mutual immanence, perhaps?), but it is also possible that they may be sublated into yet another regime of Empire. The future is indeterminately open. The ontological multitude that produces social life exists, but Hardt and Negri await whether an historical multitude will develop and cast off Empire for a grassroots democracy of direct participation.

While Hardt and Negri have been criticized for their overly immanent interpretation of Empire, they also acknowledge transcendent qualities of Empire in *Multitude*. Specifically, "biopower stands above society, transcendent, as a sovereign authority and imposes its order."[33] In *Empire*, they focus on showing the immanent aspects of Empire at work in the world instead of it being a conspiracy controlled by a few. It is everywhere and nowhere at the same time, thus opening up the possibility to attack it from anywhere by anyone.[34] In *Multitude*, they more readily acknowledge that there are elements of transcendence within Empire as it creates fluid and shifting hierarchies and boundaries to control the production of the multitude. They rightly take more seriously how the United States, G-7 countries, supranational agencies like the World Bank, International Monetary Fund, World Trade Organization, transnational business interests, and NGOs play an outsized role in Empire as a network of power.[35] Economic systems such as the goal of a free market cannot persist without political regulation and force.[36]

is this true?

The postcolonial theorist Gayatri Spivak's notion of contrasting the global vs. the planetary provides a complementary parallel with Hardt and Negri's distinction between biopower and the biopolitical, both of which align with the theory of value and relationships I have discussed in previous chapters. Analogous to Spivak's distinction between an abstracted globe and the actual planet of real relations, Hardt and Negri describe biopower as the forces of imperial interaction and control, while the biopolitical is the network of life that produces itself. For Hardt and Negri, the multitude as the biopolitical is always productive, even if they are not recognized as such. In the same manner, Spivak affirms that a member of the subaltern may be ignored by dominant perspectives and may not even be able to be heard in discourses, but she is still a productive subject, even if she has been silenced.[37]

One area where Hardt and Negri do not delve deep enough in terms of a process understanding of relational value is on ecology. Like most political theorists, they are focused on humans and their relations. Even so, they do recognize how Empire promotes ecological devastation and seeks to privatize what they call the "commons" for personal profit, such as building dams on rivers or appropriating indigenous knowledge of the earth for corporate profit.[38] Corporations claim ownership to the genes of seeds, thus contributing to a sense of their bare instrumental value.[39] Pushing beyond their potential political multitude, Spivak adds that what is needed is "a global movement for non-Eurocentric ecological justice," and even admits to dreaming "of animist liberation theologies to girdle the perhaps impossible vision of an ecologically just world."[40] Furthermore, Catherine Keller has critiqued Hardt and Negri for offering a supersessionist view of themselves vis-à-vis postcolonial theory even though they admit that they are caught up in networks of Empire just as they accuse postcolonialist theorists of being as well.[41] The postcolonial straw men they construct are too-easily dismissed.[42]

In spite of these limitations, there has been a growing consensus affirming their description of Empire. Like Hardt and Negri, the Christian thinkers Néstor Míguez, Joerg Rieger, and Jung Mo Sung agree that there is no dominant center of economic and political power today: "Empire is bigger than the United States, [but] that country has a special place in the formation of Empire today."[43] Instead of a "'strong' centre," there are "several 'loose' centers" housed in big transnational corporations and multilateral organizations.[44] However, one area of disagreement is that Hardt and Negri fail to identify the religious transcendence that motivates the biopower of Empire and its institutional support.

While Hardt and Negri emphasize how Empire's logic works immanently, Míguez, Rieger, and Sung correctly point out that there is a transcendent element of Empire at work: "[T]he fact that Empire's present means of control do not possess a specific location and are articulated in relation to productive functions do not signify in themselves that Empire does not possess or claim to have a transcendent status."[45] This status motivates people to sacrifice even when its advantages are not readily available to them. It is the "*ethos*" of Empire, its theological spirit.[46] For Empire to function as it does, it is not enough for people to submit to it: they need to be actively incorporated into Empire and want its worldview as their own.[47] *People erroneously experience its proclamation as good news.* It is this element of idolatry and sacrificial logic that justifies the violence

Illusion of Empire as good news

of Empire that these scholars rightly think Hardt and Negri miss. Namely, the process of seeking a utopian, pure free-market capitalism "orients the great strategies of political-economic action."[48] As there is not yet a perfectly free market of equal information (which is actually impossible), the mission of Empire continues indefinitely. It is the faith in the market or "market fundamentalism [that] plays a central role in the global capitalist system."[49] This is a deeper yet sympathetic analysis to John Cobb's discussion of economism, noted in Chapter 1.[50] This new Empire attempts to attract through soft power and form mimetic desires within the subordinated, with the goal of perpetual growth via the process of accumulation and consumption, and unending war upon those who resist this attraction.[51] Sung, Míguez, and Rieger wisely hold out for a positive role for transcendence, where the excluded, the economic leftovers of humanity and life, transcend Empire's enclosures and reveal its spirit of death.[52] It is my contention that the good news of our interrelated value and the unmasking of oppressive sacrifice provides a compelling alternative proclamation to the dominant narrative of Empire.[53]

Replacing Empirial Crowd News w/ real good News

Hardt and Negri's notion of the multitude offers a vision of the productive potential of the service of churching: as resistance to a totalizing economic globalization. In forming affective relationships with exploited communities (as discussed in Chapter 3), church communities are producing immaterially a new context that subverts Empire. The struggles of the multitude can be legitimately expressed in localized actions and concerns, as "each struggle remains singular and tied to its local conditions but at the same time is immersed in the common web."[54] Through its productive creativity, the multitude resists Empire and its logic of violence.[55] Empire has its own authorizing norms beyond its immanent forces, and so the diakonia of churching challenges Empire not only on the productive level but also on the level of meaning. In this way, it critiques Empire's biopower. Moreover, since the United States and its military might undergird much of Empire's practices, radical American churches have a special calling to likewise undermine proximate practices of

Empire whenever feasible. In their relevant local contexts as well as in the broader dynamics of domination and oppression, they are to speak out as a witness against them even when there is no hope that these practices can immediately be changed.

AMARTYA SEN'S CAPABILITIES APPROACH

From the critique of the idolatrous sacred unquestioned by political liberalism and the violent biopower of Empire, one might errone-ously conclude that the ecclesiological work of diakonia is liberation or bust. This, however, would be a mistake. There is also the need for addressing more proximate quality of life concerns, and for this we need the help of Amartya Sen, an Indian economist and political thinker. For those driven to resist Empire in its multifaceted forms, Sen offers the wise suggestion that people should avoid "the grand revolutionary's 'one-shot handbook.'"[56]

One of Sen's major contributions and insights is his practical, grounded perspective. It is not enough to offer a scheme that would be the ideal framework for society. Such speculations do not assist someone in determining what are the best steps by which to improve the situation that one currently faces. Rather than seek a perfect jus-tice, it is more important to diminish existing injustices.[57] He gives the following example: you may say that the Mona Lisa is the perfect painting, but when you have to decide between a Dali and a Picasso, this ideal does not help you; it does not help you compare the actual options one faces.[58] Therefore, Sen proposes a comparative approach between relevant options. I read this in terms of process thought's aims, which are always towards something that is really actualizable. Sometimes options are between bad and not-so-bad formulations. Picking the better choice may still be unpleasant and may lead to better options from which to choose in the future, making them comparatively "better," but they are still bad in the grand scale of things.[59] In doing so, Sen challenges John Rawls's theory of justice as itself internally inadequate and suggests a revision that points to the importance of capabilities over Rawls's primary goods.[60] By this, Sen is more concerned with what people are actually able to do and become in reality. Rather than having abstract *de jure* options, the *de facto* opportunities from which people can make decisions are more important.

Sen's key contribution concerns his concept of capabilities. These are actual opportunities of what people can be and do, "the freedoms that we actually have to choose between different kinds of lives."[61] These include concerns regarding education, health, accessibility, and many other areas. Sen cares about two aspects of capabilities: that people can actually choose, and that they can examine the choices available to them. In other words, he is concerned with the process of choosing itself. For example, some people need more resources in order to have the capability to fulfill a certain function.[62] Treating everyone the same actually hurts persons facing exploitation more than others. Additionally, it matters whether people have real alternatives to choose from when making decisions.[63] Without one ultimate list of multiple capabilities, he focuses on comparing among options of what people can do or be.[64] He argues persuasively that the actualization of capabilities should not be forced upon anyone. Right relations are not primarily about the mere functioning of capabilities if a center actor has coercively imposed them. Rather, what is key for justice is for them to be freely available for multiple actors to choose from.[65]

The political theorist Martha Nussbaum, one of Sen's frequent collaborators in developing the capabilities approach, has noted that even as he has attended to social justice concerns, his primary focus has been comparing different societies on quality of life measures.[66] His project is not about some absolute, transcendent ideal but rather what makes for better or worse living. Therefore, part of the value that he contributes is a complementary balance with more radical thinkers in the recognition that liberation is not the only goal that should direct churching. It is just as important to emphasize survival and quality of life.[67] Sen provides valuable resources for that project.

I interpret Sen's capabilities as a political conceptualization of Whitehead's notion of potentialities. Just as there is a difference between a conceptual possibility and a real potential, Sen wants to differentiate between theoretical opportunities of wellbeing that are available to people versus what they can actually decide to do. Whitehead makes a similar comparative quality of life claim, though he does so in a temporal comparison rather than between spatially distinct communities. For Whitehead, there is a general aim "(i) to live, (ii) to live well, (iii) to live better. In fact the art of life is *first* to be alive, *secondly*, to be alive in a satisfactory way, and *thirdly*, to acquire an increase in satisfaction."[68] Sen's notion of capabilities has a number of parallels with process thought's notion of relevant possibilities to actualize. This theory also works with notions of agency, which has parallels with the "windowless monad" of Leibniz or the empty space of final causation from which decisions arise.

In addition to offering a persuasive defense of quality of life concerns via capabilities, Sen reminds us of the need to relativize the concerns that any particular group may have. It is too easy to define other groups in terms of one's narrow location. In contrast with prevailing rhetoric of an exotic and otherworldly India, he describes its history, internal diversity, and heterogeneity before British colonialism. Rather than merely reading India in light of the West, he reads India on its own terms in such a way as to relativize the absolute claims the West has made upon it. He sees this argumentative diversity as something to be cherished. I am convinced that Sen is correct to recommend that people should resist the current neo-colonial order by rejecting subordination, but they should not reject ideas just because they come from the West. Ideas should be critically appropriated and used wherever they can further capabilities-filled living. He offers the image that people should not be "well-frogs" happily isolated from anything outside their location, which itself becomes diminished through its rigidity.[69]

The parochialism of closed groups such as nations may diminish justice, which greatly concerns Sen. They will have limited knowledge, and they will have biases. They will misread or ignore priorities that may be obvious to an outsider. He suggests Adam Smith's notion of the impartial spectator as a solution to this problem and to concerns about international justice.[70] The impartial spectator means that discussion is not restricted to the community since others can offer critiques and suggestions. Sen uses the notion of the impartial spectator to argue that if two people agree on something despite the fact that they are coming from different social locations, this strengthens the claim more than if it only came from a single perspective. "External" perspectives hold more parochial views accountable: this is what he takes away from Smith's notion of the impartial spectator.[71] One resulting implication is that there are no self-enclosed entities that are sufficient unto themselves. It is easy to misread the impartial spectator as offering a universal perspective.[72] While this may have been Smith's intention, if so, Sen is offering a counter-reading of the term. In that interpretation, the impartial spectator acts more as an indeterminate horizon for broadening perspectives.[73]

Constructively, churching is not solely interested in increasing capabilities but also in actualizing potentials for its constituent persons. However, it does not seek to actualize aims for the whole world. These aims are diverse and in part self-created by the world's constituents, and only they can actualize their own aims. The presupposition of a level of freedom or indeterminacy in the nature of reality, which Sen affirms, means that churching should not legislate how events become but *can* seek to maximize capabilities that would help reduce gross injustices. For Sen, one cannot ignore human agency, replacing it with an eye merely to consequences.[74] Churching does not worship a god who determines the mode by which actualizations occur, and it refuses to do the misguided work of enforcing what a predestining image of the divine demands. Rather, churching seeks to maximize relevant and desirable capabilities for the wellbeing of itself, others, and the whole planet.

Sen's primary limitation for churching is that he avoids advocating for a central place for faith communities in political matters

Religious
idolatry

as he tries to prevent the state from either giving preference to one religion over another or banning outright their public expression. He does this by maintaining a somewhat classic articulation of what qualifies as religious, while I want to include global economism and its meaning-making as religious idolatry. I affirm Sen's desire for state neutrality between Hinduism, Islam, and Christianity even as I interpret American state neutrality as being subservient to a greater macrotranscendent religious loyalty of economism. Despite this limitation, Sen helps prioritize part of the embodied gospel of a churching diakonia: the enhancement of real capabilities.

THEORIES OF OPPRESSION, CONFLICT, AND REPRESENTATION

Today, most people who care about a more just world, even among progressive mainline Protestant churches, conceive of justice in terms of rights and distribution. Activist churches talk about social justice, which generally means making sure that people get their fair share. The logic goes that since we are all children of God, we deserve our rights. The political theorist Iris Marion Young offers an understanding of justice different from politically liberal forms, and, like Amartya Sen, she is highly committed to the process by which decisions are made. The consequence is that Young's understanding of power shifts away from the rhetoric of distribution. People often talk about power as if it is a thing that a person or group has or lacks. However, she insightfully suggests that power is better understood as a relation.[75] By focusing on the *process* by which decisions are made, she highlights how who participates and who decides constitute the dynamics of power in those relationships.

Young identifies the problems of injustice not primarily within the framework of rights and the distribution of goods. Instead, domination and oppression are the lenses through which she thinks about injustice, where the former restricts self-determination and the latter restricts self-development.[76] Oppression itself

Not distribut
But
oppression

aspects of oppression

consists of five distinct aspects: exploitation, marginalization, powerlessness, cultural imperialism, and violence.[77] Rather than using a pluralization of labels of oppressions that are each isolated and separate entities, (such as sexism, classism, racism, etc.), she believes that applying her "five criteria to the situation of groups makes it possible to compare oppressions without reducing them to a common essence or claiming that one is more fundamental than another."[78]

Not every form of oppression exhibits all five categories. Persons may be powerless in the sense of having no say in working conditions, and face exploitation in the sense of having their work benefit another, and yet not be economically marginalized since they have steady employment. On the other hand, a woman of color living on an American Indian reservation may be marginalized from most economic activity (which is all too often equated with one's value), experience cultural imperialism from a society that measures her against a white middle-class male norm, and face violence from both a domestic partner as well as the police. As there are manifold instantiations within the logic of oppression, it is not feasible for particular expressions of churching to witness against all globalizing forms simultaneously. These dynamics of domination and oppression, and attempts at making sacred their justification, is the broadest definition of the spirit of Empire as I understand it.

It's worth noting that Young expresses a form of postmodern thought not influenced in any direct way by Alfred North Whitehead. However, her postmodern feminist perspective presents an alternative orientation that is not cosmological but nevertheless exhibits this interrelated pattern of difference.[79] Her project is assisted by a postmodern critique of the logic of identity via such theorists as Adorno, Derrida, and Irigaray.[80] Still, Young articulates a politics of relationship and differentiation, and in doing so, she fits well with the cosmology and social ontology that I have been using from Whitehead and Keller. Indeed, for Young, all normativizing theories of justice require a social ontology.[81]

Young and Whitehead mutually correct each other. There are cosmological themes that Young either misses or was not interested in where Whitehead has helped us. Likewise, Young helps us with aspects that Whitehead deemphasized, such as how the conditions of domination and oppression are expressed in a world of interrelated difference. Whitehead's dipolar position that articulates how the material and the mental are poles within entities resonates with her claim that "an ideal can inspire action for social change only if it arises from possibilities suggested by actual experience."[82] If one focuses exclusively on humans and their relationships of power, Young would be sufficient without the use of Whitehead. However, as we have seen, he makes key contributions in terms of the broader planetary and cosmological contextual framings, which we ignore at our own peril. The constructive position I am espousing, which demands variety and multiplicity, is in sync with her desire for the representation of distinct perspectives and experiences, particularly of groups that have otherwise been marginalized.[83]

Concerning politics, Young believes that political discussion needs to happen at more than one location and more than one time. There is not one arena or public sphere but multiple overlapping spheres where people gather and discuss what concerns, ideas, and hopes they have for their society. This is one of the legitimate values she sees in identity politics. People can gather outside of the dominant context in order to have their own discourses and planning outside of the rules of dominant settings. An example would be special affinity groups, such as chapters of Black Lives Matter. This does not mean that different public spheres are free from intercommunication. Indeed these overlapping spheres must communicate, but not everyone needs to be in the same conversation at the same time. This type of residential and civil clustering is what she means by "differentiated solidarity."[84] My usage of the term in Chapter 3 obviously differs from hers.

Young provides a persuasive challenge to liberal political concepts that cut out impacted voices from decision-making and offer alternative ways of giving voice in society. She does this in part by addressing internal exclusions that block people from full political participation. For example, a person or community may be formally included in discussions, but their claims or concerns are not taken seriously because of the cultural mode in which speakers present them. They may be taken as naïve, overly emotional, or simple. Rules of debate or presentation are often shaped by the dominant cultural assumptions, which in the United States are typically the presentation styles of white men. This means being dispassionate, logical, and offering step-by-step arguments from premises that the dominant group agrees to. If someone does not present this way, they are functionally excluded. As Young recognizes, being eloquent should be considered a political virtue to aspire for, but it should not be a condition to be able to speak at all. Partially motivating her advocacy of differentiated solidarity is her commitment to providing multiple avenues for people to communicate with one another.[85]

Young makes several useful suggestions to remedy instances of internal exclusion and other problems of deliberative democracy theory (which also benefits counter-imperial churching!). She suggests the steps of greeting, rhetoric, and narrative. Greeting encourages people to gather together informally before political decisions begin, share food, and introduce oneself and where one comes from. Rhetoric affirms that passion goes along with arguments and reasons. Anger can have a role especially when social injustices are severe. These activities can include unfurling banners, interrupting parliamentary procedures, shaming those who dismiss certain voices, organizing public rallies and demonstrations, and acting in guerilla theater.[86] Some of these latter examples require formal access to indoor as well as outdoor spaces.[87] Lastly, narrative or *testimonio* involves the sharing of stories from particular experiences and allows for people to hear the location from which people will be speaking.

Dominant groups frequently have biased assumptions about issues of oppression impacting other communities. Sharing stories of what has happened in one's neighborhood or family may help dismantle some of the ignorance of those listening. Young bristles at the ideal of politically liberal democratic participation and debate as essentially "polite, orderly, dispassionate, gentlemanly argument."[88] Especially when there is a structurally marginalized group whose interests are ignored in public debates, disorderliness and anger can be important methods of expression as a form of agonistic pluralism.[89]

As mentioned with regards to Rawls, churches tend to fear conflict, for it implies disunity and chaos. Therefore, most congregations are uncomfortable with its expression and seek to curtail it. However, conflict *can* be productive. The political theorist Bonnie Honig offers us a complementary perspective alongside Young on the idea of an agonistic pluralism, where agonistic means being passionate. When churches normally imagine conflict, they think in terms of antagonism, which is not the same thing. In antagonistic conflict, differences are seen as natural, perpetual, and binary exclusions, but agonistic conflict works through differences productively. Rather than seeing differences of perspective as permanent boundary markers, they are reflective of different perspectives or locations. Disturbing dominant and uncritical perspectives through offering differences of opinion are frequently necessary for the emergence of new ideas and practices.

Honig sees social movements (of which religious communities are to be part) as a form of agonistic cosmopolitanism. Rather than having to justify alliances with particular groups in a universalistic context, movements can partner with those who are *close* to them.[90] The proximity of new neighbors, not necessarily in terms of spatial nearness but relational internalization, acts as an opportunity for forms of solidarity that do not need to be justified in terms of their place in the universal. Because there is a relevant relationship, there is an opportunity of working together. This offers distinct advantages over what she calls a normative cosmopolitanism, which struggles to explain the particularity of group difference that stands in tension with its universalism. For Honig, groups can work with others precisely *because* they have particular relationships.[91] She also wisely offers space for political action that is not merely targeted at state laws but also at non-state social actors.[92]

Using Honig's notion of "agonistic cosmopolitanism," the outward life of churching can understand a key part of what it does in a new way. It is to participate in movement politics rather than seeing the political as solely focused on voting or advocating for the passage of laws, although these remain necessary features. In participating in the upbuilding of social movements, churching engages in the construction of how the world can be different. Churches can use this notion in their mission partnerships: "Why partner with Christians in Palestine and not Peru?" can be answered because churches will have ongoing relationships with some communities in one location and not in another. In this way, practitioners of churching can express a cosmopolitanism that does not have to explain away particularity. As we have seen with Hardt and Negri's multitude, agonistic cosmopolitanism is not a transcendent universalism but an immanent universalism that grows out of the productive relationships between distinct communities.

One of Iris Marion Young's strengths for my project is that she offers applicable insights and critiques to some of this chapter's previous thinkers. For example, she offers another way to interpret Amartya Sen's impartial spectator. At first, it would appear that Sen and she are mutually incompatible. She does not like universality as impartiality, but this comes primarily out of her concern that one subject will declare itself the impartial decider.[93] Though she is critical of the term "impartial," she has a different definition from that of Sen. Her problem with the idea of impartiality is that it has "no particular desires or interests in view."[94] She basically equates it with neutrality. The result is that she actually supports the content of Sen's intentions even if she would quite rightly prefer another word. She continues, "But there is another way the subject moves beyond egoism: the encounter with other people."[95] But is this not *precisely*

what Sen has in mind when he discusses the impartial spectator: allow the perspectives of others to shape and reform our own solidifications so that they loosen up and become something new? Both Sen and Young reflect a radical perspectivalism of particular loci of truth-knowledge that declares that groups need each other but can never be subsumed into one ultimate and final perspective (nor, might we say, can a planetary gospel).

Concerning representation, Young believes that there needs to be space for both direct democracy as well as forms of representation. Formal representation should not be of opinions or interests, nor should people think that representatives speak on behalf of an identity or should have a perfect correspondence to the identity they supposedly represent. Instead, what representatives should represent are social perspectives. Not every opinion or interest is legitimate, but every social perspective is legitimate.[96] We should never object to someone's experience or angle from which they observe events. Having multiple sites of representation and modes of diverse social perspectives is absolutely essential to diminish the risk of one voice pretending to speak for everyone.

For Young, participatory democracy is great for maximizing self-determination, but participation alone may not help with self-development. The latter is the ability to thrive, to have certain opportunities made available to oneself. Political self-determination alone cannot guarantee this goal, and so there is a limit to solely participatory democracy.[97] The theme of self-development aligns with Sen's capabilities approach, since her understanding of social justice includes having governments encourage equal opportunity for the development of what she calls "capacities."[98]

Young helps articulate another weakness of Hardt and Negri: their consistent disregard for any positive role for representation. For them, representation in its myriad forms is the transcendentalization of the immanently productive biopolitical. As noted earlier, they see representation as something that Empire does: it is a transcendent activity while they alternatively desire a politics of pure immanence.[99]

However, Young provides strong reasons for forms of representation that occur in multiple and overlapping locations.[100] With her, I do not see a path to a functioning purely direct democracy. Even in groups of fifty, not everyone speaks for an equal amount of time; certain people dominate conversations. This is representation by ego. The social production of the multitude produces society and can lead to expressions of self-determination, but these do not guarantee that there are equal opportunities of self-cultivation, or that resources are distributed in ways beyond those whom produce them. There need to be some forms of representation to address these issues of capabilities and resource distribution. Empire may be a form of transcendent extraction, but I remain convinced that there are ways to represent people in an equitable fashion.[101] This way, the multitude is able to participate both through its production in a direct immanent democracy as well as be represented through a differentiated representation of the multitude's social perspectives. Hardt and Negri overemphasize the role of direct democracy through their pure immanent communism, even as they rightly challenge the unjust extraction of Empire. Young's interpretation of the complex workings of oppression adds to our understanding of Empire's spirit to control all life as well.

Beyond offering a better approach to conflict, how does Young shape churching? Particularly, she offers a style of communication through difference of diverse social groups. While she presents a more formal process of deliberation, it is also a way for groups with different cultural experiences and expectations to be able to listen deeply to each other's stories and struggles. The form of churching I am advocating requires this type of listening so as to help initiate transformed outlooks for those who come from dominant social locations. Beyond her cosmological limitations, her weakness is that she lacks sufficient appreciation for the potential engagement of faith communities in their societies through radical praxis, much less that such praxis can embody faithful living.

IMPLICATIONS OF POLITICAL THEOLOGY

MENNONITE MISSIONARIES train white congregations in anti-racism awareness. Neighboring Lakota communities are seeking church partners to help resist the expansion of biker bars being built on sacred burial grounds. . . . A small group ministry brings supplies and listens in on an "Occupy" assembly gathering at an encampment in downtown Los Angeles. Building another world means building the multitude . . . Activists, farmers, and First Nation peoples protest the prospects of a tar sands pipeline and the threat of more carbon dioxide in the atmosphere. The planetary commons are not for narrow economic appropriation . . . A church sends volunteers in response to requests for tutors at a nearby elementary school of children of immigrants. The faith community deepens its ties to a population on the other side of the freeway. All children deserve the option to choose a better quality of life . . . A denomination decides to divest from businesses that profit from the suffering of Palestinians in the Occupied Territories. Resisting Empire in whatever form it takes and loving one's persecuted neighbor trumps an extra 0.5% annual retirement yield any day . . . CODEPINK activists interrupt a president's speech when he avoids addressing issues of injustice and suffering. Many others, including myself, rally for the release of prisoners, fasting and demonstrating on behalf of Guantanamo detainees whose imprisonment is a sacrifice made out of an idolatrous desire for perfect security. The multitude lives its service.

Those working within the frame of political theology have noted that we are entering a postsecular era in the West. Many scholars expected that secularity would expand as time passed, but, like Sigmund Freud's "return of the repressed," the religious has returned with a vengeance, especially within what is traditionally separated as the "political." I have not argued what the proper role of the church is in its society, politically speaking, because this assumes that there is a clear division between the fields of religion and politics. In recent decades, political theologians have been at work showing how this division is a false construction from modernity and have been deconstructing this separation, in part to explain the resurgence of religious practice as a postsecular development. This project stands within that line.

In his political theology, Jeffrey Robbins combines death-of-God radical theology with the radical democratic theory of Hardt and Negri. Robbins misreads the option for a radical process political theology by claiming that it is either radical theologically and conservative politically, or radical politically and conservative theologically.[102] I believe this book demonstrates that such a project is indeed possible. Democracy means the potential capacity of participation in decisions, not liberty or independence, and thus "democracy is rightly feared by those who have the most to lose."[103] He challenges process theology as a viable model for political theology on two accounts: its adherence to "Whiteheadian dogma" and its "Christian confessional framework."[104] While Robbins primarily critiques process and liberationist thought, Clayton Crockett's radical political theology finds a more positive stream present within both, especially in Catherine Keller's process trajectory.[105] According to Crockett's reading, the term "'potentiality' is a good contemporary postmodern name for freedom."[106] In fact, this potentiality-freedom is experienced as divinity after the death of God.[107] He follows Hardt and Negri in analyzing the multitude, and like them also problematically avoids any language of transcendence.

Besides being a theory of political philosophers, political theology is also a name for the proto-liberation theologies in Europe during the 1960s, which often challenged political regimes' idolatrous claims and acts.[108] More recently, it has been noted that the very definition of religion is unavoidably a political act, dividing the properly "political" from the "religious." The way this is done is through identifying the religious with the private, individual, spiritual side of life against the public, collective side of life. Protestantism remains the hegemonic religious model in the United States even as its numbers have waned. This means that faith communities wanting to be recognized as a legitimate religion are pressured to separate out the more political and social elements of their traditions from the more so-called religious elements. They have to become and look like denominations. This process is not my focus, but it means that Protestantism is the primary culprit in this bifurcation. It is the model that groups such as American Muslims or indigenous traditions are pressured to emulate, but what if mainline Protestants themselves got it wrong in the first place?

Living out the diakonia of counter-imperial churching requires being able to say boldly who you are and show how you are confronting the systems that ignore people's value. Otherwise, you are functionally irrelevant, both to your context in American society and to the planetary gospel that needs proclaiming in your setting. To arrive at this point, existing congregations will need this process of radicalization to include disentangling themselves from political liberalism of the Rawlsian variety, identifying the theological character of the American state, and offering a subversive (and many will say an unreasonable) counter-witness to the extent that their state and society project loyalties to globalizing Empire's *ethos* that dehumanizes and devalues others. Resisting the spirit of Empire and enhancing capabilities makes much of this diakonia counter-cultural, but it is out of a loving commitment to our planet and those that dwell on it that we take such a radical stance. The return of political theology indicates that there can be no clear division between the secular and the religious, as they are co-constituted in their very constructions. The next chapter brings us to theology proper, even as its primary thinkers deconstruct this separating barrier through their own particular politically oriented ecclesiologies.

CHAPTER 5

Prehending Missional, Processual, and Indecent Ecclesiologies

> [We are] not concerned with the survival of the church as institution, but rather with its de-institutionalization. From this perspective, church and theology may be working not to support each other but to undermine each other in order to make space for a second coming of different forms of working together, challenging systems not from within the system but from its margins, and remaining there. ~Marcella Althaus-Reid, *From Feminist Theology to Indecent Theology*

THE PREVIOUS THREE CHAPTERS have developed a counter-imperial churching's *kerygma*, *koinonia*, and *diakonia*, respectively. The concluding chapter will synthesize these elements and expand on what this actually might look like. Yet the vast majority of the thinkers and theologians I've examined thus far were not talking about churches but rather worldviews, values, and social movements. This penultimate chapter dives into church itself from the perspective of three brilliant theologians: Jürgen Moltmann, Marjorie Hewitt Suchocki, and Marcella Althaus-Reid, while also utilizing insights from the related positions of John Howard Yoder and John B. Cobb, Jr. While I will affirm much that Moltmann and Suchocki have to say *in the abstract*, Althaus-Reid is my primary ally in providing a radical critique to both of their decent, systematic approaches to theological reflection. I close this chapter by addressing ecclesial marks. Rather than affirm the classical marks through reinterpretation (one, holy, catholic, and apostolic), or inverting them (as many, secular, particular, and novel), I offer something different. I argue churching's ecclesial marks are best understood as a creatively interrelated contrast in such a way that neither set overwhelms nor becomes the final norm for the other.

JÜRGEN MOLTMANN'S MISSIONAL ECCLESIOLOGY

German theologian Jürgen Moltmann's ecclesiology is one of the most influential, liberative constructions of the 20th century, shaping much that follows him. Simply put, he casts an immense shadow. For all the significant flaws I will highlight, his thought around the coming kingdom of God and the church as engaging in God's mission for that world in particular will be key elements I will use going forward. His major work on ecclesiology comes from the 1970s, entitled *The Church in the Power of the Spirit*, in which he envisions major changes to ecclesiological structures and highlights practical changes for actual congregations. In a preface written fifteen years later, Moltmann explains how his purpose was to encourage moves away from large organizations to small-scale communities. In so doing, there would be a shift from church as "religious institution" that cares for people into more of a real community in, through, and with people.[1] Moltmann relies on three broad themes in his rethinking of church: Jesus Christ as Lord, the coming kingdom of God, and the social Trinity.

The first two traditional themes, Christ and the kingdom, are held in a dialectical continuity of past and future. In Moltmann's grand scheme, the church has a two-fold function. It acts "as witness to the promises of God, embodied in Christ's life, death, and resurrection, and in the expectation of the kingdom."[2] Scott Paeth identifies this dialectical relationship between social transformation and critique in the themes of resurrection and the cross.[3] J. Stephen Rhodes likewise affirms the dialectic, explaining that the church endures by "*remembering* what God has done and *hoping* for what God will do."[4] Whether this metanarrative works beyond the abstract remains to be seen.

Moltmann makes Christ central: "Christ is his church's foundation, its power and its hope."[5] Said in its simplest terms, "Without Christ, no church."[6] Even though Moltmann believes Jesus is its foundation, he does not believe Jesus intentionally founded the institutional church.[7] Rather, the witness of Jesus's whole life and the recognition of him as the Messiah constituted the earliest Christian faith, and only in this way did he found the church.[8] While Christ is the foundation, doctrinally, ecclesiology orients itself toward eschatology, specifically the coming kingdom of God.[9] The promise of the coming kingdom gives the church its initiative. The kingdom of God is the future for which the church works, and the church does not control this promise that God has offered. At its best, the church is "an *anticipatory sign* of the definitive reign of God."[10] Decades later, Moltmann still maintains this orientation, saying that the end of cultural Christendom provides the opportunity for the church to be reborn "as an independent and resisting community, a community with a universal mission and an all-embracing hope for the kingdom of God as the future of the world."[11]

Moltmann is driven by the idea that the church does not have a mission; God's mission has a church.[12] In broad strokes, the Holy Spirit provides the internal energy to the church, Christ goes before the church as it looks to the future, and God's mission directs it. Helpfully, the role of the church is relativized in that the kingdom, rather than the church, is to be spread throughout the world.[13] I fully agree with his claim that the church does not exist for itself, nor is it called to paternalistically look after people. Rather, it is to be in the midst of people, existing in solidarity especially with the oppressed, who are themselves "*co-subjects*" in the kingdom of God."[14] Readers

will note the latter observation's significant resonance with the koinonia from Chapter 3.

For Moltmann, the church can be like leaven in bread, producing
discord in its location and acting as the leading edge, the vanguard
of its society, towards God's promised future of justice and equality.[15]
The church cannot see itself as standing above the world,[16] but must
instead understand its relationships with groups, movements, and
organizations. It can be involved in revolutionary efforts while challenging all partial political orders that deny that universal lordship of
Jesus Christ and seeking the salvation of all spheres of life. Essentially,
the church has a destabilizing mission against the status quo for both
its members and society in light of its eschatological hope.[17]

I have suggested that churching needs to become more akin
to a spiritual social movement, but here Moltmann diverges from
that claim. He quite explicitly argues that Christian identity must
not become identical "with particular social movements."[18] As the
church is involved in this movement of history, it also self-transcends
the current moment as the Spirit leads it towards the ultimate future
goal of the kingdom. However, as I understand the planetary gospel,
it may express its language more emphatically through specific social
movements, but recognize that any one movement does not exhaust
the relational potential of the good news found in other proclamations of value and resistance. Throughout this chapter, expect to find
a pattern where Moltmann too quickly reasserts a universal unity at
the expense of particular expressions of the good news.

Another immediate example of this pattern is Moltmann's use
of the image of the trinitarian *perichoresis* as foundational to the
church's normative organization as an open community of equals.
This expresses the internal relationships of the Father, Son, and Spirit
as equals. As is the Trinity, so is the church a fellowship of equals.
Just as God opens the divine life to the world, so the church opens its
life to the world. Nevertheless, Paeth notes that it is critical to make
this analogy between church life and divine life only provisional
because of the uncertainty of the immanent nature of God.[19]

I have suggested in Chapters 2 and 3 that the relational nature of the church and humans exists through the perichoresis of the entire cosmos rather than through the divine perichoresis as foundation.[20] While we practically end up in a similar place—the inherent social quality of church koinonia and living—Moltmann's use of the immanent life of the divine as an ecclesial model reflects his more orthodox bearings. He starts with the internal interdwelling of the three divine persons before applying that relationship to creation. Specifically, the Spirit of Christ in the church corresponds to the Spirit of Life active throughout creation: "If Christ is not perceived in all the things of nature as the Wisdom of creation," affirms Moltmann, "then he is not rightly perceived in the church either."[21] While God's relationship starts in Godself, this presence expands to all creation equally. We disagree about where this incarnational stance begins: either with a divine foundation, or in the very quality of existence, divine or otherwise. Many of the differences between us rest in his foundational approach that prefers theological abstractions over the actual world.

As a messianic fellowship, Moltmann believes the church is dependent on its relationship with Christ and being involved in Christ's mission toward the kingdom of God.[22] This *missio dei* is the church's origin but extends to all of creation.[23] The salvation to which Moltmann's political church acts as a witness encompasses life to its full extent, including faith, politics, and economic life. Said another way, the undivided lordship of Christ demands that we avoid separating theological and political-social understandings of church.[24] In its proclamation and service, remembering Christ crucified enables the church to deny the national and economic values that become destructive idols. When it does so, it acts "atheistically" to the religion of political oppression among nations.[25] In line with my concept of churching, he observes that institutional church configurations that are too closely tied with oppressive power may seek to deny the legitimacy of such radical discipleship as church at all. True church fellowship as open friendship exists only through the removal of privileges, and is not done "for its own sake but only 'for others.'"[26] His discussion of privilege and the affirmation of solidarity with the oppressed, while helpful, minimizes the reality of mutual interest articulated in Chapter 3. Once again, the uncritical use of terms such as "Christ's lordship" reminds us of Moltmann's adherence to traditional theological terminology.

Yet there is much that resonates with the position I am presenting. Moltmann's kerygma parallels my understanding of the good news as affirming planetary value. Van Nam Kim sees that "for Moltmann, the Church's mission ultimately is the affirmation of life, through the practice of liberation for human beings and the rest of creatures, including nature."[27] Of course, Moltmann interprets themes of being part of God's creation through the foundationally normative prism of Christ and kingdom. Unlike a planetary gospel that grows out of its roots and connects beyond its origins, Moltmann understands the gospel as first a universal message that is then applied to different contexts. For him, proclaiming this gospel of the history of Christ and freedom for the coming kingdom is accomplished in many ways: preaching, group conversations, teaching, the celebration of sacraments, and comforting one another, to name but a few.[28] Chapter 6 will highlight a few of the complementary ways that Moltmann supports what proclamation looks like in churching minus his universalizing history.

Though Moltmann's substance-inflected position is especially frustrating as he addresses his understanding of the church's inherent nature, he again offers some practical relief: neither the activities of proclamation nor service are reserved for ordained persons. He rightly lambasts the inadequate preparation congregants receive in proclaiming the good news:

> The fact that the congregations who listen to sermons with us are hardly enabled to give any personal testimony also paralyses personal Christian life, and the development of personal conviction. Many people are quite satisfied to belong to the church, to go to church occasionally, and to agree by and

[handwritten margin note: one is general to specific; other is specific to general]

large with the church's doctrine, even if they do not know much about it, and it does not mean very much to them.[29]

"Holistic diakonia," writes Moltmann, "is healing action directed toward all of the unhealthy distortions and estrangements of human existence, whether in personal, social, or religious life."[30] Could perhaps a friendly Moltmannian position link the network of colonizing Empire with his remark on unhealthy distortions? If his idea of diakonia was restricted to the work of resisting social and political evil, and accepting that there will be counter-resistance as a consequence, Moltmann and I would be largely in agreement, but he needlessly goes further. For him, diakonia essentially means "to participate in suffering, to accept suffering, and to take on the suffering of others."[31] This is absolutely infuriating to read. This faulty emphasis claims that suffering is not merely fortuitous but essential to the church. In effect, he is asking the church to celebrate its suffering as what it means to be church. With this logic, if the church is not suffering, then it must not be the church! Moltmann forgets that abuse, exploitation, and marginalization are things to *lament* as evil, rather than being essential signs of faithfulness. It is more accurate to say that while divesting from one's privilege, affirming the value of yourself—others—and the world, and speaking truth to power is the calling of counter-imperial churching, any suffering that persons experience in light of this stance is contingent, even if it is unavoidable for those living under the conditions of Empire and especially when they resist Empire and its unholy spirit. Unavoidable suffering *does not equal* necessary suffering.

Beyond the problem of his abstract theological language, there are other weaknesses to Moltmann's ecclesiology. While Tony Jones, an Emergent Church ecclesiologist, largely recommends Moltmann's ecclesiology for the Emergent Church Movement, he claims that it is too idealistic because of Moltmann's "anthropological naiveté." This is expressed in his obliviously uncritical affirmation of new Christian charismatic movements. For example, while many charismatic communities exemplify a concern for the Spirit, they run the risk of fostering unaccountable structures and abuse among their leadership.[32] Additionally, Moltmann ignores the decline of the base community model of church in Latin America, even as Pentecostal movements that affirm a prosperity gospel have increased. This latter phenomenon directly contradicts his commitment to the poor, since they often exhibit authoritarian leadership tendencies, which circumvents his desire for a more democratic church participation.[33] The Moltmannian scholar Geiko Müller-Fahrenholz adds that "a renewal of the community from below [has] largely been rejected by the established parish communities."[34] This alone likely reflects institutional power structures within the Catholic Church suppressing alternatives since the 1980s, but the fact that Moltmann does not name and critique this phenomenon indicates that he is more interested in cherry-picking examples that fit his idealistic model than starting with the lived experience of radical discipleship communities and building his ecclesiology from the ground up.

Moltmann thinks of the church as an eschatological vanguard that prefigures the coming kingdom of God. This is only half-right: I believe that churching reflects a participatory or ethical eschatology. I am here following New Testament scholars Marcus Borg and John Dominic Crossan's understanding of the message of Jesus of Nazareth.[35] Humans cooperate with divine aims for the world, thus participating in their own divinization. Moltmann understandably does not want to say this consummation takes place through evolutionary development, as if the kingdom of God is the peak or apex of the process. Accordingly, "this future does not *de*velop out of the potential of the past, but *ad*vances towards the present—that is to say, it cannot be perceived with the category of evolution, but only with the category of the new."[36] However, he rejects that our world contributes to that coming reality at all, even though our actions participate in Christ's messianic mission towards that reality.[37] For him, God's redemption and the kingdom come from the absolute future of God. However, I believe it is better to say that our participation contextualizes and informs that coming future potentiality.

What is done in this world sets the condition for the relevant possibilities to which the world can become even as the divine lures it towards its truest (i.e., most intense and harmonious) self.

Another clear limitation with Moltmann for my project is that his focus on Europe's official church model is less directly applicable to a North American context. As Jones recognizes, Moltmann does not address the United States' implicit Christendom approach as Hauerwasians do, though the latter's atemporal church, unaffected vis-à-vis the secular world, is no solution either.[38] Paeth likewise criticizes Moltmann for focusing too heavily on a European church-state model and for thus having an inadequate analysis of how civil society impacts Christian public life. Paeth goes on to suggest that church can influence civil society for social change to occur, even though it risks becoming a civil religion if it is too sociologically oriented.[39] I believe church can avoid devolving into a form of civil religion to the extent that it maintains a friendly critique of social movements, perpetually challenges its dominant culture's assumptions, and expands its sphere of concern to other societies and to the planet itself. In effect, Moltmann's analysis would be improved by incorporating Bonnie Honig's insights from Chapter 4: political life responds not just to the state but also works with social movements for a culture's transformation.

Moltmann is a frustrating theologian to read: for pages on end there is so much to affirm, but then one finds residual dogmatic claims of the Christian tradition clogging up the works and theological abstractions that are divorced from lived experience of the planetary gospel. He is a brilliantly creative theologian, but churching does not need his systematic tone nor answers. *Ha!*

MARJORIE HEWITT SUCHOCKI'S INSTITUTIONAL PROCESS ECCLESIOLOGY

Marjorie Hewitt Suchocki is the leading process feminist theologian who has engaged with ecclesiological questions and church life.[40] In her passion for the church, many of Suchocki's books have a practical angle, such as how to pray or preach from a process perspective. As a fellow process theologian, I examine her analyses of kerygma, koinonia, and diakonia, and look particularly at her compelling understanding of institutions. While she is an innovative Whiteheadian theologian and creatively incorporates feminist thought in her work, her fundamental weakness is her inability to break free from a classical systematic theological format that first grounds the church in the nature of God and the life and work of Jesus Christ. Readers by now should recognize this structure to be a significant methodological difference from my project.

Not unlike Moltmann, Suchocki looks for an essence to the church that extends beyond contemporary settings and connects with its foundation in Jesus Christ and points also into the future. For her, ecclesiology appropriates christology, while it is also directed towards the future from God's actual harmony to the world's possible harmony.[41] Jesus's ministry of healing transformed people in his time, and the church is to do likewise in its time. This means "the church is called to witness by its life and words to a social mode of communal well-being," so politically, the church "can also be a counterforce in the wider society" to the extent that well-being is denied or undermined.[42] The sacraments of baptism and the Lord's Supper proclaim Christ and simultaneously create community, in such a way that the church "becomes once again *the anticipatory sign of God's reign* in the midst of history [emphasis added]."[43] Clearly, Suchocki's ecclesiology also appropriates eschatology.

Suchocki holds kerygma, koinonia, and diakonia together when she writes, "[T]he church is a society embodying and calling for an openness to life and mutually assured well-being, not destruction."[44] Resurrection affirms that new life is possible, that transformation can occur, and the church is called to proclaim that reality and invite its larger society into such transformation, as well. The church proclaims the gospel of the reign of God even as it is expressed in cultural and relational terms rather than propositional ones.[45]

Kerygmatically, while Suchocki recognizes that the value of entities is a critical aspect of the church's proclamation, she wisely cautions that it is impossible to make value judgments outside of one's perspective. Making decisions on the gradations of value is inevitable, and humans will only recognize a small piece of those values "into our active care and concern." The experience of universal well-being is a limit concept in terms of our perspectival appropriation. Nevertheless, she, not surprisingly, believes it is critical that we continue to insist that this value acts as a check against the all-too-easy tendency of individuals and institutions to draw the circle of concern more narrowly than what our interrelatedness warrants.[46]

Koinonia for Suchocki emphasizes the consistency between what is proclaimed and how the church lives: "In order to be true witnesses to God's fullness of action for us in Christ, we too must be living words; embodied proclamations, living in community that which we proclaim."[47] However, the church's fellowship is not itself the reign of God but only its anticipation and the way in which it is proclaimed. Declaring that it is the norm that judges all other societal arrangements and proclaiming it as a model of perfection risks the idolatrization of the church itself. Therefore, diversity and multiple cultural perspectives relativize any particular configuration of the church as does the norming reign of God.[48]

Suchocki helpfully connects the Whiteheadian relationship of the one and the many with the individual and community for the church. Individuals contribute to their community but also presuppose that very community, thus making Christianity a communal religion. Individuals respond to the gospel and the possibilities offered to them by God, but focusing only on individual responses would be a distortion. This is because the congregation's proclamation sets the conditions for the individual to respond. Ultimately, church becomes for her that community among whom faith has spaced their identities.[49] Unlike those who argue for church as a simple voluntary association of individuals, here the community gets *inside* the individuals.

As part of a larger discussion on original sin, Suchocki delves into the transmission of solidarity and the nature of institutions, which is one of her major process-feminist contributions for my understanding of koinonia. Like other feminist theologians, she notes that sin is not rebellion against God via pride. Rather, for Suchocki, it is rebellion against creation through violence. In particular, sin can pass institutionally and from generation to generation, which has significant ecclesial implications.[50] While institutions have many problems, she does not advocate for their total dissolution. They can still be systemic forces for good and expressions of the gospel, especially through institutional coalitions.[51]

Suchocki offers a very powerful process-relational analysis—which I affirm—of institutions. The preservation of any institution, including the church, enables a form of social inheritance of the privileges and sins of past generations, with the result that these forms transmit institutional sin generationally. In addition to the past sociological analyses of Walter Rauschenbusch and Reinhold Niebuhr on the effect of institutional evil on individuals, she believes that process-relational thinking can help explain certain ontological structures and their effects on individuals. The possibility of transcendence in institutions does not rely on a single unified conscience with a single body, which would make communal self-transcendence of past evil impossible, but rather relies on institutional intersubjectivity.[52]

Unlike those who idealize participation as the key to just institutions, Suchocki maintains that there are limits to participation in intersubjective relations. Only in very small groups can this be expressed through consensus and conversation. However, as groups become larger, their organizational structure becomes necessarily more complex. Thus, she leaves some space for structural hierarchies (or we might add, representation). The mission and purpose of the institution gets inside participants, even as their concerns and priorities shape institutional life. This may or may not be conscious within each individual such that institutional values are refracted between participants, strengthening their endurance. This creates a "corporate consciousness" that may ignore a person's subjectivity even though it presupposes subjectivity's ongoing activity. The real risk hierarchy poses is that it becomes easier for particular persons to hide their lack of taking responsibility and self-transcendence within a larger institution, which they may articulate in ways that seem to defend the institution.[53] Unlike Niebuhr's conclusion of the impossibility of institutional transcendence, Suchocki convincingly affirms that it is indeed possible. In fact, it is a person's responsibility to self-transcend the institutional limitations of such structures to the extent that they do evil.

Since we are "individuals-in-community," we cannot avoid having larger structures of some form or other in church koinonia. Indeed, just as organized Christian fellowship may continue patterns of violence and sin, "they are also heirs to the possibility for institutional transcendence and transformation. Communities and institutions can be far more effective against the problems of social sin, outgrowths of original sin, than can any individual acting alone."[54] Minimizing cumbersome structures is a way Suchocki rightly recognizes that we leave fewer spaces for people to avoid taking responsibility for self-transcendence, but we should still have enough structures that groups can productively cooperate with each other and hold themselves covenantally accountable. Finding ways to critique past institutional failings to which persons belong acts as a sign of hope for the larger world's structures. Church fellowship is to embody Christ, "to be love and justice, to be openness and mutuality," and to grow in these qualities.[55]

According to Suchocki, the church's diakonia promotes "inclusive well-being" and addresses the challenges of "the marginalized."[56] It does this by challenging the structures that promote ill-being in its culture, and especially in resolving its internal oppressive structures, i.e., transforming its koinonia fellowship. Friendship remains a key element in her understanding of the church's service, extending such friendship throughout the world as God has called us. To that end, she believes that it remains essential to continue sending people to

other lands and making global friendships for the purpose of valuing each other's well-being.[57] Suchocki understands this within a
religiously pluralistic context of mutual respect; friendship should
exist between followers of Christ and other religious pathways, and
this friendship she sees as a high priority.

It is especially in terms of diakonia that we begin to see one of the
primary flaws in Suchocki's ecclesiology. The problem is not with the
basic contours of her intent but in her lack of specificity. While she
offers a largely insightful process ecclesiology, especially in terms of
institutional life, my engagement with alternative political theories is
more critically explicit of this political layer and also more aggressively
seeks to reconstruct practices of churching for our time than does
her approach. The closest Suchocki comes to addressing this political
diakonia is by encouraging self-critiques within a society to the extent
to which it expresses ill-being. Yet what is this ill-being? Who are
marginalized and what does marginalization mean? Answers to these
questions are left underdeveloped as she views them as accidental or
contextual to the larger concerns of systematic ecclesiology.

Stated even more critically, while Suchocki argues for the radical openness and relativity of the church in light of God's reign,
she does not analyze the current context in which the church finds
itself in order to argue for specific alterations in its formation. Like
Moltmann, there is little planetary ground from which proclamation
and service spring. By trying to be applicable to many contexts, she
ends up lacking concreteness to any context. The closest she comes to
providing clear claims is in asking for humility of Western churches
in thinking that they are the true church in light of recent church
growth in Africa and Asia. Likewise, she is keen to reflect on the
situation of religious pluralism, as it effects how the church should
interact with other traditions and its self-understanding in light of
the salvation it has experienced in Christ. I applaud these efforts. In
truth, there is much to appreciate about Suchocki's ecclesial work.
However, all the process-relational thought in the world will not
suffice if the results remain situationally abstract.

While Suchocki does recognize that all theology, including her own, is shaped by the context and culture from which it emerges, she does not discuss the material/economic conditions which shape the possibility of Christian theologizing at all. While it is true that she mentions insights of liberation theology, and frequently notes problems in the world, these problems are understood as issues to address. This is all the more surprising given the fact that she has a very nuanced understanding of institutional sin, including its perpetuation in the church. Ironically, she wants to maintain a process ecclesiological formulation that is as much in keeping with the tradition as possible, when in fact these very formulations are conditioned by the demonic structures she is so keen to point out!

While Suchocki encourages reforms within the church, I find resources within her that would push towards a more thoroughgoing transformation of church. Respecting tradition does not necessarily mean repeating past institutional configurations of church life. In her own words, "tradition is like the crest of a wave always pushing beyond itself. Faithfulness to a tradition is not gained through treading water in repetition of some aspect of the past, but through swimming with the crest into fresh interpretations of God's gracious presence with us."[58] This might mean that denominational configurations, which themselves have not been perpetual elements of church organization, may get in the way of new models of living out Christian faithfulness. Suchocki does not make this move, and she has been active in the United Methodist Church in hopes of its internal reform, but she does leave space for others to take this step. It is time more of us did just that.

"The Church" needs a radical reconstruction into churching *because of* this institutional heritage of sin and privilege. If we want to dismantle this heritage, we cannot simply remove unjust pieces without changing the institution or creating a new institution, in keeping with her analysis of institutions. Catherine Keller wisely recognizes that this leads to a major problem:

[To the extent] religious thinkers dwell on the 'cutting edge,' they lose their traditional constituencies—and *ipso facto*, ironically, the activist potential that distinguishes *progressive* theology. Inasmuch, however, as we honor the constitutive accountability of, say, Christian theology to the church, we cannot escape the dogmatic drag, the vortex of swirling symbols and insecure institutions. This double bind disorients even the most forward-looking theologies.[59]

It is no use avoiding this double bind, and yet it could become a potential gift. What we must not do is oppose these two trajectories against each other. Rather, we can and must form new ecclesiological coalitions. Suchocki is right that institutional formations are to some extent unavoidable, but that says nothing about constructing new institutions in light of new communities. We need to push further than Suchocki while retaining the immense ecclesial value she has produced.

MARCELLA ALTHAUS-REID'S INDECENT CHURCH

Marcella Althaus-Reid provides us with a much-needed contrast to our first two theologians. Here we do not find a politically liberatory yet European systematic ecclesiology á la Moltmann, nor do we find Suchocki's process-relational construction from an American perspective devoid of political stakes. Althaus-Reid breaks us out of these paradigms: she is a destroyer of systematic worlds. Political liberation alone is not enough; feminism and relational thinking are not enough; here she adds queer and postcolonial theories, a Latin American social location, poststructuralist philosophy, and the deconstruction of the theology industry itself, all the while retaining the insights of political liberation, feminism, and relationality. If nothing else, she is *radical*.

As she takes on the religiously hegemonic context of Catholic Argentina, Althaus-Reid unsurprisingly emphasizes ecclesial deconstruction: she finds much historically, socially, ideologically, and theologically to deconstruct as it relates to LGBTQ persons. Her queer theology, using theories that deconstruct gender, sexual dualisms, and their related socio-cultural bifurcations, rightfully shakes many readers' assumptions to their depths. After reading her critiques it would be understandable for many to declare that she has nothing positive to say about ecclesiology at all! Thus, few commentators have directly addressed what constructive ecclesial comments she actually makes.[60] Nevertheless, clues are unearthed when using the framing devices of kerygma, koinonia, and diakonia. This section unfolds both her criticisms and affirmations of ecclesiology, while the chapter's final section includes some of her most original conclusions that result in the utter subversion of traditional ecclesial marks.

The majority of Althaus-Reid's ecclesial and sexual analysis is directed at either the Roman Catholic Church or liberationist Basic Ecclesial Communities (referred to as BECs).[61] Latin American liberation ecclesiologies have emphasized base communities, which have been understood through a particular lens of being poor: the virtuous poor of rural villages rather than the sexually indecent urban poor of Buenos Aires.[62] For the BECs, what mattered was political and economic liberation, while other topics were distracting secondary concerns. While recognizing the amazing work they did in the 1970s and 80s, Althaus-Reid challenges this perspective, saying, "It is not true that poor women—if conscientised—only care about fighting for economic and political liberation."[63] The BECs soft-pedaled gender and sexuality issues when they could have challenged prevailing hierarchical models and the false dichotomy of being sexual versus being political.[64] Liberation theologians were able to affirm the village poor in a procession carrying "the Virgin Mary and demanding jobs," but they could not accept transvestite Christians carrying a transvestite Christ with "a Drag Queen Mary Magdalene kissing his wounds and singing songs of political criticism"—these were not included in the preferential option for the poor.[65] Some readers might find such imagery extreme or even offensive, but this is the beauty of Althaus-Reid's planetary concreteness: it is in such moments that one finds her *indecent ecclesiology.*

Religious studies scholar Alistar Kee observes that like other postmodern critiques of various liberation theologies' ontological essentialisms, Althaus-Reid challenged Latin American liberation theology for problematically essentializing the poor as part of a modernist project of emancipation. This is one reason why the poor were declared to be asexual, because they needed to be a solid ontological unity in order to act collectively. As the urban poor experienced significant changes to their lived experience via globalization, the BECs' unity-based model and use of dependence theory proved ineffective. As the experience of the poor diversified through globalized markets while, simultaneously, historical metanarratives were ending, base communities became impossible to sustain.[66]

These essentializing or homogenizing tendencies regularly happened not only within BECs but also in how such communities were interpreted by outside observers. When Western Christian leaders or theologians would visit, Althaus-Reid was regularly essentialized as a poor virtuous woman even though she was a university student working two jobs who had her own sexual needs. For a time when liberation theology was fashionable in the West, Europe saw base communities as a return to the primitive church ecclesiastical movement, together with the romantic construction of the native, poor, down-to-earth woman.[67] Westerners would visit for a short period and then take their new knowledge back with them for a new presentation or book. While Althaus-Reid never mentions Moltmann by name, he certainly falls under the critique of Western theologians who used BECs as theological fodder for their production of new systematic books for the theological market.

One of Althaus-Reid's key queer themes I am using is indecency challenging decency, the latter being "a sexual, social, political, economic and theological system—that shapes our entire way of thinking and acting in relation to ourselves, each other, and the natural world," sometimes also called a heterosexual matrix.[68] Decency reflects a binary yet hierarchical form of thinking which she sometimes calls heteronormative. This decency predominates in an

Argentinian culture of *machismo* infused with economic exploitation and is embodied in colonizing theological discourses of the Roman Catholic Church as well as the previously mentioned assumptions of the BECs. The excluded urban poor, sex workers, and LGBTQ community/ies, have remained marginal in church life and theological reflection, and this has consequences for her ecclesiology. For Althaus-Reid, the transvestite Christ is crying outside the gates of the church with all those who have been excluded and pushed outside and may not even come back inside if invited.[69] As I read her, it is the end of the Church as we have known it, but the birth of indecent church. *Since decency is about more than just sexuality, indecency is likewise about more than sexuality.* In my interpretation of her, "indecent" and "subversive" should be understood as *synonyms*, even as the former rhetorically emphasizes sexuality and the latter emphasizes its stance towards dominant cultural assumptions. An indecent church is theologically, culturally, politically, and sexually subversive.

As one of my postmodern theological allies, Althaus-Reid rejects the notion that any one symbol can act as a universal image of sexual and political indecency. Whenever one image is lifted up as catholic, it inevitably stands on the side of sexual and political oppression.[70] Instead, many sacred images are needed that are particular to the struggles of communities.[71] In fact, the alternative images found in these faith communities challenge the decency codes of the greater *machismo* society. During the 1976–83 Argentinian dictatorship, men were beaten for not conforming to military dress or for having long hair, and women were harassed for not wearing dresses or for looking men in the eye.[72] Althaus-Reid celebrates the group called *Las Madres de la Plaza de Mayo* as women acting indecently by gathering and demanding to know what became of their disappeared children during the military junta, even as they also studied the Bible together.[73] In this group there is the kerygma, through study and naming the importance of knowing what happened to loved ones; the koinonia of mutual support; and the diakonia of challenging a regime that says that it is best to forget. Both Althaus-Reid

Les Madres as church

and I consider this a primary example of a beautifully subversive ecclesiology. It is an instance of counter-imperial churching for a planetary gospel. While base communities (or BECs) were worthwhile for a time, she approves of their displacement in favor of more popular movement constructions like *Las Madres*: they "[set] aside reductionist projects" and focus on what helps real people more than what helps "some theological market."[74]

One of the ways the kerygma is expressed for Althaus-Reid is through popular Bible readings that focus on real life while maintaining the themes of "justice, peace and love/solidarity" as interpreted by the community's struggles. In these gatherings, "women remember and re-member their communities, by continuing the traditions of giving testimony and of assuming their responsibilities as witnesses of the tragedies and struggles of our continent."[75] They proclaim not merely the challenges and injustices people face: they also include celebration and testimony to where the divine is encountered. Whether as a women's community in El Salvador, a "Widows' Group formed by Dolores or the Women's Group of Andrea in Usulatán, the reading of the Bible goes together with the reading of the *realidad* of a country at war, and the conviction that God wants God's people to live a life where human rights are respected."[76] In gatherings of worship, proclamation occurs through the collective work of the people, which involves fewer words in liturgy; instead it incorporates people's experiences like breastfeeding as well as opportunities for voluntary fasting.[77] Nowhere in Moltmann or Suchocki do we find such beautiful concreteness as liturgical breastfeeding!

 Althaus-Reid is correct that an indecent ecclesiology means that church rituals should upend society's typical power relationships.[78] In particular, she envisions rituals that subvert dominant paradigms of power: "[O]ne day the Christian liturgy might be built around the symbolic exchange of priestly clothes amongst people as an act of redistribution of power and responsibility and that the Eucharist might involve children distributing the bread amongst people."[79]

Additionally, sharing sacraments can be a way to lift up "voices of protest" rather than being understood as private communion with the divine; in this way they act as a form of indecent proclamation.[80] Gay theologian Robert Shore-Goss notes that late in her life, Althaus-Reid found personally meaningful the radically open table invitation of the Metropolitan Christian Church in Edinburgh, as well as its priority of open commensality.[81]

Those who would deny her interest in ecclesiology should note that in her last public paper, at which point she was too ill to present in person, Althaus-Reid addresses ecclesiology explicitly. Rather than proclaiming a universal and eternal grace, she believes churches should affirm a dis/grace that avoids any images of a restored essence or identity. Such a church of dis/grace must proclaim no original meanings or final closets, which results in doing redemption in reverse "without firm final destinations." This is rooted in what she calls a "Queer hermeneutics" of secrecy, which has no direct access to any transparent master narratives or totalizing teleologies and thus prevents essential beginnings or natures.[82]

Like my own approach, Althaus-Reid strives to find the divine in concrete experience, especially in what mainstream society would consider sexually deviant experience. In effect, this is grounded in her epistemology that marginalized sexual stories are "the starting points for an incarnational queer theology."[83] For example, while most people think of Eucharist as a sacrament, she is perfectly willing to consider semen as a potentially equivalent means to commune with the divine.[84] Though she would find the term distasteful, I find this to be an instance of the radically "incarnational" quality of her thought. In a context where the urban poor, LGBTQ persons, sex workers, and transvestite Christians have been declared to be without value, Althaus-Reid provocatively focuses on what they can contribute as examples that critique the liberation church and Argentinian society. Unsurprisingly, when communities find that their voice has been persistently ignored or forcibly silenced, it is often the best strategy to focus on their distinct contributions.

Like the term "indecent," the term "queer" has a definite sexual lens to it, but it does not exclusively refer to gendered sexuality. For example, Althaus-Reid affirms South American movements that "have come together as a result of many Queer alliances amongst people of different spiritualities, political ideologies and locations of race and class."[85] For her, it is critical that we "become witnesses and to participate in the act of giving testimony, of sharing our experiences of pain and joy," for doing so "makes the sharing of experiences (such as exclusion) not only translatable but also gives them the quality of salvific events."[86] In our proclamation, fellowship forms through "the process of sharing stories [whereby] we reach for the 'other' and we enrich the struggle for liberation by becoming witnesses of the suffering of the 'other.' Solidarity grows from these indecent encounters, for the 'other' is always marginal."[87] Clearly, her insights run parallel to my own, where our very earthly concerns connect us through powerful sacred bonds via our interwoven proclamation, fellowship, and service.

While affirming the singularities of existence, Althaus-Reid avoids a debilitating individualism of opaque experiences. Instead, she agrees with me that churching requires a koinonia-fellowship, for "individuals get crushed easily. The community's support and sustaining is crucial. The community carries the task of resurrection of crushed individuals all the time."[88] This fellowship of sexual difference provides a space to expose ideologies of naked power and decolonize bodies sexually, politically, and economically: this erotic desire of an orgiastic-koinonia points to a new ecclesiology.[89] In line with my earlier critiques of market fetishization, Althaus-Reid believes that solidarity beyond the market is a key part of what being indecent means: "To claim the right to love and befriend people outside the metaphysics of the market, that is, outside the pattern of profit or advantages, may be more than abnormal. In the market, solidarity is an indecent value."[90] In practice, koinonia involves "walking alongside the poor on the same road, sharing the same life experiences, observing, judging, acting and celebrating together."[91] The path is held in common even as the companions themselves remain different.

This resonates unmistakably with the themes of Chapters 3 and 4 that emphasize the need to form a solidarity that includes encountering the "other" as a network of differentiated solidarity and to agonistically work through conflict. Althaus-Reid models one aspect of that approach through her discussion of sharing stories of life struggles within a faith community. Solidarity as traditionally understood in liberation theologies is no longer appropriate or helpful if it ignores women's and queer people's experiences of sexual and gendered oppression.[92] We are in full agreement that such patriarchal, heterosexist, and transmisogynistic sameness-driven solidarity must come to an end. Any koinonia and its indecent undressing (i.e., unmasking) of both dominant sexual culture and the larger neo-liberal world order must incorporate a postcolonial understanding of complex identities, where the oppressions people experience are not always held in common but instead form a multiplicity.[93] Koinonia-living needs to move towards the ability to hear and "become witnesses in the story-sharing of multitudes."[94] For both of us, an indecent-subversive ecclesiology is always a multi-vocal practice.

When describing her indecent diakonia, Althaus-Reid expresses what a really powerful pluralistic ecclesiology can do. In subverting decent norms, both sexually and politically, Althaus-Reid defies the status quo as it relates to the consequences of economic globalization. The result "is a model of a church in permanent exile, as a protest against systems of injustice that dehumanize God's creation."[95] Devastating in her critique, like a queer-prophet, she proclaims, "The ideologues of this world care very little about presbyteries and elders or popes and bishops per se . . . [for] what they care about is that economic thought is not de-sacralized."[96] Yet this is precisely the work of marginal Christian communities, as well as the diakonia of countering Empire expressed in Chapter 4. Communities of radical discipleship do this work even if the result means that their counter-cultural stance leaves them ignored or ridiculed by dominant institutional organizations. Indecent, subversive faith communities have a critical role to play because only "people whose bodies are living parables of transgression" will be able to challenge the binaries that both church and society have supported; they ask the right questions critiquing sexual decency and neo-liberal capitalism.[97] In the service of church life, "the margins of sexuality in theology are constitutive parts of . . . the disruption of real, dissident holy praxis in the church."[98] A disruptive, dissident holy praxis is what we are seeking for counter-imperial churching.

According to Althaus-Reid, "issue-based theologies" did not recognize that confronting their heterosexist culture would help initiate a different church praxis. Without this shift, the church mimics the political-economic mode of production and its orientation to growth. By following its self-marginalization or *kenosis* of economic norms, I understand churching to not be concerned about its preservation as an institution and thus transcend the current systems and logics in which it operates. This includes ignoring the demands of the theological market: church for Althaus-Reid is to be people-centered, thus breaking the mutual dependency of decent theology for a decent church in a decent culture. In her materialist reading, the institutional church "is doomed to extinction" since no institution can persist after the "ideological discourses" that made it are exhausted.[99] I go a step further by claiming that the practice of churching can transcend the old discourse and lead to new forms of radical faithfulness to a planetary gospel.

Althaus-Reid strongly endorses new popular movements beyond BECs as "a highly positive consequence of the socio/theological decentralization of praxis," for such decentralization defies "the protectionist ethos of church ecclesiology."[100] In effect, Althaus-Reid is pointing towards a kenotic self-emptying of church where it dissolves institutionally and is reborn as a social movement. However, a problem emerges here. Ecclesiology cannot become fully immanent within indecent struggles over the long term: her own examples include a reserve of rethinking church practices, such as reading the

Bible together and singing religious songs. Such practices become relevant only because there is an institutional ecclesial framework to which such popular movements are responding. While these movements counter-culturally use the tools that are part of their material context, new ways of organizing movement groups in relation to each other would need to emerge in light of a movement's success. Althaus-Reid does none of this institutional rebuilding even though I am convinced she does recognize it as a future necessity, and it is here that Suchocki's thought serves as a necessary corrective. I believe that new institutions need to emerge out of novel spiritual social movements when old ideological discourses have run their course if their gains are to endure.[101]

Althaus-Reid's ecclesiology partially follows the model of a Radical Reformation church, particularly in her notion of addressing society while remaining culturally marginal. One of the most famous radical reformers in the second half of the 20th century was the Mennonite peace theologian John Howard Yoder.[102] Unlike typical criticisms made against the Radical Reformation, Yoder rejects the option of social withdrawal from society. Emphasizing critique and flexibility while minimizing conformity and patience, the church does not seek a "responsible involvement." Rather, its "critical independence may include an occasional radical opposition," even if that results in exclusion: they participate through critique.[103] For Yoder, the church's commitment leads it to be separated from the world to the extent that it allows its witness "to be appropriately in mission to the world." The church is to be a counter-cultural element, especially in questioning societal elites that equate Christian faith with their ideologies.[104] This parallels Althaus-Reid and points towards my second critique of her. She goes so far as to compare queer secrecy and epistemic knowing with sects, affirming the usefulness of queer theologies (and presumably ecclesiologies) using their own sectarian knowledge locations. She provocatively writes, "Hard Core Queer theologies need to continue working from their sectarian locations as cut off reflections."[105] The result appears that, at least for her, queer theologies can be relationally cut off from other epistemological locations. Here she fails to acknowledge indecent sexual practices as but one epistemological perspective for subversive incorporation. It is true that not everyone needs to be in every conversation, nor should they be invited, but at some point intersectional readings from social locations must resume. Althaus-Reid remains ambiguous on this point.

Regarding Yoder, his program fails in a number of ways as an indecent ecclesiology. Most obvious is the fact that in spite of having a postmodern sense of the particularity of the church, he overemphasizes the unity or purity of the community, in spite of rejecting the charge of purity. More damningly, Yoder admits to a high degree of homogeneity within the church vis-à-vis the world.[106] This comes in part through the desire to reach a final internal consensus, while Althaus-Reid and I are more inclined to the conflictual yet still interdependent approach of Young and Honig described in the previous chapter. With his neo-orthodoxy shining through, I read Yoder as retaining a strong resonance with aspects of Karl Barth, particularly his emphasis on "the lordship of Christ." Of course, his disparaging comments against "adult homosexuality" and his own personal sexual abuse of power would also fall under Althaus-Reid's withering critique.[107] If the ecclesiological visions Althaus-Reid and I are expressing have a resemblance to the Radical Reformation, it is quite an indecent relationship!

What Althaus-Reid's project reveals is that the ecclesiologies of Moltmann and Suchocki, along with so many other systematic thinkers, are not queer enough, neither sexually nor subversively. In effect, they are both theologically decent projects, no matter how radical their content. Moltmann's very conception for his ecclesiology as missional serves as a condemnation of its decency. Moltmann takes a missionary position on ecclesiology, but he needs to queer it up! Suchocki is considered by many to be the last great systematic process theologian, and it shows in her work. Nevertheless, I have not sought to uncritically side with Althaus-Reid over and against

Moltmann and Suchocki, and the final section on ecclesial marks will show the interrelationship of their thought.

ECCLESIAL MARKS AS CONTRASTS

The Nicene-Constantinopolitan Creed of 381 CE established the four primary marks of the church as one, holy, catholic, and apostolic, which orthodox theology has since attempted to follow. As we saw previously, Moltmann and Suchocki maintain this continuity with the tradition, and this continues with their discussions on ecclesial marks. Within the political-missional and process-relational paradigms they work from, respectively, each endeavors to give these marks the most positive interpretations possible. Though she comes to different conclusions, Althaus-Reid is like myself willing to explode this paradigm. As I review both tendencies and how these positions are argued, I intend to show that there is space for understanding ecclesial marks beyond these binary options by using the process notion of a contrast.

For Moltmann, while there may be marks in addition to the core four, such as Word and sacrament, ultimately the church is essentially one, holy, catholic, and apostolic. These are not merely distinguishing but also creedal marks, as they link together Christ, Spirit, and the coming kingdom as "inalienable signs of the true church." While he upholds these four orthodox markers, he attempts to reinterpret them in such a way as they might further his political ecclesiology as a "unity in freedom," a "holiness in poverty," a cath-olicity in "its partisan support for the oppressed," and an apostolicity in "bear[ing] the sign of the cross."[108] Those of us with liberationist concerns should admire his effort.

As with the center of Moltmann's systematic ecclesiology, these marks exist from both the messianic mission of Christ as well as the Spirit's eschatological gift. Each is grounded in Christ: church unity comes from Christ's uniting activity; church holiness comes from Christ's sanctifying activity; church catholicity comes from Christ's universal lordship; and church apostolicity comes from the mission of Christ and the Spirit. Likewise, these four marks are predicates of the coming kingdom as subject.[109] Statements about the church's unity, holiness, and catholicity are not empirical judgments but are expressions of what the church will be when justified, akin to how a person is when they are justified by faith. They point towards the kingdom and how the church is to live out its calling. Each of the marks overcomes the church's present failings: its division, sin, and particularity.[110] In this way, the four traditional marks remain normative for him.

For Moltmann, the church is one in freedom. Emphasizing the diversity of gifts within the church, Moltmann attempts to hold together the church's unity through its diversity, where difference and particularity are constitutive elements of it.[111] Because Christ is fundamentally one and Lord of all, division in the church means that Christ is divided.[112] The church's unity is shaped by the trinitarian unity, and since the Trinity is not a hierarchical relationship, the church's unity is not a monarchical one, either. The church is not trying to will itself into becoming one; rather, it is one because its unity originates in God and comes through Christ, though it will not be fully expressed until the arrival of the kingdom.[113] The church's common origin in Christ provides the unity in its diversity as members connect through the Spirit. Moltmann goes on to make a claim quite compatible with process thought, saying, "It is therefore a creative unity, in which every created being is intended to arrive at itself and to develop its own unique character, being through that very fact related to other created beings. The creative Spirit loves originals, not imitations."[114] This creative relationality is quite similar to Whitehead's idea where the many become one and are increased by one.[115] However, the rhetoric of unity remains supreme. In the midst of conflict, the church is to be united in Christ and the Spirit, and thus is united and in fellowship with the oppressed. In accepting the conflicts that will arise from such a unity, Moltmann knows that there will be tension between a unity of fellowship and a unity of service, maintaining that this tension must be held together "for unity in freedom, and freedom in unity."[116]

The church is holy for Moltmann to the extent that it acknowledges its sin and is sanctified "for the service of the kingdom of God."[117] Jesus Christ, crucified and exalted, is the poor one and so the church's fellowship with the poor reveals its holiness. Via biblical sources, Müller-Fahrenholz explains how Moltmann substantiates this conviction that this "hidden presence" resides "in the poor."[118] By taking up its cross in suffering and persecuted resistance, the church reflects the holy poverty of Christ, and is sanctified by participating in his poverty. In so doing, Moltmann argues that holy Christian poverty "is a protest against poverty" and reflects "the fellowship of the messianic mission and the hope for the kingdom."[119] Essentially, this holiness is for the world's coming future where poverty is overcome.

The church is catholic for Moltmann insofar as its "catholicity is a correlative term to its unity."[120] He affirms that the universal church enfolds every distinct, particular church.[121] While the present church is only partially catholic, in the eschatological kingdom of God, it will be fully universal. Because the lordship of Christ is universal, the church must be universal. While the church is currently particular in its location and concerns, this reflects a lack of wholeness. Normatively, it should be related to the whole and be a universal witness to the world's divisions, but for now "it is not *yet* itself the summing-up and unification of the universe [emphasis added]."[122] The *way* the church is catholic, however, is in its partisan support of the poor and oppressed, and it is their liberation that also offers salvation for oppressive communities. This means that his universalism is not neutral in conflict situations but rather takes the side of the oppressed just as "Jesus turned to the sinners, tax-collectors and lepers in order to save the Pharisees and the healthy."[123] Moltmann adds, "If God will only be 'all in all' when the rule of Christ is consummated in the rule of God, then the kingdom of glory can only be called catholic in the fullest sense at that point."[124] A major problem arises here, for his claim of the church's eschatological universality is prone to triumphalism.[125] More egregiously, while Moltmann recognizes that worldwide trade and renewed missionary zeal went hand-in-hand in the 18th and 19th centuries, his abstractions ignore the link between missional work and the violence of colonialism.[126]

The church is apostolic in a way that is different from the other three marks in Moltmann's thought. While the other three marks are to be fulfilled in the eschaton and "describe the one, all-embracing and holy kingdom of God," the church's apostolicity is the way that it continues the mission of Christ until the eschaton is reached.[127] At that point, the church will no longer need to be apostolic. Like Jesus, the church embodies the dialectic of crucifixion and resurrection.[128] Van Nam Kim notes that "the continuity of the content of the proclamation" is what makes for apostolicity, including the sacraments of baptism and the Lord's Supper.[129] While there is continuity, apostolicity is not merely a mark of legitimation but also of commission in sharing the good news of Christ, which continues in word and deed until the eschaton comes. Nevertheless, apostolic identity does not come through mere repetition of the past. As the church is oriented towards the future, it is geared towards novelty.[130] As it lives out this apostolic calling for freedom, fellowship, and mission, the church will *necessarily suffer*, which is lamentably Moltmann's fullest meaning of apostolicity.

There has been some debate about whether Moltmann's understanding of apostolic suffering is essential or simply unavoidably since there will inevitably be resistance against the mission it lives out.[131] As we saw earlier with regards to diakonia and suffering, Moltmann feels the need to push beyond what is warranted. Since the risen and crucified Christ are inseparable, and the church witnesses to both, he concludes that the church's service is expressed "as active suffering and as suffering activity."[132] He digs his hole deeper still, writing, "Fundamentally only the suffering God can help, for only he loves in a fully selfless way."[133] If suffering is necessary for God in some ultimate way, it is necessary for the church that remembers and anticipates God's work. He does recognize that suffering is inescapable to the extent that the "powers of unfreedom" resist its mission.[134] As mentioned before, if he stopped there, Moltmann would have made an apt descriptive comment, but he erroneously pushes suffering into the *prescriptive* mark of apostolicity by subsuming particular instances of suffering into his universal vision of God.

While Marjorie Suchocki uses different terminology from Moltmann, she remains beholden to the same orthodox framework of ecclesial marks. As with Moltmann, I am critical of her need to assume too much continuity with the tradition of orthodox ecclesiologies. Using the historic categories of apostolic, one, holy, and catholic, she offers a process theological interpretation on these seemingly essential marks. While I am overall critical of this approach, on the positive side, her insightful use of a process metaphysic provides a number of improvements to Moltmann's conclusions.

For Suchocki, apostolicity has both a constant and relative pole. The constant side is proclaiming "the life, death, and resurrection of Jesus Christ," which she connects with God's call for "communities of love and justice."[135] The relative side means that the way this proclamation happens must not be set in stone or become a prescription. Churches must be willing to let go of past articulations in order to be faithful to their call. Indeed, for her, the best way to be faithful to the past is through a radical openness to the future. Thus, the church's apostolic witness maintains both "constancy and openness."[136] Suchocki believes that the church is constantly called towards the future, "and even if this future is actualized, God will transcend it once again with yet another call to anticipate God's reign in new ways."[137] Thus, like Moltmann's construction, the church is perpetually novel. One key improvement made is that for Suchocki, apostolicity does not end because the kingdom of God is not a stable final destination. The church lives perpetually between the times of the reign of God as embodied in Jesus Christ but also as expressed in God's everlasting harmony from the future.[138] We should gladly affirm that suffering no longer becomes an essential component of apostolicity in her model.

The church's oneness comes not from the past but from its "shared future." Looking to the past alone will not show the church's unity. The past's diversity is the context for the church's becoming, but there is also a togetherness in relationship for future possibilities for wellbeing. The members of the church have to discern how God is calling them to live faithfully for the future together. Therefore, Suchocki holds together apostolicity and unity as interrelated elements, the former coming from the past and the latter from the future. The church is "ever formed anew" by both its given past and anticipated future.[139] Here she makes clear how past facts are the inescapable ground for the church's activity.

The present instantiation of faithful response to past context and future possibilities becomes Suchocki's third term: holiness. "If apostolicity relates to the church's continuity with the past, and unity relates to the church's creation from the future," invokes Suchocki, "then holiness is the effect of apostolicity and unity held together in the present."[140] To be a holy community is to live in light of Christ's call upon the church. From a technical process perspective, she offers another way to defend the claim that the church is essentially holy. Within God's internal process, God's consequent nature internalizes the church, which is then integrated within God's primordial nature as the living Christ's offering of initial aims. Holiness is not an either-or proposition: to the extent that initial aims are responded to more or less, the church is more or less holy. However, since God offers initial aims that are relative to the circumstances one finds oneself in, then likewise holiness must also be relative to one's context. Because of this quality, the church's holiness results in its inevitable "diversity and ecumenicity."[141]

Process theologian John Cobb's book *Spiritual Bankruptcy* functions as another ally and a critical interlocutor with Suchocki's ecclesiological construction on holiness. Cobb suggests that the church should just as much be about the work of secularizing itself (but *not* making itself secularist) in contrast to her emphasis on the church as holy. He goes so far as to say that "participation in the tradition of secularizing the Way is the most faithful form of Christianity today."[142] By secularizing, he means that the focus of Christian faithfulness should be oriented primarily towards this world and its problems.[143] While this does not mean that churches should ignore things like the otherworldly or an afterlife, these become subordinate concerns vis-à-vis the world. Elsewhere, Cobb shares with Suchocki the Moltmannian notion that the church is to be an anticipatory sign of the kingdom, what he elsewhere calls the "commonwealth of God."[144] However, he also recognizes that many churches "lack of a shared sense of the primary importance of that to which the church witnesses. As long as this sense is lacking, the church cannot convincingly call for primary commitment or loyalty. It must inevitably settle for third, fourth, fifth, or sixth place in the priority system of most of its members."[145] A secular church is oriented to the creative transformation and salvation of this world, which calls for one's primary loyalty. I would add that initial aims may be actualized, more or less, but they always occur with regards to *this* world, so they could just as readily be called secular as Suchocki calls them holy. We will return to this rhetorical decision shortly.

Suchocki's fourth and final mark of the church, catholicity/universality, is rooted in her understanding of holiness. In light of its future unity, the holiness of the church "must be expressed through diverse actualizations of holiness."[146] The catholicity of the church is not through its uniformity but through the diversity of its apostolicity. Catholicity or universality means that any culture can express Christian faith, even those that are beyond its original Palestinian and later European contexts. Because the church exists in many cultures even as it seeks to transform those cultures in light of the reign of God, a relativization process takes place. No single instantiation of church can claim to be the church universal, because it is only appropriate to a particular context. In effect, the very fact that the church exists in multiple cultures relativizes every cultural instantiation of the church. Universal validity is for the gospel itself, rather than for the particular culture's response to the gospel. Treating the church as the definitive revelation otherwise results in its idolatrization.[147]

One cannot help but be convinced that the sirens of orthodoxy are luring Suchocki to their rocky, dogmatic shores. She desires to show how process theology can be just as orthodox and Christian as other theologies with the added bonus of being intellectually compelling. Insofar as she does so, she makes a conserving move that unintentionally or not lends credence to the legitimating frame of the Christian tradition, which was formulated under the conditions of Empire. If one wants to maintain the orthodox formulations of one, catholic, apostolic, and holy church, Suchocki creatively interprets them through the lens of the process of becoming: the perspectival many become one and are increased by one through the inverted polar relations of God and World. However, she does not explain why these should be the discursive boundaries for an ecclesiological construction, as Cobb hints in calling church to be secular. Is it possible that the church should instead be considered many, secular, particular, and novel?

The traditional four marks, as expressed by Moltmann and Suchocki, reflect heterosexist ideology. As Althaus-Reid notes, "[H]eterosexuality is, after all, a way of thinking."[148] By this she means that it functions as a logical and hierarchical binary, where one side of a dualism functions as the norm for the other side. In this way, heterosexual thinking is not just about sex (though it is never not sexual), but is an ideology. The orthodox marks of the church fall under this ideology, for the one all-too-easily swallows the many. A universal frame subsumes the particular expressions. The secular is understood in terms of the holy, and the novel is understood in terms of the apostolic. Althaus-Reid manages to queer this relationship. By making ecclesial marks indecent, she converts them into a nonhierarchical pattern of difference over identity. Queer theologians recommend that we should not disregard but turn upside down certain church traditions.[149] What happens when this is done with the four creedal marks of the church? Althaus-Reid emphasizes church as Queer (particular); materialist and political (secular); avoiding one answer, approach, or formulation (many); and not seeking reform but living out new formulations (novel).

Althus-Reid's answer

We can see Althaus-Reid holding these indecent marks together when she claims that indecent theology (or church) seeks "diversity, possibility and the sense of irreducibility which comes from the experiences of people at the margins and the margins of theology itself."[150] I am reading diversity as manyness, possibility as novelty, irreducibility as particularity, and theology being produced in church communities for and by real people at the margins of life as secular. She does not systematically name these four indecent marks as such, for her method is deconstructive. Nevertheless, we can find them there, barely hidden below the surface of her writing. For example, faith communities need "different practices of dialoguing and reflecting in communities. That may also involve the theological dialogue of different communities reflecting plurality more than homogeneity."[151] Just as theology and capitalism have problems with plurality,[152] the same should be said for orthodox ecclesiologies that emerge out of historic patterns of economic and cultural domination.

his interp of Reid

Indecent church will be *novel* more than apostolic, for while many people tried to reform patriarchal structures, others have "created new ideas, organizations and institutions. Meanwhile, no matter how many Basic Christian Communities have been created and dismantled in recent years, this has only been cosmetic surgery, a face-lifting operation in the life of the church."[153] BECs erred in trying to return to some original meaning to be re-enacted rather than being open to the possibility of the unknown breaking into their old narratives.[154] Instead of affirming rupture and creativity in forming new ecclesiologies, even the militant Latin American church clings to hegemonic theological categories, or as Althaus-Reid quips: "We are still putting new patches on old wineskins."[155] To the extent that the ecclesial ideological structure is sinful, and it is clear that this is the case for her, conversion fundamentally means turning one's back on that system.[156] Both Moltmann and Suchocki incorporate the novel, but Althaus-Reid agrees with me in giving it pride of place. Her emphasis becomes not so much finding a place of inclusion for women and sexual minorities within existing institutional church structures than about radical transformation of what church means.[157]

Unlike Moltmann, who says that radical discipleship groups and mainstream church need each other,[158] Althaus-Reid is indifferent to the survival of mainstream decent religious formulations. In this way, church is about being *many* more than it is about being one. Provocatively, she is unwilling to ground her ecclesiology or its unity in Jesus Christ even as she won't utterly discount him, either. Moltmann says that "it is not faith that makes Jesus the Christ; it is Jesus as the Christ who creates faith."[159] Althaus-Reid, on the other hand, believes that women of past, present, and future—their struggles and defeats—give meaning to Christ and, in fact, *make* Jesus into the Christ.[160] Even "the consciousness of Jesus was subject to historical limitations," such as him not critiquing the cultural assumption about the uncleanliness of women's menstrual flow.[161] The difference between Moltmann and Althaus-Reid here is that while he wants to go beyond the historical Jesus by looking to the future, she is willing to subvert the perfection of Jesus, which prevents him from being a foundation in the first place for church unity.

Third, church is *secular*, for Althaus-Reid emphasizes the material, worldly, sexual bodies that are the starting point for indecent ecclesial living. It is their struggles, marginality, exclusion, and experiences of domination that her queer theology seeks to address. While she does retain a space for holiness, it is a Queer holiness that is the concrete starting point for a community.[162] The sacred is revealed in the secular, as "a Queer path of disruption made by curious amatory practices of adding people to communities of solidarity and resistance."[163] One can find the sacred, the holy, but it is *through* the secular struggle.

Fourth, church is *particular* as it uses a particular rather than universal set of epistemological experiences for its construction, as we saw in the previous section. It does not attempt to speak in a universal language nor to everyone. Althaus-Reid affirms that what we need is a "feminist epistemology, non-dualistic, non-hierarchical and relational."[164] At the same time, critiquing and leaving the church's sexual project as it is currently configured is a calling not just for queer and transgender persons but for heterosexual and cis-gender persons as well.[165] While her project is particular, it is not isolationist. Her queer, particular church is constituted by "Queer dissidents in search of paths of holiness though social practices of justice in sexual, religious and political areas of their lives."[166] In this way, she points towards the interrelationship of orthodox and subversive marks, which will conclude this chapter.

By incorporating Althaus-Reid's critique, the paradigm of the traditional four marks becomes neither normative nor adequate. Moltmann and Suchocki try to negotiate a way for the terms to be interrelated, but the results are disappointing. One side of the ledger (one, holy, catholic, and apostolic) always dominates the other side (many, secular, particular, and novel) regardless of how generously they interpret the terms. The only realistic justification is out of fidelity to historic dogma. For them, *the orthodox terms are ultimately not up for debate but only how they will be interpreted.* While one rationale may be fealty to ecumenical partnerships with confessional and creedal traditions in order to promote mutual recognition as true church, this exhibits a circular logic. One becomes forced to affirm marks such as unity because the many (and supposedly divided) churches demand a unity. However, by inverting orthodoxy's logic through Althaus-Reid's concerns, we uncover a case for the very opposite of the traditional ecclesial marks. But where does that leave us? I suggest we understand these two sets of marks in terms of a dipolar continuity of mutually contrasting terms.

We have seen in Chapter 2 how dipolarity works within an occasion as well as between the divine and the world, and in Chapter 3, we saw Catherine Keller's four dyads concerning the human as one/many, private/public, body/soul, here/now. However, can this dipolar structure express the character of churching in terms of ecclesial marks? One could be tempted to misread the relationship of the traditional and subversive marks in a number of ways. One could choose one set as normative over the subordinated set as does the orthodox tradition. Second, one could add them together so that there would be eight marks and we need both sets. Third, one could affirm a total relativism where we have eight marks and you choose your favorites among them. However, none of these options would make the marks anything more than a plural list of self-enclosed entities and thus miss the interrelationship between them. The marks do not exist in a static pattern, but in a relationship that is itself a process that issues forth in novelty. Following Whitehead, what was previously an opposition can become a more intense contrast.[167]

First, churching is both many and one: many people come together into one network, relating to one another, but that very unity is then offered back to the many without becoming a rigid relationship. In any given moment in the activity of churching, the physical pole feels the many which condition and invite its becoming, while the mental pole feels the one real potential it can become. It is neither simply one diverse group nor many individual ones, for the one and the many become a multiplicity, a multitude of relating together in differentiated solidarity, never as an enclosed unity, but as an open-ended many-one that is offered to the novel many.

Second, churching is both holy and secular: holy in reflecting the divine aims for itself and the world, and responding to the divine, but secular in that the value produced in its life and work is always to, for, and with the world. It turns initial aims into indeterminate aims, which are both holy and secular: gifts of creativity from the divine, but made determinate by the creative decisions of those entities for the intensification of value. This aligns with saying that churching is called to proclaim a planetary gospel. It is sacred good news for the world, addressing actual problems in life.

Third, churching is both universal and particular: it is universal in terms of its unavoidable interrelatedness with other churching moments and activities of practicing the way of Jesus, but it is particular in that this interrelatedness is felt in a specific way and from a specific perspective. Every particular location *universally* acts this way, but in so doing, it does this as a pure *singularity* of decision. Again, readers should see this as aligned with a planetary gospel that speaks to distinct, particular situations but then grows from those many positions into a web of connection. The gospel becomes universal only from the bottom up across relationships.

Fourth, churching is both apostolic and novel: apostolic in that it feels past churching practices not merely as a constraint but as potential patterns to faithfully actualize again, but novel in that it is directed towards the not-yet horizon of how its world can maximize the potential for intensity and harmony in creative non-actualized forms. Churching is thus most faithfully apostolic when it is most appropriately novel for its relevant world.

One—many; holy—secular; universal—particular; apostolic—novel. Each side of each pair is reinterpreted through the other without becoming the other as they interact as contrasts and instances of creative becoming. And these acts are themselves instances of the divine presence in the world, the divine matrix of intercommunication and creativity: not the face, but the backside of the divine within the world, as experienced by Moses.

It has been too easy for churches to claim only one side of this polarity. The traditional focus has been on the left side of the poles: one—many; holy—secular; catholic—particular; and apostolic—novel. At its best, the right side of the ledger has been included but only insofar as it is subsumed by the left side.[168] This logic still falls until the power of the One. Of the three major ecclesiologies we have explored in this chapter, and unlike the vast majority of ecclesiologies, only Althaus-Reid significantly breaks this mold. Because her approach is so striking in its nonconformity, its *indecency*, to many eyes it may appear that she has not constructed an ecclesiology at all. Or one might be inclined to conclude that she has constructed an anti-ecclesiology. But this is true only if one takes as normative the traditional creedal marks of the church. As we have seen,

Althaus-Reid dwells much more positively on the right side of the ledger: many, secular, particular, and novel.

While I consider the ecclesial marks as best understood as a dipolar contrast, from a rhetorical perspective it is appropriate in many instances to emphasize the subversive side of the polarity. This is because it is the side that has been underserved and interpreted historically in a secondary relationship of marginality. Church is both one and many, in their interrelationship, but simply saying this does not break the mindset that cannot help but think of *The Church*, with its many parts. In this way, rhetorically using the subversive side of the contrast can help people think about church anew in such a way that the traditional marks do not become the unspoken mental norms. If church is really particular, this rhetorical subversion is a legitimate calling for counter-imperial churching to undertake as a planetary gospel is proclaimed in myriad expressions. The rhetorical emphasis on particularity motivates my removal of the definitive clause "the" before "church" within my project. In its place, one can more appropriately say "a church," "churches," the condition of being "church," or my favorite, the process of "churching." Church is best understood as one-many, holy-secular, catholic-particular, and apostolic-novel, held together in an intense creative contrast.

While these dipolar marks describe what church *is*, the final chapter will describe what churching *does* by reiterating Chapters 2 through 4 and offering more specificity to their broad claims. This follows the New Testament description of church as kerygma, koinonia, and diakonia, all of which were present in Moltmann, Suchocki, and Althaus-Reid. Nevertheless, in the final analysis, a counter-imperial process ecclesiology is more interested in exploring the practice of churching than in what the nature of the church *is*. In this way, ecclesiology and missiology become non-different, inextricably woven together in a contrast of mutually enriched perspectives. Churching should help us more faithfully and creatively follow the way of Jesus for our hurting world. At its best, that is what church has always sought to do.

CHAPTER 6

Living Out a Counter
Imperial Ecclesiology

It is not a harmless churchy balance of love and justice that
we need, but an *ekklesia* (community) of just love, an eros
that readies us for deadly dangers and for delightful sur-
prises. ~Catherine Keller, *God and Power*

WEAVING THE STRANDS

IN THE COURSE OF THIS BOOK, our journey has been through
many areas: the problem of American ecclesial communities and
their larger planetary context, the insights of process thought in
reformulating a theory of value in contrast to neo-liberal economic
value, rethinking human interrelationships and mutual interest, the
importance of encounter for dismantling privilege and fostering
transformation, political theory alternatives to idolatrous political
liberalism in the United States, and ecclesiologies of mission and
indecency. These have been read through the traditional Christian
themes of kerygma, koinonia, and diakonia, but why should a radical process ecclesiology attempt to demonstrate this relationship?
Whitehead offers one important justification: practically speaking,

[handwritten: summary]

157

to the extent that one can refer to tradition with integrity, the like-lihood of effectiveness increases.[1] We cannot jettison the material context, the many, the apostolic tradition of churching in our effort to construct the novel integrating practices we are seeking. Without reference to the past, it becomes much more difficult for people to positively prehend the potentials being offered to them. Even more critically, I cannot help but call upon a Christian framework: it is my context, and I demand from it compelling answers to the questions I have been raising. In doing so, I have been reworking the tradition as a way to increase the likelihood that others will want to participate in this project in their contexts.

A transcendental kerygma is expressed in Chapter 2: all have value for themselves, for others, and for the world through a process of cumulative interpenetration, and thus we are called to affirm the difference of others. Koinonia is practicing differentiated solidarity in light of our mutual interest from Chapter 3; it is also forming indecent intentional communities through Marcella Althaus-Reid while still being open to larger institutional structures using Iris Marion Young's defense of representation in Chapter 4 and Marjorie Hewitt Suchocki's analysis in Chapter 5. Diakonia is resisting the spirit and values of Empire expressed as domination and oppression, seeking liberation and doing mission á la Jürgen Moltmann, and expanding Amartya Sen's capabilities for quality of life in the face of idols of sacrifice and neo-liberal globalization. This chapter will weave together these tasks into a novel contrast by summarizing elements of what has come before while also expanding its analy-sis, lifting up concrete instantiations to follow, and connecting its conclusions with other thinkers who make similar moves even as it acknowledges differences of emphasis.

A close articulation to my own project comes in the latter half of Joerg Rieger and Kwok Pui-lan's *Occupy Religion: A Theology of the Multitude*. Rieger and Kwok believe the core of their theology of the multitude comes from experiences of otherness and (horizontal) transcendence, whether these are through "religious" experiences or not, and from avoiding their suppression into "a transcendence that backs up the status quo."[2] Like Rieger and Kwok, I affirm an "open invitation to all members of the body of Christ to participate in ministry, instead of limiting ministry to the clergy."[3] Here, priesthood is a function or role within the community rather than a special calling. Buildings are strictly optional, for in an ecclesiology of the multitude, one aptly challenges the division of sacred and secular space and time, for "sacred space is not bound by a place or dwelling."[4]

NO special leader or place

Similar to my differentiated solidarity, their deep solidarity at its best is a mark of the church's faithfulness to participating in what the divine is doing in the world.[5] Again, Rieger and Kwok describe this type of solidarity by rethinking what it means to "follow Jesus" or practice "discipleship": rather than "refer[ring] to involvement in service projects; rather, these terms refer to joining in solidarity with the least of these and acknowledging and reinforcing their agency. In short, discipleship means becoming a productive agent in relationship with other productive agents."[6] Thus, the spiritual practice of encounter should mean that radical disciples affirm the presence of those the dominant society sees as untouchables. It is not merely a toleration of someone's presence but rather an embracing of people's difference. Reflecting on those differences together and on how they have been constructed is a spiritual practice to transform oneself and how one relates to others. Bernard Lee helpfully describes this form of discipleship as an apprenticeship.[7]

with Not service to

As Rieger and Kwok aptly note, privileges are often doled out so that those receiving them will continue to follow the status quo. However, those with privileges can use them to undermine the ongoing distribution of privileges. For example, "instead of using their privileges to create power differentials, members of the middle class can use their knowledge, expertise, and connections to strengthen [a justice] movement."[8] This functions as a long-term divestment of privilege. Prayer helps us prepare to be open to this self-divestment and process these experiences of encounter, enabling us to celebrate these connections, and urging people to claim their self-respect when objectified by others. When we reflect together on our shared stories, and listen deeply to each other in ways that seek to feel another's feelings, we can become creatively *different* from what was otherwise not possible.

My construction maintains a friendly yet critical distance from the emerging church movement (ECM). Like the ECM, it challenges the use of traditional religious space and time. It seeks active participation among worship attendants, such as the use of prayer stations. It is more decentralized than pastor-driven churches and is open to forms of postmodern philosophy. It directs itself to younger persons and holds a place for kenotic thinking. However, Rieger and Kwok aptly express a major critique concerning the ECM: though there are many good things happening, as a whole it "lacks a focus on issues of class and fails to see postmodernism as the cultural logic of late capitalism," i.e., it misses its privileged place in globalizing Empire.[9] Catherine Keller likewise furthers an implicit critique of this approach of many emergent communities when she says, "It is not (as some postmodern theisms imply) that Christianity can stand here at its ancient gate, innocent of the aggressions of the West, ready to receive refugees from secular modernity."[10] I am not convinced that many in the ECM are prepared to take seriously the spiritual practice of divesting from their privilege, prioritize encountering others, or put world-loyalty ahead of church renewal efforts.

Like myself, Catherine Keller recognizes the limitations to resistance as an end in itself. She says, "We have a chance not just to resist the garish monocultures of the newest empire, but to stir alternative desires. Some who resist nobly, however, do not relay the vibrancy. Let us honor but not emulate them. For without the message of the rhythmic spirit, without the drumbeat and the tides, the good tidings run dry."[11] Thus, through my encounter with her, I believe the key is to offer a kerygma of alternative planetary desires and dreams that expresses the differentiation of values for themselves, each other, and the world. As Whitehead and other process thinkers have indicated, this expresses the three-fold character of the universe.[12] Creatively aiming for transformative desires, and seeing this possibility as genuinely *good news for ourselves and for our world*, is the ground through which resistance occurs. Its vibrancy is in the power of desires for novel becoming rather than the desire of acquisitive Empire. As has been repeatedly noted, all entities are internally complex, including humans. One must not conclude that setting one's will against Empire as analyzed in Chapter 4 will be enough:

> In Christian circles in the United States in particular, resistance against Empire is often seen as a conscious rejection that requires personal commitment, resolve, and a strong will. More subtle thinkers point out that resolve is not enough and that we need to form habits, which come from inhabiting particular traditions.[13]

There must be no intellectual dualism of pure church and demonic Empire, for Empire is in us; it is our condition. At best, we can rephrase that New Testament insight for our time, saying *we are in the System but not of the System*.

It is dangerous to define oneself against Empire, for it risks creating a new dualism or essentialized binary. As Keller wisely states, "It is tempting to take up a righteous apocalyptic stance of anti-imperialism. However, within its Northern Hemisphere context at least, the church will do better with counter-imperialism, along with an honest dose of Niebuhrian irony, for Christianity long ago lost its innocence."[14] While resisting Empire is an essential task of diakonia, one should not pretend that it is the only problem facing our planet nor the cause of all problems.[15] Empire as the overriding spirit of domination and oppression is not the sole material condition in which we develop ourselves ecclesiologically. Markets themselves are not the problem but rather the problem is when people attempt to make them the absolute measure of value. However, in this time, and in this world of globalizing Empire, if the values that churching aspires to are undermined, i.e., intrinsic value and interrelationship, encountering the other and divesting of inequitable power relations, then churching must include resistance to Empire in its manifold forms. By practicing differentiated solidarity, churching says no to the spirit of Empire and subverts the logic of instrumental value and necessary sacrifice.

We have seen how we are each a locus of distinct value even as we are related to one another. As Keller notes: "For the plurality of our relations to a complex world requires attunement each to our own complexity: the multiplicity of the world is both within and without. So this sort of fluid positionality is a kind of spiritual practice, always as internal as it is external, as personal as it is political."[16] *Becoming open to change is the call of those experiencing unjust privileges; seeking some stability, endurance, and preservation of value is the call for those swept up in the flux of becoming.* Their different locations demand diverse responses, while recognizing their interdependence through encounters demands of them a dose of apophatic humility. Keller affirms Ivone Gebara's claim that "we believe in the dimension of 'not-knowing,' a fundamental dimension of our being, a not-knowing that makes us more humble and at the same time more combative, in order to gain respect for differences and the possibility of building an interdependent society."[17] This apophatic humility is consistent with Tony Jones's "epistemic humility," and being combative resonates with Bonnie Honig's "agonism."

Churching does not exist merely for its own sake, nor is it practiced simply to fulfill the perceived spiritual desires of individual persons. It is valuable in its own right, but it *persists* as a vehicle that counters all idolatries for the sake of the good news of divine liberation and wellbeing for all creation-values. Churching cannot be done alone, for transformation can only occur to the extent that there are other superjects to prehend. Kerygma points towards both self-love and a critique of structures and practices that negate that intrinsic-relational love for wellbeing. Within the context of the United States, this unavoidably includes a basic critique of the dual idolatries of neo-liberal globalization and American-exclusive loyalties. Such a witness will therefore bleed into diakonia, or service, with the goal of moving participants to become living, verbal witnesses of repentance (*metanoia*) and the dismantling of the complex dynamics of domination and oppression.

In my project, kerygma is the proclamation of a planetary gospel grounded in our interwoven value relations and the call to live these out in differentiated solidarity with one another. In a parallel way, Dorothee Sölle believes that the proclamation of the kingdom of God gives birth to the church, and its service is towards that kingdom for the liberation of the oppressed.[18] Just as every concrescence for value is a concrete growing together, Sölle's kerygma is a concrete rather than a timeless universal.[19] For her, kerygma is encouragingly understood as "preaching, teaching, instruction" not just doctrinal content but also "a call to new life and to conversion" such that it "is always a matter of bearing witness, testifying to the truth."[20] Discipleship goes together with the message that we proclaim, for we are ourselves the product of the message and invite others to recognize this reality and live differently with others in light of it.

Sölle appropriately sees koinonia as "communion with God and communion between its members . . . grow[ing] out of the church's message and diakonia," which functions as solidarity with others.[21] From the previous chapters' presentations, one can say that this communion is part of the nature of reality as a cosmic process of becoming, where we are unavoidably interconnected. Through encountering others in all their related difference, we can take up a differentiated solidarity of relationship over sameness.

Like my affirmation of the praxis of encounter, Jung Mo Sung agrees that face-to-face encounters are where we have spiritual experiences of grace, but he warns us of the risky "temptation for us to withdraw into communitarian environments and into local, microsocial struggles."[22] Likewise, it is a mistake "to desire that large religious, economic, and political institutions function like our small communities; or to struggle for the project of a society that is simply the quantitative amplification of our communitarian relations," for this ignores the fact that new qualities emerge from the microsocial to the macrosocial.[23] This complements Iris Marion Young's previous insight that while self-determination can happen without institutions, self-cultivation needs institutional support. We see here an instance of diverse thinkers—an American postmodern feminist political philosopher and a Brazilian neo-liberationist theologian—making a complementary point from different locations. Along with Suchocki's analysis, we have ever-expanding and overlapping evidence that there will need to be some institutional alignments of churching. To reject this would be to transcendentalize the critique and could easily lead to denigrating partnerships that may otherwise help further differentiated solidarity. There can be no simple escape to small groups as the final normative model for society, for what works in ecclesial small groups will not always work on a large scale for either church communities or society in general.[24]

As long as humanity endures on this earth, there will always need to be institutions. Michael Hardt and Antonio Negri's desire for no representation goes too far in dismissing all forms of representation or, in other words, all forms of institutionalization. Separate "manys" need structures and patterns through which they can relate. Churching does not become a spontaneous anarchy of just particular manys any more than the planetary gospel stops at its originating roots; they remain "many—one" and "particular—universal" in their creative becoming. Many institutions need to be understood as partial, fragmentary, and subject to revision or replacement when they no longer serve their function of structuring larger networks. Wherever there are gatherings of those following the way of Jesus beyond small-scale groups of consensus-making and reciprocity, there will need to be larger organizing frameworks that help coordinate these networks. Decentralized institutions with many modules of decision-making are preferred without an exclusive centralized leadership, whether of bishops, clergy, or CEOs.

While there many be a non-difference between churching and socio-cultural life as holy and secular, there is not an easy identity where churching dissolves into the life of society as a form of absolute immanence: they remain dipolar. In like manner, Sölle says that resisting the institutionalization of Spirit is not faithful but comes more "from the extreme individualism which dominates our culture."[25] It is too much to seek a totally free and spontaneous self-organizing process of churching. Self-organization happens, but its occurrence will not guarantee that the particular form of self-organization will be just.

While many elements of this construction emphasize the local congregation and its practices, we must be careful not to worship the local. Sung suggests that the significant risk of postmodern thinking is the almost "exclusive valorization of local and specific works without linkage with more comprehensive social and political projects."[26] This would be akin to a planetary gospel misinterpreted as contextual but not interconnected with others. Must we choose between transforming our planetary society vs. practicing concrete actions of solidarity?[27] No, for a process worldview shaped by liberationist, postcolonial, and radical political sensibilities cannot make this false separation. As I have shown, the microcosm is within the macrocosm and the macrocosm is in the microcosm; it is a planetary gospel we affirm. Through this reciprocal polarity, churching gatherings can oscillate in their orientation between the local and the cosmic, dipolarly expressed as the "planetary," without establishing a dualism or trying to actualize every relationship in every activity in a totalizing project.

Likewise, are the activities of churching done for the purpose of liberation or to improve the quality of daily life? This debate has occurred throughout many contextual theologies in recent decades, from Latin American Liberation Theology to Black and Womanist theologies.[28] From Amartya Sen and process thought's emphases on maximizing relevant possibilities for actualization, we see an emphasis on quality of life. However, hopes and efforts for liberation and r/evolutionary shifts can also emerge when patterns change. The question that quality of life discussions ask is "whose quality of life?" This is where encounter becomes so critical, such as in helping tutor the children of immigrants (even as one learns from them and organizes with their families for better schools), because it relativizes and expands the edges of churching communities' sphere of concern. Again, we need both together to find the fullest meaning of churching.

Churching exists within the dipolar framework of mysticism and activism or, as described in Chapter 5, of the holy and secular. We should not simply be activists running around crying out for justice from one issue to the next. Yet critically, spiritual communion cannot be disentangled with *this world of planetary relations*. Discerning initial aims towards greater value requires a listening and waiting that cannot be predictably programmatized.[29] These ideals are always towards the world rather than away from it. The subjectivity of interrelated mutual immanence is the spiritual-political project of churching, of encountering, so that mutual interest becomes manifest and self-transcendence becomes possible. One can divest oneself from unjust power differentials and privileges as one counters Empire's totalizing attempts to extract value from life and relationships. This is not done through force of will, but in building new contexts for novel subjective actualizations and potentialities. By transforming desires and aims, the novel *becomes*. Listening for the call and henceforth responding by constructing a world organized around the capability of choosing more intensity and harmony necessitates a certain level of social activism and organizing as a way of life.

Following John Cobb, this secularizing tendency in Christianity is not a problem, for it is done out of affirming the sacred value of all planetary life. Unlike Karl Barth's concern for Nazi civil religion, "it is not secularizing Christianity that weakens resistance to demonic forces. What prevents appropriate resistance is assimilation into the culture that should be resisted."[30] Mainline Protestant communions must recognize that it has become a contextual necessity of churching to say "no" to the system of Empire in which they find themselves immersed, as did the original Kairos Document's condemnation of apartheid South Africa and the Confessing Church's challenge to the

Third Reich of Germany.[31] In doing so, we will counter-culturally stand in solidarity with anyone or thing experiencing abuse and expendability amidst Empire. In doing so, churching affirms planetary value and seeks to maximize the potential becoming for that value for itself, others, and the world. Churching seeks to be a space in which participants may actualize themselves in light of the divine primordial vision while their secular (and holy) living makes certain potentials more relevant and desirable, increasing capabilities liberation from oppression to be realized.

We must remember that a planetary gospel of counter-imperial churching is, following Marcella Althaus-Reid, inherently particular. It requires a certain concreteness for it to sing. It will resist particularly relevant instantiations of oppression on behalf of a planetary affirmation of value that has been denied, all the while building connections across differences. One powerful contemporary, indecent example in the United States is the Black Lives Matter movement, or BLM.

While some Christians lamentably distrust the Black Lives Matter movement, I'm convinced that it incarnates key elements of what I've been calling "churching." Such ruthless particularity shows that churching always responds to a crisis in our world and addresses an audience that hungers to hear it.

BLM expresses the three elements of churching. First, it focuses on proclaiming the value and dignity of black lives. Its very name articulates this. BLM takes up God's preferential option for the oppressed in contrast to the institutions that deny this. Some people are put off by such specificity—don't all lives matter? Isn't all life sacred? #AllLivesMatter is not the gospel because it does not respond to a pressing problem. It tries to universalize the answer. While it is a "true" statement metaphysically, it is also completely irrelevant and contributes nothing as a response to Black oppression. It actually obscures the problem. It forgets that the planetary gospel *always* addresses concrete problems. The problem is not that everyone is a target of the police; hands are not reaching for weapons when persons like myself, a white man, interact with them. #AllLivesMatter drains the specificity out of the good news. *A generic gospel is no gospel at all.* We don't see white people being killed or systemically harassed by the state in equivalent ways. When our society acts in ways that show that black lives do matter, then everyone will be better off (an expression of mutual interest). BLM knows that salvation comes first through those pushed to the bottom of society.

Second, BLM practices a fellowship of intersectional solidarity. It lifts up stories of those murdered and abused and works to form a community of love. BLM's founders are three Black women, two of whom are Queer and the third being the daughter of immigrants. They themselves embody the interconnection of multiple issues, identities, perspectives, and a prophetic challenge which the Queer theologian Marcella Althaus-Reid said needs to come from "people whose bodies are living parables of transgression." When your very being is considered unacceptable in society, you can provide a radical critique countering a violent status quo. Implicitly, BLM invites all of us to hear these parables and convert from our society's oppression. BLM has an obvious spiritual core with liturgical elements in their events, including call and response chants, as well as check-ins at the end of actions that build relationships of support.[32] The latter are almost identical to cabin sharing at church camp along the lines of "highs and lows."

Finally, BLM does the gospel service of resisting evil and oppression, particularly resisting state violence perpetrated against people of color in our communities done to maintain white supremacy. Extrajudicial killings, police harassment, and intimidation of Black people is a this-worldly anti-gospel, a particular incarnation of Empire's sacrificial logic. Black activists' indecent tactics of disruption and critiques of respectability uncover the lie of a politically liberal discourse. Althaus-Reid and Young would cheer them on.

No movement is perfect, but those who seek to follow Jesus can humble themselves and listen to, not talk at, BLM. We can learn much from them, and in so doing practice a differentiated solidarity.

BLM reminds us that *the gospel is less about proclaiming faith in Jesus than living the faithfulness of Jesus.* Our churchy language itself can get in the way. Given all the pain people have caused in Jesus's name, sometimes the gospel is best expressed without Jesus being mentioned altogether. But for those of us who seek to walk in his way, such a confessional withdrawal is done out of loyalty to that way itself. The mystics among us might even call it apophatic churching!

BLM is not the only gospel, for there are as many gospels as there are proclamations countering bad news and oppression in our world. To think otherwise would suggest a fragmented, siloed gospel rather than an interdependent one. But in the United States, I believe *it is one of the most essential practices of gospel living today.*

While these groups fulfill the function of churching in their particular proclamations, solidarities, and resistance, readers will rightfully ask, "Is that it?" BLM has strong religious undercurrents of African indigenous traditions, especially Yoruba. Explicit churching can learn much from them: there is more gospel in their lived activities than most institutional churches. But something is missing. An explicit theological affirmation is what I am seeking. I don't expect Black Lives Matter organizers to claim their work as the way of Jesus, though I wouldn't contradict that assertion if they made it. In our work of practicing solidarity and proclaiming a planetary gospel, *someone* needs to make the theological leap and connect what for many remains unbridgable. When that is done, there you find not just the pattern of churching but an actual affirmation of that process at work in people.

In some ways, it comes down to the following question: "What about Jesus?" Does counter-imperial churching have no need of him? To varying degrees, the ecclesiologies of Chapter 5 ground themselves in the life and work of Jesus. Jürgen Moltmann and Marjorie Suchocki both utilize Jesus/Christ/Jesus Christ/etc. in their ecclesial interpretations. Marcella Althaus-Reid, on the other hand, sees him as an important yet historically limited figure. Both positions are appropriate to the extent that they are interpreted in light of a kerygma of universal value relations and production through the divine matrix. It is possible to reject Christ as Lord without making Jesus superfluous to an ecclesial project. As this book is neither a systematic theological project nor a Christology, it is only at this late stage that we can finally "come to Jesus."[33]

For this project, Jesus functions primarily epistemologically. He does not initiate the process cosmology nor is he the source for solidarity. Yet unlike a simplified caricature of the medieval theologian Abelard, I do not understand Jesus to be solely a moral example, for through a social ontology one could say that Jesus, or better yet, *his way*, gets inside us whenever we positively prehend it. And what was this way? As Cobb aptly recognizes, "Jesus was crucified as a threat to [the Roman] empire."[34] There are costs to resisting Empire: loss of privilege, of status, and even sometimes of life.

Confessionally, I am inspired to this position because of the witness of Jesus. However, I am not interested in claiming that Jesus constituted this possibility of value production, as if it was not possible before his life and ministry. Rather, he reveals it in a *novel, particular* way that becomes *universally* decisive for churching. He is epistemologically revelatory, but in a hidden way, given that the production of value is an open-ended rather than a closed or totalizing process that swallows up creative becoming as objectifiable.[35] This prevents us from making Jesus into the foundation for churching's kerygma. Could it be that perhaps the most faithful way to follow Jesus is to let go of him on behalf of the divine commonwealth that he pointed towards, as does the Black Lives Matter movement? Rather than Cobb's Logos-Christology that equates the Christ as creative transformation,[36] Christians can say that they have encountered creative transformation through the epistemic lens of Jesus without exhaustively identifying him with it as such. The scripture that embodies this quality is Mark 7:24–30 where Jesus meets the Syrophoenician woman.[37] Christ challenges our certainties and totalizing values,[38] and epistemologically reveals this openness through Jesus's own upending of narrow certainties.

Ecclesially, Jesus is no longer understood as the head of the church. If the church had a head, this would set up an overarching unity that would overwhelm the diversity, which would violate churching's dipolarity. A headless church removes the logic of the One,[39] the unity that overwhelms the differences. We would never want to impose the church's unity in the way Dietrich Bonhoeffer does with Christ as its head.[40] In fact, Bonheoffer goes so far as to say that the members of the church are not connected to each other directly but only through Christ.[41] Nevertheless, we still have a way of discussing the relationality of the body to itself as a related multiplicity, a many—one. In 1 Corinthians 12:12–26, Paul maintains that there is one body, but he indicates it has a dynamic quality such that it is not a hierarchical unity: "On the contrary, the members of the body that seem to be weaker are indispensable, and those members of the body that we think less honorable we clothe with greater honor, and our less respectable members are treated with greater respect."[42] Paul is making the move towards a dynamically related body. If we go one step further, we can avoid any essentializing unity or single ultimate perspective and see the connections as happening in each and for each other, thus approaching the church as a body without organs,[43] or an entirely living nexus,[44] in which roles are not essentialized but arise from multiple located perspectives.

Catherine Keller describes Jesus as a revealed mystery, even "the parable of God," which is a wonderful image.[45] If parables are revelatory without a single meaning ever becoming final, and they open up the potential for new understandings and ways of living and responding to one's situation, then this title is thoroughly appropriate. Jesus becomes a window through which the divine reflects; he is a luminous darkness, a revealed mystery, a parable.[46] Jesus's life and ministry reveal the divine character and concern for the world with words and deeds that his followers encounter as an ongoing potential of creative transformation. But the point of a parable is not its inner hidden meaning. It moves beyond itself even as it is the starting point for reflection. Likewise, one does not need to be concerned about Jesus's inner nature or relationship with the divine primordial nature. Any ontological answers would necessarily turn to speculative theology, which may be interesting, but they are of secondary importance to how Jesus functions for this ecclesiology's kerygma. Beyond himself, Jesus invites us to look to the divine commonwealth: itself an ever-present yet open-ended horizon. To seek and to affirm the divine commonwealth is to affirm the maximization of planetary value through the cumulative interpenetration of the world's becoming, challenging those systems and patterns that deny or exploit this value. To love oneself and one's neighbor as oneself is to affirm each as mutually interested values for themselves, for others, and for the world.[47]

One of the original contributions of Jürgen Moltmann was the centrality of eschatology and the idea of *anticipation*, which we also saw Marjorie Suchocki utilize. Part of eschatology's importance is that beyond resistance, it addresses the novel.[48] This novel becoming is never-ending, because it comes from the inexhaustible fullness of the divine life, ever urging on new value-productions even after intense aims for transformation are realized. In this interpretation, I am following an orthodox process theological position as well as the neo-liberationist position of Jung Mo Sung.[49]

The faith that churching practices "is the confidence to act in the face of an open-ended future, thus to act in great humility and in great love" that participates in the "planetary struggle for 'justice, peace and the integrity of creation.'"[50] Even when we recognize how our selves and others are complexly constituted, neither practicing differentiated solidarity through encounter nor mutual interest are enough to change the dominant power of Empire. But this is practiced not out of certainty of victory but faithfulness to maximizing divine-planetary value. As Sung incisively indicates, "We need people and groups who incarnate those values in their lives and religious and social practices and who, in that way, serve as models of desire, as catalysts of new social and religious movements."[51]

When discussing the kingdom of God, or *basileia tou theou*, I prefer the term *the divine commonwealth*.[52] This divine commonwealth is a never-ending process of value creation, specifically as the ongoing struggle to recognize and maximize value wherever possible. This includes not only liberation from oppression but seeking endurance of value as survival and quality of life. There is never a moment in which one arrives at a final point and says it is finished, because there is always more yet to come. The struggle for just relations is never complete, as the process of becoming is never complete. As Sung declares, "[T]he value and validity of Liberation Christianity are not based on the promise to build utopia but on the justice of the struggle itself."[53] Even as certain struggles achieve better relations, there will be new challenges:

> The choice to keep working, 'in spite of all this' is not the fruit of an irrational or meaningless choice, much less the result of a sacrificial choice...It is something positive that maintains [one] in her choice: the humanizing experience that arises from an encounter with the poorest people and friendship with them.[54]

In my appropriation of Keller, the faith that churching practices "is the confidence to act in the face of an open-ended future, thus to act in great humility and in great love.[55]

CONCRETE RECOMMENDATIONS TO ACTUALIZE

As I begin to wrap up my explication of counter-imperial churching for a planetary gospel, I feel the need to move to the quite particular. Yet in doing so, what seems obvious from my social location will undoubtedly feel arbitrary for some readers. "How wrong you are, Timothy! That's not what it would look like in my setting at all!" And how right you may certainly be. The following recommendations describe a number of spiritual practices and organizational implications that radical discipleship for today entails. Again, these are not meant as reform efforts for existing congregations but more as recommended parameters when thinking about churching with others. It will be too detailed for some, while feeling like a mere sketch for others. I request some grace in readers recognizing that these are the most tentative of suggestions that would best be considered within a community that determines its own needs and ways of expressing a planetary gospel.

Today, self-conscious churching will look more akin to mission centers that work for the transformation and salvation of the world with their loci of activity emerging out of their web of relevant relationships. The new church effort Urban Mission in Pomona, California, is one pertinent example. That community avoided instituting worship as the center of its life. Instead, it sought to find out what were the spiritual, physical, and social needs of the primarily working-class Latino community in which it found itself. It was one of several ministries offered. With multiple bi-vocational ministers, one focuses on healthy eating and ecological living, while another specializes in ministries of re-entry and restoration for the formerly incarcerated, and another leads engagement with the real needs of the community.

Whether connecting across the street or with partners halfway around the planet, churches are to realize creative possibilities for the salvation of their world. The practices of solidarity, resistance, discernment, community, and celebration of sacred plurality departs from focusing on recruiting reluctant Sunday School teachers and distributing the interest income from the endowment to various charities. Instead of misdirecting the institutional churches' priorities at survival and repetition, novel faithfulness may mean letting go of cherished traditions like Sunday School altogether and replacing them with activities that people are genuinely excited about in light of their experiences of resisting injustice, encountering the other through differentiated solidarity, and practicing divine listening for new sacred directions to their ministries.

One method of practicing encounter in faith communities is through small group gatherings in which people share their faith journeys, struggles, and hopes, even as they are invited to critically reflect on their experiences. One important element of such gatherings is that groups are not homogeneous. If they are, sharing runs the risk of having people experience a group as a replication of sameness and identity. With heterogeneity, and skillful guided facilitation, differences can be heard for what they are without too quickly shifting to find the common in another's voice. For example, a starting point in deconstructing internalized racial prejudice among white Americans is not by arguing that race is a socio-cultural power construction (which is accurate if efficaciously irrelevant) but by *being with* people who identify with a different race and hearing their stories, hopes, and struggles, followed by critical reflection in light of the kerygma and larger structural patterns. In this way, when you see a group of teenagers walking down the street, you can draw on your small group experiences, thus making an inculturated negative reaction to the racialized other less likely and efforts to dismantle white supremacy more fruitful. If unconscious racism today is in part uncomfortableness around people of a different race, the way out is partially through encounter and incorporating into one's vision new experiences and new possibilities for solidarity.[56] At other times, like-groups need to cluster together to process their own feelings to avoid emotional manipulation of others who are specifically targeted for oppression.

Thus solidarity and storytelling become spiritual practices that groups can undertake in order to reconstruct and deconstruct who they have been, the types of relational patterns they have expressed, in order to become something different—increasing the relational intensity and harmony of disparate perspectives and experiences. If we want and expect people to change, we must change their surroundings and those with whom they regularly engage and then offer them tools to critically reflect on their encounters.[57]

In addition to her utterly subversive style, Marcella Althaus-Reid does suggest at least one practical suggestion for existing congregations. For the growing number of progressive mainline Protestant congregations, becoming "Open and Affirming" (ONA) has been a sign of inclusive welcome. These congregations are in a situation significantly different from the one Althaus-Reid wrote of in the early and mid-2000s, where LGBTQ rights were not even speakable in "decent" company. Since then, a growing number of countries in the Americas have expanded protections for the LGBTQ community, including Argentina and the United States. However, within mainline congregations, there rhetorically persists a homosolidarity of "identity," where LGBTQ persons are "no different" from the rest of "us." It seems that among such congregations, relationship is contingent on the relating of like to like. However, Althaus-Reid suggests we move towards an ecclesiology that breaks through such a pattern. For her, accepting or including without "welcoming the different" is part of the logic of hegemony, something an indecent faith practice must reject.[58] Welcoming the difference of LGBTQ persons cannot simply be one more issue to consider. The logic of heteronormativity is revealed in the encounter with the sexually marginalized, whom churches so often seek to reincorporate under a decent (and unified) banner.

As explained in Chapter 4, mainline Protestants struggle with working constructively through conflict.[59] The preferred model going forward is one where the diverse priorities and concerns of a community are expressed with an attitude that moves towards consensus without seeking uniformity. However, this requires at least two things: one, that people are not afraid of disagreeing and hearing distinct perspectives on things they care about, and two, that participants develop their own theological thinking by being practicing theologians. You need to work through your anxiety around conflict, pray for Al-Qaeda during worship, and be ready to discuss such statements afterwards. When people are not sure about what they believe and are committed to, and why, they are much more hesitant to discuss these things with others. They will tend to fall back on the dominant culture for their justifications, which typically will not provide adequate resources in thinking and living out a radical faith.[60]

Not at all ??

Churching is not a refuge for the lost, a place for private solace, or a community of the saved separated from the remainder of the world. It is a means by which divine values and desires are reflected and revealed for the world. In that way it could appropriately be called a sacrament. This follows Andrew Blume, who claims that the church is a sacrament of Christ, for a sacrament is manifest and Christ is present "to the extent that the church—as a community and not necessarily as an institution—does reflect God's love in action."[61] This does not define the character of the institution, but rather describes events of churching. Just as experiencing Jesus's priorities was to know the priorities of the divine character, so experiencing churching is to know likewise. By churching, we manifest and witness to how the divine is working in the world. In process language, we point to the real potentialities being offered for the world to actualize in light of entities' relevant contexts. As Blume explains, traditional church sacraments are *foci* for understanding the larger divine incarnational reality of "purposeful love in action."[62]

Same as Bryon Stone

Like Bernard Lee,[63] I support developing intentional communities, but they cannot be understood as dependent on strong-willed individuals who seek to resist evil. As shown in Chapter 3, we cannot forget that human beings are complex,[64] being especially intertwined with processes of internalized colonization. Furthermore, thinking of communities as voluntary, strong-willed collectives does not necessarily challenge the problematic notion of autonomy and may in fact be a symptom of it. Nevertheless, one of the primary ways to resist Empire is "simply to live, individually and in communities, in a countercultural way" like early churches.[65] It is for this reason that I support Moltmann's emphasis on adult baptism, however optional, and I agree with him that infants should receive blessings (and we should add: animals, too).[66] Rather than being a non-committal group, churching emphasizes each person's "call to liberating service."[67] Baptism into this commitment is not for the dedicated volunteer but for one responding to an invitation to live differently.

Being part of an alternative community should be intentionally done, even as you recognize the need for ongoing grace in light of your internalized oppressions and oppressive practices.

Those familiar with the Catholic Worker Movement will see parallels with my recommendations. During the communal worship time at one such center, in the Boyle Heights neighborhood of Los Angeles, they replace a sermon with an interactive discussion framed by scripture and some guiding questions. After singing and prayer, the participants share a potluck meal with informal discussions around the table. There is an element of decentralization to this collection of activists: they are accountable to each other, even as they maintain a strong spiritual focus to the heart of their life together.

Intentional communities are helpful and an encouraged option, but what is more important is that real relationships of accountability, learning, and listening are fostered. Dominant American culture makes this very difficult to achieve, and communities that opt for alternative configurations (as well as any supposedly purity-driven intentional communities) will need to be persistently discerning in how they are warped and misshaped by Empire's logic and demonic values within them. There is no pure position; this demonic spirit of domination and oppression will find ways into us in spite of ourselves.

Jesus's ministry reflects various ways people experienced the Divine, including through his teaching, healing, and table fellowship with peasants and expendables in Galilee. This suggests that there can be novel sacraments wherever divine love is encountered, including practices that have been discussed throughout this book; i.e., listening to the stranger, kenotically divesting yourself of privileges to be in solidarity with another, proclaiming the value of the planet and its inhabitants, and working against their degradation. They can all equally be sacraments of divine disclosure and love. Life together includes the spiritual practices of interstitial centering and contemplative prayer, encounter, and the ways we prepare for this in worship gatherings through songs, stories, scripture, and prayers. Those who desire to hew more closely to the activities that Jesus and his disciples performed could practice foot (or hand) washing as an experience of spiritual welcome and intimacy.

In practice, resisting Empire and America's use of military hegemony for its enforcement means taking a stance of nonviolence. Counter-imperial churching asks of us to find creative third alternatives beyond silent withdrawal and violent resistance. If we are each values for ourselves and each other, and our task is to proclaim this and resist all that needlessly destroys them, then taking a nonviolent stance regarding social transformation is critical. In this way, churching attempts to reflect the divine invitation to creative transformation. Taking deliberatively violent action consistently results in the internalization of that violence, while persistent pressure and engagement, even in the face of no guarantee of victory, is the best stance of a radical church.[68] Items that support American exceptionalism, or function to justify our violence as redemptive, such as the American flag, have no business in churching (except for perhaps being one among dozens of flags from around the world, especially those with whom communities have deep ongoing partnerships).

Creative resistance includes the indecent proposals that Iris Marion Young says persons in dominant positions find improper or out of order, like interrupting a leader's speech when he evades accountability. Likewise, churching actions can be another form of prayer as people disrupt unjust proceedings, create dramas, sing songs, lead chants, engage in civil disobedience (such as getting arrested for trespassing with Walmart workers), organize marches and rallies, and occupy buildings significant to the economic engine as well as government institutions. A warning is warranted: following the way of Jesus requires you to spiritually prepare yourself for the consequences!

Emphasizing the counter-imperial aspects of churching does not result in rejecting all "religious practices and beliefs."[69] This is particularly true for things like worship and prayer, which are ways to internalize the kerygma and create koinonia. Diverse communities will find a variety of ways to express the particulars of appropriate worship, for just as we encounter divinity through a multitude of initial aims, we respond in a multiplicity of ways. This may or may not include a "sermon," though many postmoderns like myself strongly prefer formats that offer the opportunity for response and dialogue, either during or after designated worship times. A process-liberationist worship liturgy should include participatory elements such as the sharing of prayer concerns, potential for movement (such as with prayer stations), a flexible space, the singing of songs, and the sharing of both apostolic and novel sacraments. These should be used to help people draw connections with their own lived experiences—of struggle, friendship, or privilege—while also giving them resources to survive in the face of domination and oppression even when there is no evidence that things will get better.

Regarding the Eucharist, Althaus-Reid and I both support a radically open table regardless of religious persuasion.[70] One must not first believe before being invited to eat, but one first eats in order to encounter radical love.[71] Moltmann recognizes that "there should be no congregational assemblies for worship without table fellowship, no proclamation of the gospel of the Kingdom without eating and drinking in the Kingdom with Jesus!"[72] Moltmann also encourages Agape meals, which I agree are critically important for what they teach and the form of interrelationship they proclaim.

A poststructuralist process ecclesiology will affirm a spirituality of moment-by-moment mindfulness that does not predetermine its direction.[73] Value is produced in the empty space, so one ecclesial spiritual practice will be akin to contemplative or centering prayer.[74] It is the interstitial inbetweenness of spirituality, "a *planetary spirituality of the interstices.*"[75] Keeping the space of becoming open reduces the human proclivity to think that humans can direct other entities in their becoming. This connects with what was said in Chapter 2 on the notion of indeterminate initial aims that open up a space for creativity, which is the non-difference of the world and the divine.

Solidarity and spirituality necessarily go hand in hand. The goal is to feel the feelings of others, to relativize our own perspectives, to be able to hear each other more deeply, to sit within the matrix of relationships, to remain in that indeterminacy so that something novel, a contrast that we could not see before, can emerge. Rather than having a definitive telos prejudging our interactions, we try to sit in that empty space, to allow for a new synthesis to emerge, to become the process of decision.[76] It takes concerted spiritual practice and prayerful openness to become moved to participate in solidarity with those struggling against very unique challenges, like white churches resisting the cultural imperialism of biker-bars on sacred Lakota land in South Dakota.

Resisting Empire does not have to be a dour affair. In such public displays of faithfulness, one of my favorite examples is the Pasadena Palm Sunday peace parade. Carrying palm fronds, singing songs of peace, and walking from an oppressed neighborhood in town to the center of an outdoor shopping district, the event has a joyful character. There is even a "donkey" for children to ride at the head of the procession (technically a pony). While the theme is different each year, the central confrontation revolves around the power of Sophia-Christ confronting the personified powers of domination and oppression. Sophia is represented through a 12-foot tall puppet with moveable arms worn on a person's back. One year, She confronted the power of Mammon, or the infinite accumulation of wealth incarnate, and freed those imprisoned from its power in dramatic theater. Mammon was not obliterated but transformed as the jail holding captives released balloons at the moment of liberation for those held in its grasp. This was very political in its implications, but the event was not about politics per se. It was about our world. It was about diakonia. It challenged Empire and economism with powerful symbols that were spiritually evocative without being didactically burdensome. It reflected some of the best of what counter-imperial churching looks like in a single event, and it was fun.

What would it mean for churching to include activists who are deeply grounded in spirituality and creating community in their efforts to construct a more equitable world? What kind of theology would they need? How would they understand themselves and what they did together? Would they not be a community of/in process? In part, it is for them that I have been constructing this vision of counter-imperial churching. This reconstructed church will look more akin to churches that have followed in the tradition of what is often called the Radical Reformation. That is, they will act as counter-witnesses (*martyria*) to the general direction of the dominant culture through the testimony of their lives and the values they seek to actualize. This church will not try to be all things to all people but is intended for those who are seeking to make a deep commitment to an alternative way of living, of connecting, and of resisting.

A politically oriented, indecent ecclesia can attract social justice activists who are currently alienated from churches and their own spiritual lives. Ecclesially, this can be an element of mutual interest. Rather than fret about dwindling numbers of dollars and participants, there are faithful alternatives. As Keller suggests, perhaps it is time that "we who repent the spectacular failure of Christendom to do justice, practice kindness or walk humbly with our God, are ready for new and stranger coalitions."[77] If ecclesiology normatively means supporting Christendom, then paraphrasing James Cone, we had better get on with it and kill ecclesiology altogether! But I think we need not go quite so far as declaring this project ultimately an anti-ecclesiology, for would this not give Christendom even in its death throes the normativity it has so desperately claimed as its own? As the church historian Gary Dorrien has noted, Keller offers the idea of "pitching theology to environmentalists, radical feminists, liberation movements, and antiglobalization activists."[78] And why not provide an ecclesiology for them? Diverse groups attempting to prevent a new pipeline for oil can understand their struggle as a spiritual one, where affirming planetary value has kerygmatic value. As an institution seeking its own preservation, "the Church" needs to end and accept its own process as subject-superject: to die to itself and become a living movement as an interrelated value-network of solidarity and resistance.

CONCLUSIONS

While some people may misread my ecclesiological construction as an attempt at a universally normative ecclesiology, I would prefer to describe it as *a*, rather than *the*, model for ecclesiological reconstruction. It has particularly emphasized an American setting, while churching is certainly beyond the limits of the United States' frame. It has been a perspectival approach, even as it has made gestures across differences. I have sought to remain in conversation with various relationally different perspectives and disciplines, including liberation theology, process thought and theology, postcolonial thought and theology, alternative ecclesiological formulations, and political theory. The world needs a counter-imperial ecclesiology rooted in the American location even if the particular model I have offered is found to be wanting. The United States needs a genuine ecclesial alternative.[79]

I want it to be inconceivable and nonsensical for someone to say, "I'm heading off to church now." This inappropriately makes church into an object, or an identity, with clear inside and outside boundaries. Questions like "Are you a member?" point to the church as a club. To what extent is churching willing to subvert the dominant ethos of its location, particularly when that ethos dominates and oppresses both people and the Earth? Our Jesus-inspired spiritual institutions need a thoroughgoing dismantling even as I have reconstructed churching. It may be that what emerges will not be called by the same name, or even look or feel like "church" anymore. But it will also not be an *ex nihilo* creation: it will be a repetition with a difference, a novel concrescence from past actualizations. "The church" should no longer be considered a noun, an entity, an object to which we relate to in a subject-object form. Rather, churching is the activity or process of actualizing and practicing discipleship with others in the way of Jesus. It is an event! We do not simply mimic the activities of Jesus, fetishizing them. Rather, they become a repetition with a difference, novelty bursting forth from the newly emerging creative possibilities offered to us.

We need new communities in order to create a new cultural context. Certain ideals cannot be actualized unless there exists the necessary material conditions for their achievement. This is one of Marcella Althaus-Reid's abiding insights. If mainline Protestant communities were founded in the material context of colonial pioneer expansion and the development of bourgeois capitalism, then they will *necessarily* reflect those material foundings. If those foundings are explicitly repudicated and organizing happens through their negative prehension, they would be in some very real way a new creation. As we continue living into a globalizing world racked with massive power differentials yet increased opportunities for encounter, of ecological instrumentalization and planetary solidarity, new ecclesial formations need to emerge. As Rieger and Kwok state beautifully, "We cannot ask people to believe that another world is possible without creating an environment where people can have a moment to experience and live into it."[80] The formation of new ecclesial communities works to create a new context and offers new possibilities that were not previously envisionable.

At a more basic level, we need to find new ways to talk about following Jesus's way. The terms of our parents and grandparents don't sing to those with ears under the age of forty, and they don't address our context. What was at one time fresh and vital has ossified and become stale. This goad, this aim for transformation has reoccurred persistently through the ages. Now is a time to prehend it again.

Famously, the Social Gospel movement of the early 20th century Progressive Era focused on the awful conditions of labor, the poor, and urban slums. Its followers rightly believed that the gospel was not just for your personal uplifting but should uplift the whole society. They promoted labor laws and unionization and were committed to the idea that Christians were called to help bring the Kingdom of God into reality here on earth. A few of this movement's flaws were its general avoidance of addressing racism and segregation, its middle-class audience, and its optimistic view of progress as slowly but surely inevitable. Contemporary terms like "progressive

Christianity" have similar problems: too white, too optimistic, too middle-class, too American.

Taking a cue from the Social Gospel movement, I have suggested an alternative phrase: "the planetary gospel." Like the former, it points to *this life and world as the audience for the good news*. It has a core biblical term in it, which is certainly a plus. Remembering Gayatri Spivak, the planetary is different from the global. You can hold a globe or observe it from afar. A globe is an abstraction. But the planetary is right here, right now, the material that makes up you, your context, and your web of relations. It is both incarnationally present to your setting *and* to the web that ties us all together in common through our diverse contexts.

A planetary gospel offers good news to the lived situations we find ourselves in. Gospel just means good news, particularly the good news that Jesus brings or reveals. But good news only sounds like good news when it addresses the *bad news* of our world. Baldly stated, any supposed gospel that is abstracted from its actual context, whatever that may be, *is meaningless*. At the intersection of our lived, embodied struggles of countering globalizing Empire and our proclamation we find the good news of Jesus.

Just as we are each in specific contexts, we are also part of a larger planetary network of relationships and interdependence. We need to learn from and listen to our siblings in other contexts so as to see how the planetary gospel addresses their situation and avoid equating our context with the only context. By doing so, we practice that good news of compassion and justice for our world that Jesus revealed and continues to reveal in our planetary living. May it be so!

Endnotes

CHAPTER ONE

1   I'd like to thank radical biblical theologian Ched Myers of the Bartimaeus Institute for introducing this term to me.

2   John B. Cobb, Jr., "Democratizing the Economic Order," in *The American Empire and the Commonwealth of God: A Political, Economic, Religious Statement*, David Ray Griffin, John B. Cobb Jr., Richard A Falk, and Catherine Keller (Louisville: Westminster John Knox Press, 2006), 97.

3   Cobb, "Democratizing the Economic Order," 91.

4   Jung Mo Sung, *Desire, Market and Religion,* Reclaiming Liberation Theology (London: SCM Press, 2007), 1.

5   Obviously, much more needs to be said about Empire, and Chapter 4 will delve more deeply in interpreting this globalizing phenomenon.

6   Catherine Keller, "The Love of Postcolonialism," in *Postcolonial Theologies: Divinity and Empire*, ed. Catherine Keller, Michael Nausner, and Mayra Rivera (St. Louis: Chalice Press, 2004), 221.

7   Catherine Keller, *God and Power: Counter-Apocalyptic Journeys* (Minneapolis: Fortress Press, 2005), 21.

8   For an example of this approach, see John B. Cobb, Jr., ed., *Progressive Christians Speak: A Different Voice on Faith and Politics* (Louisville: Westminster John Knox Press, 2003).

9   As George Pixley indicates, "The clearest instances of resistance in distinction from reform occur when people are powerless to change the system." George Pixley, "The Bible's Call to Resist," in *Resistance: The New Role of Progressive Christians*, ed. John B. Cobb, Jr. (Louisville: Westminster John Knox Press, 2008), 25.

10   Cobb, *Resistance*, 55–164.

11   Mark Lewis Taylor, "Spirit and Liberation: Achieving Postcolonial Theology in the United States," in *Postcolonial Theologies: Divinity and Empire*, ed. Catherine Keller, Michael Nausner, and Mayra Rivera (St. Louis: Chalice Press, 2004), 40.

12   John B. Cobb, Jr., "A Challenge to the Church," *Creative Transformation* 18.4 (Fall 2009): 7.

13   Pixley, "Bible's Call to Resist," 22.

14   See Kairos Palestine 2009, "A moment of truth: A word of faith, hope, and love from the heart of Palestinian suffering," http://www.kairospalestine.ps/sites/default/Documents/English.pdf (accessed July 27, 2013).

15   Pixley, "Bible's Call to Resist," 23. Unless otherwise noted, all italicized words or phrases found within quotations are original to the quote.

16   See World Alliance of Reformed Churches, *Accra Confession: Covenanting for Justice in the Economy and the Earth* (Accra, Ghana: 24th General Council, 2004). A copy of the confession can be found here: http://www.ucc.org/justice/globalization/pdfs/Accra-new-final.pdf.

17   World Alliance of Reformed Churches, *Accra Confession*, pt. 5.

18   Ibid., pts. 6–13.

19   Ibid., pt. 16.

20   It is also noteworthy that both the Accra Confession and the Kairos Palestine 2009 document were written by more hierarchical ecclesial structures than will be emphasized in this book. I do not intend to present my project as universally normative for Christians

throughout the planet. Readers can see clear differences between myself and the Accra Confession in my theological analysis, especially when it comes to God's sovereignty, the relationship of justice and unity, the analysis of empire, and the assurance of the victory of peace and justice.

21 *1968 Year Book and Directory of the Christian Church (Disciples of Christ)*, ed. Howard E. Dentler (Indianapolis: Christian Church (Disciples of Christ), 1968), S-310.

22 This is based on a comparison of the denominational annual yearbooks from 1968–2012. The most recent consulted edition is as follows: *Yearbook and Directory of the Christian Church (Disciples of Christ), 2012*, ed. Howard E. Bowers (Indianapolis: Office of the General Minister and President, 2013), 550.

23 *Yearbook and Directory, 2012*, 550.

24 *2011 United Church of Christ Yearbook* (Cleveland: United Church of Christ, 2011), 693. The calculated years are from 2000 through 2010. In 2000, membership was 1.377 million, and in 2010, it was 1.058 million. This amounts to a decline of 319 thousand in ten years, or 31,900 per year.

25 In effect, the rate of decline of these denominations mimics the demographic reductions of the city of Detroit, which has dropped from 1.8 million in the 1950s to 700,000 residents by 2013.

26 *Yearbook and Directory of the Christian Church (Disciples of Christ), 2011*, ed. Howard E. Bowers (Indianapolis: Office of the General Minister and President, 2012), 68.

27 Marcella Althaus-Reid describes how Westerners came to Argentina to gaze at basic ecclesiastical community gatherings. See Marcella Althaus-Reid, *Indecent Theology: Theological Perversions in Sex, Gender, and Politics* (London: Routledge, 2000), 26.

28 Keller writes, "With its imperial success, the church . . . absorbed an *idolatry of identity*: a metaphysical Babel of unity, an identity that homogenized the multiplicities it absorbed, that either excluded or subordinated every creaturely other, alter, subaltern." Keller, *God and Power*, 115.

29 See Craig L. Nessan, *Beyond Maintenance to Mission: A Theology of the Congregation* (Minneapolis: Fortress Press, 1999).

30   Dorothee Sölle writes, "If church *de facto* consists in sitting still for an hour on Sunday without getting to know anyone else, the unity of kerygma, diakonia, and koinonia is destroyed." Dorothee Sölle, "The Kingdom of God and the Church," in *Thinking About God: An Introduction to Theology*, trans. John Bowden (London: SCM Press, 1990), 144.

31   John Howard Yoder, *The Original Revolution: Essays on Christian Pacifism* (1971; repr., Scottdale, PA: Herald Press, 2003), 65.

32   This commitment came along with the simultaneous goals of creating 1,000 new congregations, transforming 1,000 existing congregations, and developing leaders in the church by 2020. See Richard L. Hamm, *2020 Vision for the Christian Church (Disciples of Christ)* (St. Louis: Chalice Press, 2001).

33   However, the Disciples of Christ decided in 2005 to switch the order and priority of the stance to pro-reconciliation/anti-racism. At its core, this was a marketing strategy to make its white congregations feel more comfortable and less confrontational with the project, and reflected Disciples' fetishization of unity and avoidance of conflict. Without the primary and more difficult work of rooting out racism in its systemic and institutional forms, reconciliation is premature, counterproductive, and an expression of the underlying privilege that needs dismantling.

34   Cobb, "Challenge to the Church," 6.

35   John B. Cobb, Jr., *Spiritual Bankruptcy: A Prophetic Call to Action* (Nashville: Abingdon Press, 2010), 175–76.

36   Norman Pittenger helpfully comments that one should not try to separate the Church from its activity, for the activity itself is the Church. This is very close to how I am using the term "churching." Inspiration for the term "churching" comes from my friend, Caoimhe Ora Snow, who posted a note on her Facebook wall one day concerning a worship service at the progressive-emergent congregation (a)Spire Ministry to which we were both members: Gone Churchin'. Norman Pittenger, *The Pilgrim Church and the Easter People* (Wilmington, DE: Michael Glazier, 1987), 79.

37   Why Jesus should be used at all is reserved for the final chapter.

38   For a sample, see Alfred North Whitehead, *Religion in the Making* (1926; repr., New York: Fordham University Press, 2011), 12–13, 45,

55; and Alfred North Whitehead, *Adventure of Ideas* (1933; repr., New York: Free Press, 1967), 11.

39 For examples, see Alfred North Whitehead, *Dialogues of Alfred North Whitehead*, ed. Lucien Price (1954; repr., Boston: David R. Godine, 2001), 88, 124, 125, 144, 169.

40 One notable exception is Randall C. Morris, *Process Philosophy and Political Ideology: The Social and Political Thought of Alfred North Whitehead and Charles Hartshorne* (Albany: State University of New York Press, 1991). While he connects Whitehead with British liberal socialism, Morris does not address imperialism.

41 Alfred North Whitehead, *Science and the Modern World* (1925; repr., New York: Free Press, 1967), 48.

42 Whitehead, *Science and the Modern World*, 24.

43 Paul W. Kahn, *Political Theology: Four New Chapters on the Concept of Sovereignty* (New York: Columbia University Press, 2011), 5–6.

44 Of course, a good argument can be made that such purely instrumental appropriation would be merely a superficial use of process thought that strikes against the heart of a process worldview.

45 As far back as 1925, Whitehead also noticed this phenomenon: "Religion is tending to degenerate into a decent formula wherewith to embellish a comfortable life." Whitehead, *Science and the Modern World*, 188.

46 See Lewis Smythe, "The Role of the Church in Changing Persons and Society," *Lexington Theological Quarterly* 6, no. 3 (July 1971): 81–91.

47 Examples include Norman Pittenger, *The Christian Church as Social Process* (Philadelphia: Westminster Press, 1971); and Bernard Lee, *The Becoming Church: A Process Theology of the Structure of Christian Experience* (New York: Paulist Press, 1974). To my knowledge, Pittenger wrote the first book on process theology and the church.

48 Pittenger, *Pilgrim Church and the Easter People*, 48.

49 K. Brynolf Lyon, "Companions on the Way: Creating and Discovering the Congregational Subject," *Encounter* 63, no. 1–2 (Winter/Spring 2002): 148.

50 Lyon, "Companions on the Way," 149–57.

51 Daniel J. Ott, "The Church in Process: A Process Ecclesiology" (PhD diss., Claremont Graduate University, 2006), ii.

52 Ott, "Church in Process," 11.

53 Ibid., 184.

54 Sölle, "Kingdom of God and the Church," 141.

55 See James Cone, *A Black Theology of Liberation*, 20th anniv. ed. (Maryknoll, NY: Orbis Books, 2008), 129–32.

56 Clark M. Williamson and Ronald J. Allen, *The Vital Church: Teaching, Worship, Community, Service* (St. Louis: Chalice Press, 1998), 4.

57 Williamson and Allen consider it the most important yet ironically the most neglected task. Williamson and Allen, *Vital Church*, 4.

58 Clark M. Williamson, "Companions on the Way: The Church," in *Way of Blessing, Way of Life: A Christian Theology* (St. Louis: Chalice Press, 1999), 276.

59 Bernard Lee, "Reconstructing Our American Story: Intentional Christian Communities." *Chicago Studies* 26, no. 1 (April 1987): 16.

60 Sölle, "Kingdom of God and the Church," 147. She mentions testimony as bound up with kerygma; they are separated only when divorced from discipleship.

61 Williamson and Allen, *Vital Church*, 45.

62 Ibid., 107, 120–21.

63 Jesus's radical ministry is central to my thinking, but Christianity has historically twisted itself by overemphasizing the internal person of Jesus. How could he do the amazing things he did: who was he on the inside, and how are he and God related? As important as these questions are, a better approach, for me, is to look not so much at the *person of Jesus* but at the *priorities of Jesus*. His was the way of compassion and justice for our world. He invites us to follow him and to embody, in our own lives, relationships, and practices, divine love for the world. As a result, a discussion of Jesus himself will be deferred to the concluding chapter.

64 Philip Clayton, *Transforming Christian Theology: For Church and Society* (Minneapolis: Fortress Press, 2010), 40–42.

65 Taylor, "Spirit and Liberation," 52.

66 George Pixley, "Latin American Liberation Theology," in *Resistance: The New Role of Progressive Christians*, ed. John B. Cobb, Jr. (Louisville: Westminster John Knox Press, 2008), 173.

67 Pixley, "Latin American Liberation Theology," 182.

68 Alfred North Whitehead, *Process and Reality*, corrected edition, ed. David Ray Griffin and Donald W. Sherburne (New York: Free Press, 1978), 5.

69 With process thought, there is a double move of deconstruction and reconstruction. Actual entities are superjects beyond themselves and their own values: what they become is not all that can be. Any totalizing moves are undone in the becoming of novelty. At the same time, there are reconstructions through the prehension of completed entities into a new concrescence.

70 It is worth noting that many of these persons either studied with Catherine Keller or have participated in Drew's Transdisciplinary Theological Colloquia organized by her.

71 Cobb, *Resistance*, vii.

72 As Cobb correctly realizes, "Those who are successful in the American empire think in terms of what supports the status quo. If the world is to be saved, we must develop policies on entirely different principles." Cobb, *Spiritual Bankruptcy*, 181.

73 Cobb, *Spiritual Bankruptcy*, 110. He accurately notes, "*Homo economicus* is imaged as a self-enclosed individual who relates to others in the market by making agreements that are considered by all participants to be individually beneficial."

CHAPTER 2

1 John B. Cobb, Jr. and Lewis Ford represent these two options with the former remaining closer to Whitehead's original position and the latter revising them. See John B. Cobb, Jr., *A Christian Natural Theology: Based on the Thought of Alfred North Whitehead*, 2nd ed. (Louisville: Westminster John Knox Press, 2007), 8, 21; and Lewis S. Ford, *Transforming Process Theism* (Albany: State University of New York Press, 2000), 213, 367.

2 David Ray Griffin, *Reenchantment without Supernaturalism: A Process Philosophy of Religion*, Cornell Studies in the Philosophy of Religion (Ithaca, NY: Cornell University Press, 2001), 3–4.

3   Catherine Keller, "Introduction: The Process of Difference, the Difference of Process," in *Process and Difference: Between Cosmological and Poststructuralist Postmodernisms*, ed. Catherine Keller and Anne Daniell (Albany: State University of New York Press, 2002), 12.

4   John B. Cobb, Jr., "Who Is a Whiteheadian?" Process and Faith, entry posted March 2007, http://processandfaith.org/writings/ask-dr-cobb/2007-03/who-whiteheadian (accessed April 30, 2013).

5   While I am using the terms cosmology and metaphysics fairly interchangeably, they are technically distinct, with the former being the conditions of the existing world, while the latter are the conditions for any conceivable world. See Philip Rose, *On Whitehead*, Wadsworth Philosophers Series (Belmont, CA: Wadsworth, 2002), 3.

6   Alfred North Whitehead, *Adventure of Ideas* (1933; repr., New York: Free Press, 1967), 236.

7   Alfred North Whitehead, *Process and Reality*, corrected edition, ed. David Ray Griffin and Donald W. Sherburne (New York: Free Press, 1978), 21.

8   Rose, *On Whitehead*, 20.

9   Ibid., 35.

10 Whitehead, *Process and Reality*, 150.

11 Rose, *On Whitehead*, 30.

12 Ibid., 37.

13 Whitehead, *Adventure of Ideas*, 195.

14 Rose, *On Whitehead*, 79–80.

15 Alfred North Whitehead, *Modes of Thought* (1938; repr., New York: Free Press, 1968), 93.

16 Rose, *On Whitehead*, 39.

17 Alfred North Whitehead, *Science and the Modern World* (1925; repr., New York: Free Press, 1967), 69.

18 Whitehead, *Process and Reality*, 222.

19 Ibid., 23.

20 Ibid., 26.

21 Ibid., 226.

22 Rose, *On Whitehead*, 40.

23 For example, one can start with extension and move back through concrescence, prehension, and ingression. See Gilles Deleuze, *The Fold: Leibniz and the Baroque*, trans. Tom Conley (Minneapolis: University of Minnesota Press, 1993), 77–80.

24 Rose, *On Whitehead*, 42.

25 Ibid., 42.

26 Ibid., 51.

27 Whitehead, *Process and Reality*, 258.

28 There are many other subcategories within Whitehead's philosophy that lie beyond the scope of this book. For a fuller list and description of Whitehead's categories, see John B. Cobb, Jr., *Whitehead Word Book: A Glossary with Alphabetical Index to Technical Terms in* Process and Reality (Anoka, MN: Process Century Press, 2015).

29 Whitehead, *Process and Reality*, 348.

30 Roland Faber, "De-Ontologizing God: Levinas, Deleuze, and Whitehead," in *Process and Difference: Between Cosmological and Poststructuralist Postmodernisms*, ed. Catherine Keller and Anne Daniell (Albany: State University of New York Press, 2002), 222.

31 John B. Cobb, Jr., "God as the Power of the Future," Process and Faith, entry posted January 2012, http://processandfaith.org/writings/ask-dr-cobb/2012-01/god-power-future (accessed March 9, 2013).

32 This conclusion is implied in Marjorie Hewitt Suchocki, "The Dynamic God," *Process Studies* 39, no. 1 (Spring 2010): 39–58.

33 Whitehead, *Process and Reality*, 224.

34 Roland Faber, *God as Poet of the World: Exploring Process Theologies*, trans. Douglas W. Stott (Louisville: Westminster John Knox Press, 2008), 96–97.

35 Rose, *On Whitehead*, 62–63.

36 Whitehead, *Modes of Thought*, 168.

37 Whitehead, *Adventure of Ideas*, 201.

38 Whitehead, *Modes of Thought*, 164.

39 Whitehead, *Process and Reality*, 7.

40 Whitehead, *Adventure of Ideas*, 134.

41 Faber, *God as Poet of the World*, 76.

42 Marjorie Hewitt Suchocki, *The End of Evil: Process Eschatology in Historical Context* (1988; repr., Eugene, OR: Wipf & Stock, 2005), 88.

43 Faber, *God as Poet of the World*, 79.

44 Ibid., 80.

45 In this way, it is not unlike the Buddhist realization that Emptiness implies Buddha-nature and vice versa.

46 Deleuze, *The Fold*, 81.

47 Whitehead, *Adventure of Ideas*, 201.

48 Alfred North Whitehead, *Religion in the Making* (1926; repr., New York: Fordham University Press, 2011), 137.

49 Faber, *God as Poet of the World*, 170–74.

50 Whitehead, *Process and Reality*, 7.

51 Ibid., 88.

52 Faber, *God as Poet of the World*, 184.

53 Ibid., 212.

54 Ibid., 102.

55 Ibid., 164.

56 Catherine Keller, *The Face of the Deep: A Theology of Becoming* (London: Routledge, 2003), 219.

57 Roland Faber, "Emptiness and Nothingness," (class lecture, Mysticism and Process Theology, Claremont School of Theology, Claremont, CA, February 22, 2011).

58 Whitehead, *Process and Reality*, 225.

59 For Moses's encounter with the divine backside, see Exodus 33:18-23, NRSV.

60 Whitehead, *Religion in the Making*, 86–87.

61 Whitehead, *Modes of Thought*, 102.

62 Whitehead, *Religion in the Making*, 91.

63 Marjorie Hewitt Suchocki, "Prayer in Troubled Times: A Process Perspective" (Center for Process Studies lecture, Claremont School of Theology, Claremont, CA, October, 2010).

64 Monica A. Coleman, *Making a Way Out of No Way: A Womanist Theology* (Minneapolis: Fortress Press, 2008), 86.

65 Whitehead, *Adventure of Ideas*, 252.

66 Brian G. Henning, *The Ethics of Creativity: Beauty, Morality, and Nature in a Processive Cosmos* (Pittsburgh: University of Pittsburgh Press, 2005), 3.

67 Henning, *Ethics of Creativity*, 6.

68 Ibid., 100.

69 Ibid., 6–7.

70 Whitehead, *Religion in the Making*, 84–85.

71 Ibid., 83. Thus, the destruction or degradation of the other hurts us, as well.

72 Judith Jones, "Intensity and Subjectivity, *Handbook of Whiteheadian Process Thought,* vol. 1, ed. Michel Weber and Will Desmond (Frankfurt, Germany: Ontos Verlag, 2008), 281.

73 Ibid., 283.

74 Whitehead, *Process and Reality*, 112.

75 Whitehead, *Modes of Thought*, 14.

76 Whitehead, *Process and Reality*, 100.

77 Whitehead, *Modes of Thought*, 111.

78 Charles Birch and John B. Cobb, Jr., *The Liberation of Life: From the Cell to the Community* (1981; repr., Denton, TX: Environmental Ethics Books, 1990), 205.

79 Birch and Cobb, *Liberation of Life*, 2.

80 Ibid., 78.

81 Ibid., 139.

82 Ibid., 234.

83 Ibid., 238.

84 I will elaborate on this further when discussing Amartya Sen's

thought in Chapter 4.

85   Birch and Cobb, *Liberation of Life*, 173.

86   Ibid., 174.

87   Ibid., 274.

88   Henning, *Ethics of Creativity*, 4.

89   Ibid., 39.

90   Griffin, *Reenchantment without Supernaturalism*, 97.

91   Whitehead, *Process and Reality*, 167.

92   Henning, *Ethics of Creativity*, 48.

93   These include persons such as Jorge Luis Nobo and Nancy Frankenberry.

94   Henning, *Ethics of Creativity*, 52–55.

95   Whitehead, *Adventure of Ideas*, 193.

96   Henning, *Ethics of Creativity*, 58–64.

97   Whitehead, *Process and Reality*, 104.

98   Luke Higgins, "Becoming through Multiplicity: Staying in the Middle of Whitehead's and Deleuze-Guattari's Philosophies of Life," in *Secrets of Becoming: Negotiating Whitehead, Deleuze, and Butler*, ed. Roland Faber and Andrea Stephenson (New York: Fordham Press, 2010), 147–150.

99   One can see a strong resonance here with a postcolonial theory of hybridity. See Wonhee Anne Joh, *Heart of the Cross: A Postcolonial Christology* (Louisville: Westminster John Knox Press, 2006), 59, where she states that radical postcolonial hybridity "stresses that identity is not the combination of right parts, an accumulation or a fusion of various parts, but an energy field of different forces. Thus, hybridity's 'unity' is not measured by the sum of all its parts. New possibilities, in fact 'newness,' enters the space between fixed identities by way of interstitial openings." I read this as the entrance of novelty through initial aims for concrescing entities.

100 Whitehead, *Modes of Thought*, 120.

101 The relationship of Jesus of Nazareth with this good news will be addressed in Chapter 6.

102 Birch and Cobb, *Liberation of Life*, 123.

103 Ibid., 151.

104 Ibid., 153.

105 Nathan Ingraham, "Fungus network lets plants alert each other to defend themselves against aphid attacks," http://www.theverge.com/2013/5/10/4318740/fungus-network-lets-plants-alert-each-other-to-defend-themselves (accessed May 15, 2013).

106 Birch and Cobb, *Liberation of Life*, 149.

107 John Sweeney referencing a comment from Marjorie Suchocki (informal conversation, Center for Process Studies, Claremont, CA, August, 2014).

108 Roland Faber, "Ecotheology, Ecoprocess, and Eco*theosis*: A Theopoetical Intervention," *Salzburger Theologische Zeitschrift* 12 (2008): 89.

109 While it is technically true that such concern could theoretically reach all the way out to the entire cosmos, most of those relationships are relatively trivial even as many establish the condition for the maintenance of life on our planet. If and when we have significant encounters with life outside our planetary context, this qualification would likely need revision. As of 2017, these remain tantalizing possibilities, but more as pure possibilities than real potentials for actualization.

110 Of particular note is the edited collection that came out of the 2007 Drew Transdisciplinary Theological Colloquim. See Stephen D. Moore and Mayra Rivera, eds., *Planetary Loves: Spivak, Postcoloniality, and Theology* (New York: Fordham University Press, 2011).

111 Gayatri Chakravorty Spivak, *Death of a Discipline* (New York: Columbia University Press, 2005), 73.

112 Whitehead, *Process and Reality*, 20.

CHAPTER 3

1   Catherine Keller, *From a Broken Web: Separation, Sexism, and Self* (Boston: Beacon Press, 1986), 1–2.

2   Keller, *From a Broken Web*, 4–13.

3   Ibid., 18.

4   Ibid., 161. Unless otherwise stated, all direct quotations that include italics are in the original quote.

5   Ibid., 190.

6   Ibid., 27.

7   Ibid., 183–86.

8   Ibid., 201-06.

9   Ibid., 162–227.

10 Ibid., 5–6.

11 Ibid., 91.

12 Ibid., 232–43.

13 Catherine Keller, "The Apophasis of Gender: A Fourfold Unsaying of Feminist Theology," *Journal of the American Academy of Religion* 76, no. 4 (December 2008): 925.

14 Keller, "Apophasis of Gender," 928.

15 Ibid., 914.

16 Ibid., 918–27.

17 Nicholas of Cusa, *Nicholas of Cusa: Selected Spiritual Writings,* trans. and ed. H. Lawrence Bond (New York: Paulist Press, 1997), 140.

18 Cusa, *Nicholas of Cusa,* 161.

19 At this "fold" in her career, Keller rarely speaks positively of what she affirms outside of poetic-mystical language. However, in a footnote she acknowledges that she remains complicit with Carter Heyward's "relational ontology of the self," of which Keller's earlier work is a profound exemplification. See Keller, "Apophasis of Gender," 923.

20 Keller, "Apophasis of Gender," 927.

21 Ibid., 919–22.

22 Ibid., 923.

23 Ibid., 925-28.

24 Catherine Keller, "The Love of Postcolonialism," in *Postcolonial Theologies: Divinity and Empire,* ed. Catherine Keller, Michael

Nausner, and Mayra Rivera (St. Louis: Chalice Press, 2004), 237.

25 Wonhee Anne Joh, *Heart of the Cross: A Postcolonial Christology* (Louisville: Westminster John Knox Press, 2006), 53–54.

26 Jea Sophia Oh, *A Postcolonial Theology of Life: Planetarity East and West* (Upland, CA: Sopher Press, 2011), 59.

27 Jung Mo Sung, *The Subject, Capitalism, and Religion: Horizons of Hope in Complex Societies* (New York: Palgrave Macmillan, 2011), 36–43.

28 Sung, *Subject, Capitalism, and Religion*, 54–58. One major difference is that Sung limits this self-creativity to social systems like the market, and remains silent about the self-creativity of "nature." This latter notion is a distinct strength of Whiteheadian thought.

29 Brian G. Henning, *The Ethics of Creativity: Beauty, Morality, and Nature in a Processive Cosmos* (Pittsburgh: University of Pittsburgh Press, 2005), 62.

30 1 Corinthians 12:26, NRSV.

31 James Cone, *A Black Theology of Liberation*, 20th anniversary ed. (Maryknoll, NY: Orbis Books, 2008), 103.

32 Cone, *Black Theology of Liberation*, 107.

33 As we saw in the previous section, Keller describes this reassertion of identity in terms of patriarchy.

34 Alfred North Whitehead, *Adventure of Ideas* (1933; repr., New York: Free Press, 1967), 265.

35 Monica A. Coleman, *Making a Way Out of No Way: A Womanist Theology* (Minneapolis: Fortress Press, 2008), 80–81.

36 Coleman, *Making a Way Out of No Way*, 81.

37 Justice will be defined in Chapter 4 using the thought of Iris Marion Young, taking care to avoid distributionist simplifications of the term.

38 Alfred North Whitehead, *Religion in the Making* (1926; repr., New York: Fordham University Press, 2011), 87.

39 Alfred North Whitehead, *Modes of Thought* (1938; repr., New York: Free Press, 1968), 109.

40   Marjorie Hewitt Suchocki, *The Fall to Violence: Original Sin in Relational Theology* (New York: Continuum, 1994), 70–71.

41   Roland Faber, *God as Poet of the World: Exploring Process Theologies*, trans. Douglas W. Stott (Louisville: Westminster John Knox Press, 2008), 311.

42   For more on middle axioms, see John Howard Yoder, *The Christian Witness to the State*, Institute of Mennonite Studies Series, no. 3 (Newton, KS: Faith and Life Press, 1964), 32–33.

43   Joerg Rieger and Kwok Pui-lan, *Occupy Religion: Theology of the Multitude* (Lanham, MD: Rowman & Littlefield, 2012), 18.

44   Rieger and Kwok, *Occupy Religion*, 28.

45   Ibid., 68.

46   I will discuss Young's position in Chapter 4.

47   Catherine Keller, *God and Power: Counter-Apocalyptic Journeys* (Minneapolis: Fortress Press, 2005), 148.

48   Suchocki, *Fall to Violence*, 101.

49   Whitehead, *Adventure of Ideas*, 285.

50   Ibid., 285.

51   Ibid., 289.

52   Thomas Jay Oord, *The Nature of Love: A Theology* (St. Louis: Chalice Press, 2010), 17–28.

53   Oord, *Nature of Love*, 56–63.

54   Charles Birch and John B. Cobb, Jr., *The Liberation of Life: From the Cell to the Community* (1981; repr., Denton, TX: Environmental Ethics Books, 1990), 164.

55   Birch and Cobb, *Liberation of Life*, 164.

56   Ibid., 165.

57   Ibid., 165.

58   Ibid., 206.

59   Ibid., 206.

60   Ibid., 247.

61   Ibid., 329–30.

62 Jung Mo Sung, *Desire, Market and Religion,* Reclaiming Liberation Theology (London: SCM Press, 2007), 45.

63 Sung, *Desire, Market and Religion,* 49.

64 Faber, *God as Poet of the World,* 226.

65 Marion Grau, *Rethinking Mission in the Postcolony: Salvation, Society, and Subversion* (London: T&T Clark, 2011), 265.

66 Grau, *Rethinking Mission,* 266.

67 This knowledge comes from personal experience and conversations with people of the Yakama and Lakota nations.

68 Grau, *Rethinking Mission,* 276.

69 Ibid., 288.

70 Ibid., 22–23.

71 Ibid., 280.

72 Joerg Rieger, "Theology and Mission Between Neocolonialism and Postcolonialism," *Mission Studies: Journal of the International Association for Mission Studies* 21, no. 2 (2004): 213.

73 Rieger, "Theology and Mission," 214.

74 Ibid., 214.

75 Whitehead, *Adventure of Ideas,* 157.

76 Rieger, "Theology and Mission," 218.

77 Ibid., 222.

78 Mayra Rivera, *The Touch of Transcendence: A Postcolonial Theology of God* (Louisville: Westminster John Knox Press, 2007), 2. The touch of transcendence could also be read as the non-difference between God and world in the gift of the initial aim to becoming actualities that is both their truest self and the immanence of God from a process perspective as seen in Chapter 2.

79 Rivera, *Touch of Transcendence,* 82.

80 Suchocki contrasts a horizontal with a vertical transcendence. See Suchocki, *Fall to Violence,* 42–43.

81 Matthew 25:40, NRSV.

82 Sung, *Desire, Market and Religion,* 130–31.

83 Ibid., 134.

84 Sung, *Subject, Capitalism, and Religion*, 30.

85 Ibid., 32.

86 Ibid., 126.

87 Whitehead, *Adventure of Ideas*, 259.

88 Sung, *Subject, Capitalism, and Religion*, 138.

89 Oh, *Postcolonial Theology of Life*, 118.

90 It also impacts the distribution of books, dissertations, and articles in a globalized theological market.

91 Barbara J. King, "Jared Diamond, A New Guinea Campfire, and Why We Should Want to Speak Five Languages," National Public Radio, entry posted January 10, 2013, http://www.npr.org/blogs/13.7/2013/01/10/168878237/jared-diamond-a-new-guinea-campfire-and-why-we-should-want-to-speak-five-languag (accessed May 25, 2013).

92 Sung, *Desire, Market and Religion*, 74.

93 Luke 14 tells the parable of inviting the poor, the blind, and the lame to a banquet table. From a reader-response perspective following this chapter's analysis, it could easily mean that you must have a meal with people that you want to work with. But this is the standard: you eat with people, you get to know them, you let their concerns become your concerns and *then* you can work with them on the issues that impact them. You don't try to help out with a colonialist mentality without knowing them. For example, you don't want members of a congregation to volunteer to work against racialized mass incarceration if they don't know people who are or have been incarcerated. You first have a meal with them: you encounter the other!

CHAPTER 4

1 John Rawls, *A Theory of Justice* (Cambridge: Belknap Press of Harvard University Press, 1971), 3.

2 In his earlier work, Rawls characterizes his own conception of justice as the "priority of the right over the good." Rawls, *Theory of*

Justice, 31.

3   John Rawls, *Political Liberalism*, expanded ed. (New York: Columbia University Press, 2005), 141.

4   Rawls, *Political Liberalism*, xxxvii.

5   Ibid., 48–50.

6   Ibid., 446.

7   Ibid., 450.

8   Ibid., 144.

9   Ibid., 459.

10 Ibid., 215.

11 I am inclined to believe that the things that are most important are those that are the hardest to achieve agreement upon, because they challenge dominant loyalties and ultimate values.

12 Paul Kahn, *Political Theology: Four New Chapters on the Concept of Sovereignty* (New York: Columbia University Press, 2011), 1.

13 Kahn, *Political Theology*, 2.

14 Ibid., 7.

15 Ibid., 15.

16 Ibid., 11.

17 Ibid., 18.

18 By mainline Protestant, I refer to what is often called the "Seven Sisters." While they consist of precursor denominations, in their current forms they are the following organizations: United Methodist Church, Presbyterian Church (USA), Episcopal Church, Evangelical Lutheran Church of America, American Baptist, United Church of Christ, and Christian Church (Disciples of Christ).

19 I observed this when the Disciples of Christ's national gathering (called General Assembly) did not condemn the Iraq War until 2007. By that time, there was a clear national majority that had turned against the conflict. Yet even then, this was done with much handwringing and reinforced language of how our resolution was not a condemnation of the United States armed forces, heroes and patriots all.

20 In contrast, the first section of Chapter 3 examines a process social ontology.

21 Subsequent thinkers in this chapter will challenge a Rawlsian fetishization with distribution in favor of productive relationships when theorizing on justice.

22 I am not arguing for the presence of the latter in sanctuaries, either.

23 Michael Hardt and Antonio Negri, *Empire* (Cambridge: Harvard University Press, 2000), xii.

24 Hardt and Negri, *Empire*, xiii.

25 Ibid., 445.

26 Ibid., 38.

27 Michael Hardt and Antonio Negri, *Multitude: War and Democracy in the Age of Empire* (New York: Penguin Press, 2004), 15.

28 Hardt and Negri, *Multitude*, 167.

29 Ibid., 146.

30 This is not unlike Whitehead's recognition that evil draws upon and destroys the value upon which it depends as mentioned in Chapter 2. See Alfred North Whitehead, *Religion in the Making* (1926; repr., New York: Fordham University Press, 2011), 82–84.

31 Hardt and Negri, *Empire*, 294.

32 Hardt and Negri, *Multitude*, 340. See also Michael Hardt and Antonio Negri, *Commonwealth* (Cambridge: Harvard University Press, 2009), 344, where they write: "[T]he parallel coordination among the revolutionary struggles of singularities is possible, but it is by no means immediate or spontaneous."

33 Hardt and Negri, *Multitude*, 94. This is a correction from their earlier work, and even otherwise adept critics often ignore this transition.

34 Hardt and Negri, *Empire*, 58.

35 Hardt and Negri, *Multitude*, 59.

36 Ibid., 168.

37 Gayatri Chakravorty Spivak, *A Critique of Postcolonial Reason: Toward a History of the Vanishing Present* (Cambridge: Harvard

University Press, 1999), 308–09.

38 Hardt and Negri, *Multitude*, 282–84. See also Hardt and Negri, *Commonwealth*, viii.

39 Hardt and Negri, *Multitude*, 112–13.

40 Spivak, *Critique of Postcolonial Reason*, 380, 382.

41 Catherine Keller, *God and Power: Counter-Apocalyptic Journeys* (Minneapolis: Fortress Press, 2005), 121.

42 I am pleased to discover that their more recent work does at least briefly acknowledge insights of postcolonial work. See Hardt and Negri, *Commonwealth*, 78.

43 Néstor Míguez, Joerg Rieger, and Jung Mo Sung, *Beyond the Spirit of Empire: Theology and Politics in a New Key*, Reclaiming Liberation Theology (London: SCM Press, 2009), 28.

44 Jung Mo Sung, *Desire, Market and Religion*, Reclaiming Liberation Theology (London: SCM Press, 2007), 78.

45 Míguez, Rieger, and Sung, *Beyond the Spirit of Empire*, 66. When Hardt and Negri do mention transcendence, it is consistently described as the negative activity of Empire as opposed to the pure immanence of the multitude.

46 Ibid., 1.

47 Ibid., 19.

48 Ibid., 72.

49 Ibid., 84.

50 In 2011, process and liberationist theologians met and identified a number of areas of resonance. See "Power and Empire: A Process-Liberation Conversation" (conference, Center for Process Studies, Claremont, CA, October 10–12, 2011).

51 Míguez, Rieger, and Sung, *Beyond the Spirit of Empire*, 89.

52 Ibid., 22.

53 Sung, Míguez, and Rieger are not the first to locate a spiritually transcendent dimension in systems. For a brilliant analysis of the spiritually demonic element of the systemic powers, see Walter Wink, *Engaging the Powers: Discernment and Resistance in a World of Domination* (Minneapolis: Fortress Press, 1992).

54 Hardt and Negri, *Multitude*, 217.

55 Ibid., 63–95.

56 Amartya Sen, *The Idea of Justice* (Cambridge: Belknap Press of Harvard University Press, 2009), 100.

57 Sen, *Idea of Justice*, ix.

58 Ibid., 16.

59 See Alfred North Whitehead, *Process and Reality*, corrected edition, ed. David Ray Griffin and Donald W. Sherburne (New York: Free Press, 1978), 244.

60 Sen, *Idea of Justice*, 64.

61 Ibid., 18.

62 Ibid., 66.

63 Ibid., 230.

64 This is in contrast to Nussbaum's discreet list of ten capabilities. See Martha C. Nussbaum, *Creating Capabilities: The Human Development Approach* (Cambridge: Belknap Press of Harvard University Press, 2011), 33-34.

65 Sen's argument that capabilities are for individuals mimics the logic of value-entities in Chapter 2 of this work. Only entities have intrinsic value, though they have profound instrumental value for others and the world. See Sen, *Idea of Justice*, 246.

66 Martha C. Nussbaum, *Frontiers of Justice: Disability, Nationality, Species Membership* (London: Belknap Press of Harvard University Press, 2006), 70.

67 This has obvious resonances with womanist theologies. See Delores S. Williams, *Sisters in the Wilderness: The Challenge of Womanist God-Talk* (Maryknoll, NY: Orbis Books, 1993), 175; and Monica A. Coleman, *Making a Way Out of No Way: A Womanist Theology* (Minneapolis: Fortress Press, 2008), 94.

68 Alfred North Whitehead, *The Function of Reason* (1929; repr., Boston: Beacon Press, 1971), 8.

69 Amartya Sen, *The Argumentative Indian: Writings on Indian History, Culture and Identity* (New York: Picador, 2005), 86.

70 Sen, *Idea of Justice*, 44–45.

71 Ibid., 246, 45.

72 Ibid., 118.

73 Ibid., 70.

74 Ibid., 23. Process thinkers would rightly add that one should not dismiss any agency, whether human or otherwise.

75 Iris Marion Young, *Justice and the Politics of Difference* (Princeton: Princeton University Press, 2011), 31.

76 Young, *Justice and the Politics of Difference*, 37.

77 Ibid., 9.

78 Ibid., 64.

79 Wonhee Anne Joh notes that Young's 'unassimilated Otherness' "resonates with Whitehead's related entity." Wonhee Anne Joh, *Heart of the Cross: A Postcolonial Christology* (Louisville: Westminster John Knox Press, 2006), 151.

80 Young, *Justice and the Politics of Difference*, 98.

81 Ibid., 25.

82 Ibid., 241.

83 Ibid., 187.

84 Iris Marion Young, *Inclusion and Democracy* (Oxford: Oxford University Press, 2000), 197.

85 Young, *Inclusion and Democracy*, 171–72.

86 Ibid., 53–65.

87 From Marcella Althaus-Reid's perspective, many of these activities could rightly be called "indecent." See Chapter 5 for her notion of indecency.

88 Young, *Inclusion and Democracy*, 49. May we kill it in churching, too!

89 Ibid., 49. An example of this was when Medea Benjamin, the CODEPINK activist, interrupted President Obama during his speech on Guantanamo prisoners and their hunger strike in May 2013. Many news commentators responded that it was improper for her to do so: Young would say that they were uncritically supporting decent political order and rhetoric.

90 Bonnie Honig, *Emergency Politics: Paradox, Law, and Democracy* (Princeton: Princeton University Press, 2009), 122-23.

91 Many people may rightly recognize this book itself as a work of agonistic cosmopolitanism. The particularity of Christianity, with its images, themes, and specific social location are put to work out of a cosmological commitment to the entire planet, life, and people. Its location does not have to be explained away, for its recognition is the very condition for its radical praxis.

92 Honig, *Emergency Politics*, 134.

93 Young, *Justice and the Politics of Difference*, 105.

94 Ibid., 106.

95 Ibid., 106.

96 Young, *Inclusion and Democracy*, 146.

97 Ibid., 180–86.

98 Ibid., 187.

99 The one late exception is where they suggest their openness to institutional organization beyond direct participation to the extent that such institutional configurations are open-ended, contestable, and conflictual. See Hardt and Negri, *Commonwealth*, 357.

100 Young, *Inclusion and Democracy*, 133.

101 Likewise, Míguez, Rieger, and Sung reject the communist ideal of a stateless free association of producers as being impossible. Míguez, Rieger, and Sung, *Beyond the Spirit of Empire*, 103–05.

102 Jeffrey W. Robbins, *Radical Democracy and Political Theology*, Insurrections: Critical Studies in Religion, Politics, and Culture (New York: Columbia University Press, 2011), 1–11.

103 Robbins, *Radical Democracy and Political Theology*, 71.

104 Ibid., 194, ft. 17.

105 Clayton Crockett, *Radical Political Theology: Religion and Politics after Liberalism* (New York: Columbia University Press, 2011), 55.

106 Crockett, *Radical Political Theology*, 3.

107 Ibid., 17.

108 One political theologian in particular, Dorothee Sölle, was a helpful

resource in this project's broad paradigm of kerygma, koinonia, and diakonia, which was expressed in Chapter 1.

CHAPTER 5

1 Jürgen Moltmann, *The Church in the Power of the Spirit: A Contribution to Messianic Ecclesiology*, trans. Margaret Kohl (Minneapolis: Fortress Press, 1993), xiii.

2 Scott R. Paeth, *Exodus Church and Civil Society: Public Theology and Social Theory in the Work of Jürgen Moltmann* (Burlington, VT: Ashgate, 2008), 49.

3 Paeth, *Exodus Church and Civil Society*, 24.

4 J. Stephen Rhodes, "The Church as the Community of Open Friendship," *Asbury Theological Journal* 55, no. 1 (Spring 2000): 43. Unless otherwise noted, all italicized quotations are from the respective cited author.

5 Moltmann, *Church in the Power of the Spirit*, 5.

6 Ibid., 66.

7 Van Nam Kim, *A Church of Hope: A Study of the Eschatological Ecclesiology of Jürgen Moltmann* (Lanham, MD: University Press of America, 2005), 40–41.

8 Kim, *Church of Hope*, 45–46.

9 Moltmann, *Church in the Power of the Spirit*, 205.

10 Ibid., 27.

11 Jürgen Moltmann, *Sun of Righteousness, Arise!: God's Future for Humanity and the Earth*, trans. Margaret Kohl (Minneapolis: Fortress Press, 2010), 17.

12 Moltmann, *Church in the Power of the Spirit*, 10.

13 Ibid., 11.

14 Rhodes, "Church as the Community of Open Fellowship," 42.

15 Moltmann, *Church in the Power of the Spirit*, 49.

16 Rhodes, "Church as the Community of Open Friendship," 43.

17 Ibid., 44.

18   Paeth, *Exodus Church and Civil Society*, 27.

19   Ibid., 45.

20   Alfred North Whitehead, *Adventure of Ideas* (1933; repr., New York: Free Press, 1967), 168–69. Whitehead notes that while classical theologians offered a form of mutual immanence in the divine nature, they "never made this advance into general metaphysics." The same problem is true for Moltmann.

21   Moltmann, *Sun of Righteousness, Arise!*, 69.

22   Ibid., 137–38.

23   Moltmann, *Church in the Power of the Spirit*, 10–11.

24   Ibid., 5–15.

25   Ibid., 154.

26   Ibid., 107.

27   Kim, *Church of Hope*, 392.

28   Moltmann, *Church in the Power of the Spirit*, 206.

29   Jürgen Moltmann, *The Spirit of Life: A Universal Affirmation*, trans. Margaret Kohl (Minneapolis: Fortress Press, 1992), 186.

30   Jürgen Moltmann, "Diaconal Church in the Context of the Kingdom of God," in *Hope for the Church: Moltmann in Dialogue with Practical Theology*, ed. and trans. Theodore Runyon (Nashville: Abingdon, 1979), 27.

31   Moltmann, "Diaconal Church in the Context of the Kingdom of God," 31.

32   Those aware of Jones's own abuse of power and domestic abuse will surely find his criticism an example of the pot calling the kettle black.

33   Tony Jones, *The Church Is Flat: The Relational Ecclesiology of the Emerging Church Movement* (Minneapolis: JoPa Group, 2011), 149–51.

34   Geiko Müller-Fahrenholz, "In the Fellowship of the Spirit of God," in *The Kingdom and the Power: The Theology of Jürgen Moltmann* (London: SCM Press, 2000), 105.

35   See Marcus Borg, *Jesus: Uncovering the Life, Teachings, and Relevance of a Religious Revolutionary* (New York: HarperOne, 2008),

259–60, and John Dominic Crossan, *The Birth of Christianity: Discovering What Happened in the Years Immediately After the Execution of Jesus* (San Francisco: HarperSanFrancisco, 1998), 273–89, 317.

36 Moltmann, *Sun of Righteousness, Arise!*, 222.

37 Moltmann, *Church in the Power of the Spirit*, 65.

38 Jones, *Church Is Flat*, 153–55. As John Cobb recognizes, a more radical church will have similar practices but provide a different analysis and motivation from postliberal Hauerwasians. Three primary differences are that they will pursue actions when they can make a positive difference, will form alliances with others of diverse persuasions, and will offer an alternative picture not just for church but also for the world. See John B. Cobb, Jr., ed., *Resistance: The New Role of Progressive Christians* (Louisville: Westminster John Knox Press, 2008), xiii.

39 Paeth, *Exodus Church and Civil Society*, 112–49.

40 In fact, we have already found her to be of great help in Chapter 2 for cosmological questions and in Chapter 3 regarding mutual interest, solidarity as social ontology, and the difference between horizontal and vertical transcendence.

41 Marjorie Hewitt Suchocki, *God, Christ, Church: A Practical Guide to Process Theology*, rev. ed. (New York: Crossroad, 1989), 129–38.

42 Suchocki, *God, Christ, Church*, 123.

43 Ibid., 160. Such language unmistakably mimics Moltmann.

44 Ibid., 121.

45 Ibid., 133–39.

46 Marjorie Hewitt Suchocki, *The Fall to Violence: Original Sin in Relational Theology* (New York: Continuum, 1994), 70–73.

47 Suchocki, *God, Christ, Church*, 139.

48 Ibid., 165–66.

49 Ibid., 133–37.

50 Suchocki, *Fall to Violence*, 161.

51 Marjorie Suchocki, *Divinity and Diversity: A Christian Affirmation of Religious Pluralism* (Nashville: Abingdon Press, 2003), 118.

52 Suchocki, *Fall to Violence*, 113–20.

53 Ibid., 120–22.

54 Ibid., 157.

55 Suchocki, *God, Christ, Church*, 149.

56 Suchocki, *Divinity and Diversity*, 79.

57 Ibid., 109, 115.

58 Marjorie Hewitt Suchocki, *In God's Presence: Theological Reflections on Prayer* (St. Louis: Chalice Press, 1996), 11.

59 Catherine Keller, *The Face of the Deep: A Theology of Becoming* (London: Routledge, 2003), 229.

60 One of the primary exceptions is by Robert Shore-Goss, "Dis/Grace-full Incarnation and the Dis/Grace-full Church: Marcella Althaus-Reid's Vision of Radical Inclusivity," in *Dancing Theology in Fetish Boots: Essays in Honour of Marcella Althaus-Reid*, 1–16, ed. Lisa Isherwood and Mark D. Jordan (London: SCM Press, 2010).

61 Her family was Methodist and she was part of a fundamentalist church before returning to a Methodist community and working with BECs. Néstor Míguez (informal group discussion, Buenos Aires, Argentina, July 11, 2013). She also participated in Quaker, Anglican, and Metropolitan Community Church groups while living in Scotland.

62 Marcella Althaus-Reid, *Indecent Theology: Theological Perversions in Sex, Gender, and Politics* (London: Routledge, 2000), 64–66.

63 Althaus-Reid, *Indecent Theology*, 129.

64 Ibid., 132.

65 Ibid., 25. The language of "transvestite" may concern readers within the United States, for in that context transgender women are often violently misgendered by being labeled men in women's clothing. However, in a number of Latin American countries, such as Mexico, there are strongly distinct communities that self-identify as transgender, transsexual, and transvestite. I am giving Althaus-Reid the benefit of the doubt that she is speaking in the latter category and not in the misgendering category.

66 Alistar Kee, "Queering Ontologies: A Critique of Three Liberation

Theologies," in *Dancing Theology in Fetish Boots: Essays in Honour of Marcella Althaus-Reid*, ed. Lisa Isherwood and Mark D. Jordan (London: SCM Press, 2010), 138–39.

67 Althaus-Reid, *Indecent Theology*, 26, 32.

68 Rosemary Radford Ruether, "Talking Dirty, Speaking Truth: Indecenting Theology," in *Dancing Theology in Fetish Boots: Essays in Honour of Marcella Althaus-Reid*, ed. Lisa Isherwood and Mark D. Jordan (London: SCM Press, 2010), 255.

69 Althaus-Reid, *Indecent Theology*, 116.

70 For example, the Virgin Mary only appears to ask for a new temple to be built and never appears to demand houses or a free hospital be built for the poor, or to condemn human rights abuses. See Althaus-Reid, *Indecent Theology*, 60.

71 There are other images people already turn to: some Brazilian transvestite Christian communities interpret the Virgin Mary as a divine drag queen; some groups invoke the name of *Santa Librada*, the transvestite Christ who assists people who have to cross legal boundaries for the sake of survival, while others focus on the Deceased Correa, who died on a journey with her infant but whose breasts continued to lactate so that the infant survived, who is also invoked for those taking journeys. See Althaus-Reid, *Indecent Theology*, 79–85.

72 Ibid., 105, 188.

73 Ibid., 193. As of July 2013, they continue to meet in Buenos Aires's central plaza every Thursday at 3:30 p.m.

74 Ibid., 35.

75 Marcella Althaus-Reid, *From Feminist Theology to Indecent Theology* (London: SCM Press, 2004), 106. It is indeed curious that even at a queer/liberation/postcolonial conference in Buenos Aires given in her memory in 2013, no presentation mentioned this book but instead focused almost exclusively on her more famous work, *Indecent Theology*.

76 Althaus-Reid, *From Feminist Theology to Indecent Theology*, 119.

77 Ibid., 121.

78 Joerg Rieger and Kwok Pui-lan, *Occupy Religion: Theology of the*

Multitude (Lanham, MD: Rowman & Littlefield, 2012), 127.

79   Marcella Althaus-Reid, *The Queer God* (London: Routledge, 2003), 123.

80   Althaus-Reid, *Queer God*, 122.

81   Shore-Goss, "Dis/Grace-full Incarnation and the Dis/Grace-full Church," 10–11.

82   Marcella Althaus-Reid, "Hard Core Queer: The Church as Dis/grace" (paper presented at "Queering the Church" conference, Boston University School of Theology, Boston, MA, April 18–19, 2007), 2–7.

83   Shore-Goss, "Dis/Grace-full Incarnation and the Dis/Grace-full Church," 8–9.

84   Hugo Córdova Quero, informal conversation, Buenos Aires, Argentina, July 11, 2013. Quero is a Queer postcolonial theologian living in Argentina, and Althaus-Reid directed his dissertation until her death from cancer in 2009.

85   Althaus-Reid, *Queer God*, 148.

86   Marcella Althaus-Reid, "From Liberation Theology to Indecent Theology," in *Latin American Liberation Theology: The Next Generation*. ed. Ivan Petrella (Maryknoll, NY: Orbis Books, 2005), 25.

87   Althaus-Reid, "From Liberation Theology to Indecent Theology," 25.

88   Althaus-Reid, *Indecent Theology*, 130.

89   Althaus-Reid, *Queer God*, 168.

90   Althaus-Reid, "From Liberation Theology to Indecent Theology," 33.

91   Althaus-Reid, *From Feminist Theology to Indecent Theology*, 18.

92   Althaus-Reid, *Indecent Theology*, 91.

93   Ibid., 168–69.

94   Althaus-Reid, "From Liberation Theology to Indecent Theology," 26.

95   Althaus-Reid, *From Feminist Theology to Indecent Theology*, 28.

96   Ibid., 111.

97 Althaus-Reid, *Indecent Theology*, 179.

98 Althaus-Reid, *Queer God*, 161.

99 Althaus-Reid, *From Feminist Theology to Indecent Theology*, 111–12.

100 Althaus-Reid, *Indecent Theology*, 171.

101 Ivan Petrella agrees that this is the trajectory Althaus-Reid sets out. See Ivan Petrella, "Liberation Theology after Marcella," in *Dancing Theology in Fetish Boots: Essays in Honour of Marcella Althaus-Reid*, ed. Lisa Isherwood and Mark D. Jordan (London: SCM Press, 2010), 204.

102 In his own sexual misconduct and abuse of power, Yoder reveals that all theology is indeed sexual, though not necessarily liberative or healthy, especially when closeted and expressing power differentials.

103 John Howard Yoder, *The Priestly Kingdom: Social Ethics as Gospel* (Notre Dame: University of Notre Dame Press, 1984), 11.

104 Yoder, *Priestly Kingdom*, 85.

105 Althaus-Reid, "Hard Core Queer," 6.

106 Yoder, *Priestly Kingdom*, 96, 162.

107 Ibid., 11, 101.

108 Moltmann, *Church in the Power of the Spirit*, 338–41.

109 Ibid., 338–39.

110 Ibid., 22–25.

111 Moltmann, *Spirit of Life*, 184.

112 Moltmann, *Church in the Power of the Spirit*, 343.

113 Kim, *Church of Hope*, 54–64.

114 Moltmann, *Spirit of Life*, 233.

115 Alfred North Whitehead, *Process and Reality*, corrected edition, ed. David Ray Griffin and Donald W. Sherburne (New York: Free Press, 1978), 21.

116 Moltmann, *Church in the Power of the Spirit*, 345–47.

117 Ibid., 354.

118 Müller-Fahrenholz, "Fellowship of the Spirit of God," 83, 89.

119 Moltmann, *Church in the Power of the Spirit*, 355–56.

120 Ibid., 348.

121 Kim, *Church of Hope*, 79.

122 Moltmann, *Church in the Power of the Spirit*, 349.

123 Ibid., 352.

124 Ibid., 350.

125 Müller-Fahrenholz, "Fellowship of the Spirit of God," 102.

126 Moltmann, *Church in the Power of the Spirit*, 9.

127 Ibid., 358.

128 Jones, *Church Is Flat*, 132.

129 Kim, *Church of Hope*, 84.

130 Moltmann, *Church in the Power of the Spirit*, 359–60.

131 For example, Müller-Fahrenholz suggests that apostolicity comes through witnessing to the kingdom and resisting principalities and powers, which results in the cross and consequent suffering. See Müller-Fahrenholz, "Fellowship of the Spirit of God," 83.

132 Moltmann, *Church in the Power of the Spirit*, 361.

133 Moltmann, "Diaconal Church in the Context of the Kingdom of God," 28.

134 Moltmann, *Church in the Power of the Spirit*, 361.

135 Suchocki, *God, Christ, Church*, 139.

136 Ibid., 141.

137 Ibid., 191.

138 Ibid., 189.

139 Ibid., 144–45.

140 Ibid., 146, 48.

141 Ibid., 148–50.

142 John B. Cobb, Jr., *Spiritual Bankruptcy: A Prophetic Call to Action* (Nashville: Abingdon Press, 2010), 12. Later, Cobb writes, "To secularize a tradition is to bring it effectively to bear on the real problems of human beings and society in a healing and creative way."

In effect, the otherworldly or afterlife are not dismissed but they become subordinated concerns.

143 Cobb, *Spiritual Bankruptcy*, viii.

144 John B. Cobb, Jr., "Commonwealth and Empire," in *The American Empire and the Commonwealth of God: A Political, Economic, Religious Statement*, David Ray Griffin, John B. Cobb Jr., Richard A Falk, and Catherine Keller (Louisville: Westminster John Knox Press, 2006), 144.

145 John B. Cobb, Jr., *Reclaiming the Church: Where the Mainline Church Went Wrong and What to Do about It* (Louisville: Westminster John Knox Press, 1997), 8.

146 Suchocki, *God, Christ, Church*, 150.

147 Ibid., 164–67.

148 Althaus-Reid, *From Feminist Theology to Indecent Theology*, 63.

149 Althaus-Reid, *Queer God*, 8.

150 Althaus-Reid, *From Feminist Theology to Indecent Theology*, 143.

151 Althaus-Reid, *Queer God*, 17.

152 Althaus-Reid, *Indecent Theology*, 177.

153 Althaus-Reid, *From Feminist Theology to Indecent Theology*, 74.

154 Althaus-Reid, *Indecent Theology*, 24.

155 Althaus-Reid, *From Feminist Theology to Indecent Theology*, 74.

156 Ibid., 3.

157 Ibid., 97.

158 Moltmann, *Church in the Power of the Spirit*, 99, 326.

159 Ibid., 197.

160 Althaus-Reid, *From Feminist Theology to Indecent Theology*, 56.

161 Ibid., 6.

162 Althaus-Reid, *Queer God*, 4.

163 Ibid., 149.

164 Althaus-Reid, *From Feminist Theology to Indecent Theology*, 82.

165 Ibid., 100.

166 Althaus-Reid, *Queer God*, 165.

167 John B. Cobb, Jr. and David Ray Griffin, *Process Theology: An Introductory Exposition* (Louisville: Westminster John Knox Press, 1976), 99-100. Concerning creative transformation, Cobb and Griffin write, "Growth is not achieved by merely adding together elements in the given world in different combinations. It requires the transformation of those elements through the introduction of novelty. It alters their nature and meaning without suppressing or destroying them."

168 This is particularly true with other process ecclesiologies. To the extent that they discuss ecclesial marks, they always emphasize the marks of one, holy, catholic, and apostolic. See Clark M. Williamson, "Companions on the Way: The Church," in *Way of Blessing, Way of Life: A Christian Theology* (St. Louis: Chalice Press, 1999), 256–59, and those process ecclesiologies reviewed in Chapter 1. In contrast, I say that churching is holy to the extent that it seeks to discern initial aims, but these are always directed for and in relation to itself, others, and the world; therefore it is just as true to say it is secular!

CHAPTER 6

1 Alfred North Whitehead, *Adventure of Ideas* (1933; repr., New York: Free Press, 1967), 171. He writes, "But it is a question for discussion why the more radical schools should not cut entirely free from any appeal to the past, and concentrate entirely upon the contemporary world and contemporary examples. The summary answer is that in so far as such an appeal to tradition can be made with complete honesty, without any shadow of evasion, there is an enormous gain in popular effectiveness."

2 Joerg Rieger and Kwok Pui-lan, *Occupy Religion: Theology of the Multitude* (Lanham, MD: Rowman & Littlefield, 2012), 75.

3 Rieger and Kwok, *Occupy Religion*, 124.

4 Ibid., 117.

5 Rieger and Kwok call this "theopraxis." Ibid., 86.

6 Ibid., 78.

7   Bernard Lee, "Reconstructing Our American Story: Intentional Christian Communities." *Chicago Studies* 26, no. 1 (April 1987): 17.

8   Rieger and Kwok, *Occupy Religion*, 70.

9   Ibid., 123.

10 Catherine Keller, *The Face of the Deep: A Theology of Becoming* (London: Routledge, 2003), 230.

11 Keller, *Face of the Deep*, 231.

12 Alfred North Whitehead, *Religion in the Making* (1926; repr., New York: Fordham University Press, 2011), 48.

13 Néstor Míguez, Joerg Rieger, and Jung Mo Sung, *Beyond the Spirit of Empire: Theology and Politics in a New Key*, Reclaiming Liberation Theology Series (London: SCM Press, 2009), 137.

14 Catherine Keller, *God and Power: Counter-Apocalyptic Journeys* (Minneapolis: Fortress Press, 2005), 20.

15 Jung Mo Sung agrees: "Today one of the favorite scapegoats is neoliberalism and its representatives. It seems that neoliberalism is the cause of everything bad that exists in the world, even those things that had existed before neoliberalism and that will continue to exist following the end of the neoliberal hegemony." Jung Mo Sung, *The Subject, Capitalism, and Religion: Horizons of Hope in Complex Societies* (New York: Palgrave Macmillan, 2011), 142.

16 Keller, *God and Power*, 148.

17 Ivone Gebara, *Out of the Depths: Women's Experience of Evil and Salvation*, trans. Ann Patrick Ware (Minneapolis: Fortress Press, 2002), 132.

18 Dorothee Sölle, "The Kingdom of God and the Church," in *Thinking About God: An Introduction to Theology*, trans. (London: SCM Press, 1990), 137.

19 Sölle, "Kingdom of God and the Church," 146.

20 Ibid., 141.

21 Ibid., 142–44.

22 Sung, *Subject, Capitalism, and Religion*, 47.

23 Ibid., 48.

24 Ibid., 87.

25 Sölle, "Kingdom of God and the Church," 137.

26 Jung Mo Sung, *Desire, Market and Religion,* Reclaiming Liberation Theology (London: SCM Press, 2007), 53.

27 Sung, *Desire, Market and Religion,* 54.

28 Ibid., 102. Delores S. Williams, *Sisters in the Wilderness: The Challenge of Womanist God-Talk* (Maryknoll, NY: Orbis Press, 1993), 196.

29 At his best, Moltmann sees this as well: "Mysticism does not mean estrangement from action; it is a preparation for public discipleship." Jürgen Moltmann, *The Spirit of Life: A Universal Affirmation,* trans. Margaret Kohl (Minneapolis: Fortress Press, 1992), 209.

30 John B. Cobb, Jr., *Spiritual Bankruptcy: A Prophetic Call to Action* (Nashville: Abingdon Press, 2010), 50.

31 David Ray Griffin, "Resurrection and Empire," in *The American Empire and the Commonwealth of God: A Political, Economic, Religious Statement,* David Ray Griffin, John B. Cobb Jr., Richard A Falk, and Catherine Keller (Louisville: Westminster John Knox Press, 2006), 155–56. Griffin considers this moment as likely creating a *status confessionis.*

32 One closing call and response that I hear each time goes as follows: "It is our duty to fight for freedom . . . it is our duty to win . . . we must love each other and support each other . . . we have nothing to lose but our chains."

33 Keller likewise delays discussing Christ until near the end of her book of constructive theology. See Catherine Keller, *On the Mystery: Discerning Divinity in Process* (Minneapolis: Fortress Press, 2008), 133–55.

34 Cobb, *Spiritual Bankruptcy,* 27.

35 As Whitehead notes, "The essence of Christianity is the appeal to the life of Christ as a revelation of the nature of God and of his agency in the world." Whitehead, *Adventures of Ideas,* 167.

36 Monica A. Coleman, *Making a Way Out of No Way: A Womanist Theology* (Minneapolis: Fortress Press, 2008), 92–93.

37 In this story, Jesus begins with a horizon of concern that excludes

the woman and her daughter. However, he experiences creative transformation through his encounter with her and finally responds. Soon after this encounter Jesus travels to the Gentile side of the Sea of Galilee to feed the multitude, where before he had restricted this ministry to the Jewish people. This claim is similar to Althaus-Reid's understanding of Jesus's historical limitations, but emphasizes that he reflects an openness to creative transformation. Brian McLaren makes much the same point concerning Matthew's version of the story. See Brian D. McLaren, *Everything Must Change: Jesus, Global Crises, and a Revolution of Hope* (Nashville: Thomas Nelson, 2007), 155–58.

38 John B. Cobb, Jr., *Lay Theology* (St. Louis: Chalice Press, 1994), 93.

39 Laurel C. Schneider, *Beyond Monotheism: A theology of multiplicity* (London: Routledge, 2008), 1–5.

40 Dietrich Bonhoeffer, *The Cost of Discipleship* (1937; repr., New York: Touchstone, 1995), 243.

41 Dietrich Bonhoeffer, *Life Together: The Classic Exploration of Christian Community*, trans. John W. Doberstein (New York: HarperOne, 1954), 25.

42 1 Corinthians 12:22–23, NRSV.

43 Gilles Deleuze and Félix Guattari, *A Thousand Plateaus: Capitalism and Schizophrenia*, trans. Brian Massumi (Minneapolis: University of Minnesota Press, 1987), 30.

44 Alfred North Whitehead, *Process and Reality*, corrected edition, ed. David Ray Griffin and Donald W. Sherburne (New York: Free Press, 1978), 103–05.

45 Keller, *On the Mystery*, 155.

46 William Herzog offers the distinct position that the parables of Jesus "were not meant to be stories with either a clear moral or a single meaning . . . [but] were meant to be discussion-starters, whose purpose was to raise questions and pose dilemmas for their hearers" about their lives and the larger realities in which they were caught. William R. Herzog II, *Parables as Subversive Speech: Jesus as Pedagogue of the Oppressed* (Louisville: Westminster/John Knox Press, 1994), 259.

47 If that is the case, proclaiming, teaching, and witnessing to these

values are ways to reflect not so much faith in Jesus but *the faith-fulness of Jesus.* Cobb, *Spiritual Bankruptcy,* 29.

48 Míguez, Rieger, and Sung, *Beyond the Spirit of Empire,* 131.

49 For a deeper analysis of eschatology in terms of a non-totalizing revolution which includes an analysis of both Catherine Keller and Jung Mo Sung, see the article: Timothy Murphy, "Reconceiving Revolution: Towards Micro-Revolutions of Becoming," *Claremont Journal of Religion* 2, no. 2 (Spring 2013): 87–113. Accessed November 8, 2013. http://claremontjournal.com/wp-content/uploads/2013/06/Reconceiving-Revolution-Towards-Micro-Revolutions-of-Becoming-by-Timothy-Murphy.pdf.

50 Keller, *God and Power,* 151.

51 Sung, *Subject, Capitalism, and Religion,* 93.

52 There has been a long and ongoing debate on the appropriateness of English terms for the basileia. Some prefer kingdom, empire, or reign. For their limitations, see Melanie Johnson-Debaufre, "The *Basileia Theou* and the Space/s of Utopian Politics," paper presented at the Twelfth Transdisciplinary Theological Colloquium, Common Good(s): Economy, Ecology, and Political Theology, Drew Theological School, Madison, NJ, February 10, 2013. While John Cobb prefers "Commonwealth of God," I have chosen the word "divine" over "god" because of the tendency to objectify the latter in English. The result is "the divine commonwealth."

53 Sung, *Desire, Market and Religion,* 146.

54 Ibid., 148.

55 Keller, *God and Power,* 151.

56 In light of the kerygma, a koinonia of encounter and love for creative transformation involves two sides for the postcolonial process position of Clayton Crockett and Jay McDaniel: "On the one hand, love involves listening for hybridity in the other, with a willingness to be creative[ly] transformed by [the] singular hybridity of the other person. This creative transformation can best occur through empathy: perspective taking, active concern, and also 'feeling the feelings' of others. But it also requires a conscious bracketing or 'negative prehending' of existing stereotypes: an active forgetting which has an apophatic quality of its own. This can be called relational

unknowing or compassionate forgetting." Clayton Crockett and Jay McDaniel, "From an Idolatry of Identity to a Planetization of Alterity: A Relational-Theological Approach to Hybridity, Sin, and Love," *Journal of Postcolonial Theory and Theology* 1, no. 3 (November 2010): 15. Accessed November 15, 2013. http://postcolonialjournal.com/Resources/Crockett%20JPTT%20Dec%2027.pdf.

57 In a similar fashion, people become LGBTQ-affirming not because of arguments but from experiencing something different and being offered some conceptual tools to make sense or meaning out of it.

58 Marcella Althaus-Reid, "From Liberation Theology to Indecent Theology," in *Latin American Liberation Theology: The Next Generation.* ed. Ivan Petrella (Maryknoll, NY: Orbis Books, 2005), 28.

59 One scripture passage that can be understood as affirming a notion of productive conflict comes from one of Jesus's more unsettling sayings. In Matthew 10:34 (NRSV), Jesus says, "Do not think that I have come to bring peace to the earth; I have not come to bring peace, but a sword." There will not be easy agreement or consensus, but conflicts will emerge, even within the same household! The peace of passive acquiescence gives way towards a process leading to a contestable consensus.

60 I once led a meeting among a pro-LGBTQ church group and suggested that it would be helpful for us to explore how our faith helps us affirm and welcome LGBTQ persons. I was quite surprised when a member immediately chimed in with "I don't consider this a religious issue at all; this is about rights!" John Cobb explains this tendency when he writes: "Secularizing churches made up of people who are not encouraged to be reflective about their faith have little chance of avoiding enculturation into an increasingly secularist environment." See Cobb, *Spiritual Bankruptcy*, 130.

61 Andrew C. Blume, "Towards a Process Sacramental Ecclesiology," *Process Studies* 37, no. 1 (Spring-Summer 2008): 48–49.

62 Blume, "Towards a Process Sacramental Ecclesiology," 42, 45.

63 Lee, "Reconstructing Our American Story," 11–24.

64 Brynolf Lyon also incorporates this insight, as is mentioned in Chapter 1.

65 John B. Cobb, Jr., ed. *Resistance: The New Role of Progressive*

Christians (Louisville: Westminster John Knox Press, 2008), xii.

66 Jürgen Moltmann, *The Church in the Power of the Spirit: A Contribution to Messianic Ecclesiology,* trans. Margaret Kohl (Minneapolis: Fortress Press, 1993), 240. Of course, people who have already been baptized do not need to be re-baptized. At any rate, baptism is not a requirement for participation in churching or for leadership, though it is a potentially powerful event of divine encounter and response.

67 Moltmann, *Church in the Power of the Spirit,* 242.

68 For more on the relationship between process thought and pacifism, see Justin Heinzekehr, "Pacifism from a Process Perspective: Redefining Process Ethics through an Anabaptist Lens," MA Thesis, Claremont School of Theology, 2011; Daniel A. Dombrowski, *Christian Pacifism* (Philadelphia: Temple University Press, 1991); and Timothy Murphy, "The Pacifism of Duane Friesen: Engaged Realism, Process Thought, and Critical Assessment," *Process Studies* 42, no. 1 (Spring-Summer 2013): 110–31.

69 Cobb, *Spiritual Bankruptcy,* 163.

70 We could even go one step further and welcome attending animals beyond the human to Holy Communion, such as with blessed doggie treats. Instead of saying, "The bread of life and cup of blessing," one could say, "Good dog! Good dog!" This is one of many ways animals can more fully be church, encountering and proclaiming good news.

71 Chapter 5 provided several other helpful recommendations for concrete indecent churching practices by Althaus-Reid and will not be repeated here.

72 Jürgen Moltmann, "The Life Signs of the Spirit in the Fellowship Community of Christ," in *Hope for the Church: Moltmann in Dialogue with Practical Theology,* ed. and trans. Theodore Runyon (Nashville: Abingdon, 1979), 55.

73 Luke Higgins, "Becoming through Multiplicity: Staying in the Middle of Whitehead's and Deleuze-Guattari's Philosophies of Life," in *Secrets of Becoming: Negotiating Whitehead, Deleuze, and Butler,* ed. Roland Faber and Andrea Stephenson (New York: Fordham Press, 2010), 154.

74 Keller says as much when she writes, "For the plurality of our

relations to a complex world requires attunement each to our own complexity: the multiplicity of the world is both within and without. So this sort of fluid positionality is a kind of spiritual practice, always as internal as it is external, as personal as it is political." Keller, *God and Power*, 148.

75 Keller, *God and Power*, 130.

76 This is close to a Quaker spirituality of waiting on the Spirit.

77 Keller, *Face of the Deep*, 230.

78 Gary Dorrien, *The Making of American Liberal Theology: Crisis, Irony, & Postmodernity, 1950-2005*, vol. 3 of The Making of American Liberal Theology (Louisville: Westminster John Knox Press, 2006), 512.

79 I would like churching to be an alternative in faithful praxis not unlike the way the news organization Democracy Now! is an alternative to corporate media in the United States. Thus, churching is an alternative to a corporatized, commercialized, christendomized church. Radical churching is to Democracy Now! as mainline Protestant Christianity is to the mainstream media.

80 Rieger and Kwok, *Occupy Religion*, 123.

Bibliography

1968 Year Book and Directory of the Christian Church (Disciples of Christ). Edited by Howard E. Dentler. Indianapolis: Christian Church (Disciples of Christ), 1968.

2011 United Church of Christ Yearbook. Cleveland, OH: United Church of Christ, 2011.

Althaus-Reid, Marcella. *From Feminist Theology to Indecent Theology: Readings on Poverty, Sexual Identity and God*. London: SCM Press, 2004.

———. "From Liberation Theology to Indecent Theology." In *Latin American Liberation Theology: The Next Generation*, edited by Ivan Petrella, 20-38. Maryknoll, NY: Orbis Books, 2005.

———. "Hard Core Queer: The Church as Dis/grace." Paper presented, "Queering the Church" conference, Boston University School of Theology, Boston, MA, April 18-19, 2007.

———. *Indecent Theology: Theological Perversions in Sex, Gender, and Politics*. London: Routledge, 2000.

———. *The Queer God*. London: Routledge, 2003.

Birch, Charles, and John B. Cobb, Jr. *The Liberation of Life: From the Cell to the Community*. 1981. Reprint, Denton, TX: Environmental Ethics Books, 1990.

Blume, Andrew C. "Towards a Process Sacramental Ecclesiology." *Process Studies* 37, no. 1 (Spring-Summer 2008): 39–54.

Bonhoeffer, Dietrich. *The Cost of Discipleship*. 1937. Reprint, New York: Touchstone, 1995.

____. *Life Together: The Classic Exploration of Christian Community.* Translated by John W. Doberstein. New York: HarperOne, 1954.

Borg, Marcus. *Jesus: Uncovering the Life, Teachings, and Relevance of a Religious Revolutionary.* New York: HarperOne, 2008.

Bracken, Joseph A. "Ecclesiology and the Problem of the One and the Many." *Theological Studies* 43, no. 2 (June 1982): 293–311.

Brock, Rita Nakashima, and Rebecca Ann Parker. *Saving Paradise: How Christianity Traded Love of This World for Crucifixion and Empire.* Boston: Beacon Press, 2008.

Cargas, Harry James, and Bernard Lee, eds. *Religious Experience and Process Theology: The Pastoral Implications of a Major Modern Movement.* New York: Paulist Press, 1976.

Clayton, Philip. *Transforming Christian Theology: For Church and Society.* Minneapolis: Fortress Press, 2010.

____. "An Upside-Down Politics and an Inside-Out Church: Moving Occupy From Tent to Pew." Presentation, annual meeting of the American Academy of Religion, Chicago, IL, November, 2012.

Cobb, John B., Jr. "A Challenge to the Church." *Creative Transformation* 18, no. 4 (Fall 2009): 2–7.

____. *A Christian Natural Theology: Based on the Thought of Alfred North Whitehead.* 2nd ed. Louisville: Westminster John Knox Press, 2007.

____. "Commonwealth and Empire." In *The American Empire and the Commonwealth of God: A Political, Economic, Religious Statement,* by David Ray Griffin, John B. Cobb Jr., Richard A Falk, and Catherine Keller, 137–50. Louisville: Westminster John Knox Press, 2006.

____. "Democratizing the Economic Order." In *The American Empire and the Commonwealth of God: A Political, Economic, Religious Statement,* by David Ray Griffin, John B. Cobb Jr., Richard A Falk, and Catherine Keller, 86–102. Louisville: Westminster John Knox Press, 2006.

____. "God as the Power of the Future." Process and Faith, posted January 2012, http://processandfaith.org/writings/ask-dr-cobb/2012-01/god-power-future (accessed March 9, 2013).

____. *Lay Theology.* St. Louis: Chalice Press, 1994.

____, ed. *Progressive Christians Speak: A Different Voice on Faith and Politics.* Louisville: Westminster John Knox Press, 2003.

____. *Reclaiming the Church: Where the Mainline Went Wrong and What to Do about It.* Louisville: Westminster John Knox Press, 1997.

____, ed. *Resistance: The New Role of Progressive Christians.* Louisville: Westminster John Knox Press, 2008.

____. *Spiritual Bankruptcy: A Prophetic Call to Action.* Nashville: Abingdon Press, 2010.

____. *Whitehead Word Book: A Glossary with Alphabetical Index to Technical Terms in* Process and Reality. Anoka, MN: Process Century Press, 2015.

____. "Who Is a Whiteheadian?" Process and Faith, posted March 2007, http://processandfaith.org/writings/ask-dr-cobb/2007-03/who-whiteheadian (accessed April 30, 2013).

Cobb, John B., Jr., and David Ray Griffin. *Process Theology: An Introductory Exposition.* Louisville: Westminster John Knox Press, 1976.

Cobb, John B., Jr., and W. Widick Schroeder, eds. *Process Philosophy and Social Thought.* Chicago: Center for the Scientific Study of Religion, 1981.

Coleman, Monica A. *Making a Way Out of No Way: A Womanist Theology.* Minneapolis: Fortress Press, 2008.

Cone, James. *A Black Theology of Liberation.* 20th anniversary edition. Maryknoll, NY: Orbis Books, 2008.

Crockett, Clayton. *Radical Political Theology: Religion and Politics after Liberalism.* New York: Columbia University Press, 2011.

Crockett, Clayton, and Jay McDaniel. "From an Idolatry of Identity to a Planetization of Alterity: A Relational-Theological Approach to Hybridity, Sin, and Love." *Journal of Postcolonial Theory and Theology* 1, no. 3 (November 2010): 1–26. Accessed November 15, 2013.

http://postcolonialjournal.com/Resources/Crockett%20JPTT%20
Dec%2027.pdf.

Crossan, John Dominic. *The Birth of Christianity: Discovering What
Happened in the Years Immediately After the Execution of Jesus.* San
Francisco: HarperSanFrancisco, 1998.

Culp, Kristine A. "Revisioning the Church: Toward a Process
Ecclesiology." Master's thesis, Princeton Theological Seminary, 1982.

Cusa, Nicholas. *Nicholas of Cusa: Selected Spiritual Writings.* Translated
and edited by H. Lawrence Bond. New York: Paulist Press, 1997.

Davies, Mark Y. "Towards an Ecologically Sensitive Ecclesiology:
Ethical and Ecclesiological Implications of John Cobb's Process
Theology." MDiv thesis, Candler School of Theology, 1992.

Deleuze, Gilles. *The Fold: Leibniz and the Baroque.* Translated by
Tom Conley. Minneapolis: University of Minnesota Press, 1993.

Deleuze, Gilles, and Félix Guattari. *A Thousand Plateaus: Capitalism
and Schizophrenia.* Translated by Brian Massumi. Minneapolis:
University of Minnesota Press, 1987.

Dombrowski, Daniel A. *Christian Pacifism.* Philadelphia: Temple
University Press, 1991.

Dorrien, Gary. *The Making of American Liberal Theology: Crisis, Irony,
and Postmodernity, 1950–2005.* Vol. 3 of *The Making of American
Liberal Theology.* Louisville: Westminster John Knox Press, 2006.

Faber, Roland. "De-Ontologizing God: Levinas, Deleuze, and
Whitehead." In *Process and Difference: Between Cosmological and
Poststructuralist Postmodernisms,* edited by Catherine Keller and
Anne Daniell, 209–34. Albany: State University of New York
Press, 2002.

———. "Ecotheology, Ecoprocess, and Eco*theosis*: A Theopoetical
Intervention." *Salzburger Theologische Zeitschrift* 12 (2008): 75–115.

———. "Emptiness and Nothingness." Class lecture (Mysticism and
Process Theology), Claremont School of Theology, Claremont,
CA, February 22, 2011.

———. *God as Poet of the World: Exploring Process Theologies.* Translated
by Douglas W. Stott. Louisville: Westminster John Knox Press,
2008.

Ford, Lewis S. *Transforming Process Theism*. Albany: State University of New York Press, 2000.

Gebara, Ivone. *Out of the Depths: Women's Experience of Evil and Salvation*. Translated by Ann Patrick Ware. Minneapolis: Fortress Press, 2002.

Grau, Marion. *Rethinking Mission in the Postcolony: Salvation, Society, and Subversion*. London: T&T Clark, 2011.

Griffin, David Ray. *Reenchantment without Supernaturalism: A Process Philosophy of Religion*. Cornell Studies in the Philosophy of Religion. Ithaca, NY: Cornell University Press, 2001.

____. "Resurrection and Empire." In *The American Empire and the Commonwealth of God: A Political, Economic, Religious Statement*, by David Ray Griffin, John B. Cobb Jr., Richard A Falk, and Catherine Keller, 151–57. Louisville: Westminster John Knox Press, 2006.

Hamm, Richard L. *2020 Vision for the Christian Church (Disciples of Christ)*. St. Louis: Chalice Press, 2001.

Hardt, Michael, and Antonio Negri. *Commonwealth*. Cambridge: Harvard University Press, 2009.

____. *Empire*. Cambridge: Harvard University Press, 2000.

____. *Multitude: War and Democracy in the Age of Empire*. New York: Penguin Press, 2004.

Heinzekehr, Justin. "Pacifism from a Process Perspective: Redefining Process Ethics through an Anabaptist Lens." MA thesis, Claremont School of Theology, 2011.

Henning, Brian G. *The Ethics of Creativity: Beauty, Morality, and Nature in a Processive Cosmos*. Pittsburgh: University of Pittsburgh Press, 2005.

Herzog, William R., II. *Parables as Subversive Speech: Jesus as Pedagogue of the Oppressed*. Louisville: Westminster/John Knox Press, 1994.

Higgins, Luke. "Becoming through Multiplicity: Staying in the Middle of Whitehead's and Deleuze-Guattari's Philosophies of Life." In *Secrets of Becoming: Negotiating Whitehead, Deleuze, and Butler*, edited by Roland Faber and Andrea Stephenson, 142–56. New York: Fordham Press, 2010.

Honig, Bonnie. *Emergency Politics: Paradox, Law, and Democracy.* Princeton: Princeton University Press, 2009.

Hough, Joseph C., Jr., and Barbara G. Wheeler., eds. *Beyond Clericalism: The Congregation as a Focus for Theological Education.* Atlanta: Scholars Press, 1988.

Isherwood, Lisa, and Mark D. Jordan, eds. *Dancing Theology in Fetish Boots: Essays in Honour of Marcella Althaus-Reid.* London: SCM Press, 2010.

Joh, Wonhee Anne. *Heart of the Cross: A Postcolonial Christology.* Louisville: Westminster John Knox Press, 2006.

Johnson-Debaufre, Melanie. "The *Basileia Theou* and the Space/s of Utopian Politics." Paper presented at the Twelfth Transdisciplinary Theological Colloquium, Common Good(s): Economy, Ecology, and Political Theology, Drew Theological School, Madison, NJ, February 10, 2013.

Jones, Judith. "Intensity and Subjectivity." Edited by Michel Weber and Will Desmond. Vol. 1 of *Handbook of Whiteheadian Process Thought.* Frankfurt, Germany: Ontos Verlag, 2008.

Jones, Tony. *The Church Is Flat: The Relational Ecclesiology of the Emerging Church Movement.* Minneapolis: JoPa Group, 2011.

Kahn, Paul W. *Political Theology: Four New Chapters on the Concept of Sovereignty.* New York: Columbia University Press, 2011.

Kairos Palestine 2009. "A moment of truth: A word of faith, hope, and love from the heart of Palestinian suffering." http://www.kairospalestine.ps/sites/default/ Documents/English.pdf (accessed July 27, 2013).

Kee, Alistar. "Queering Ontologies: A Critique of Three Liberation Theologies." In *Dancing Theology in Fetish Boots: Essays in Honour of Marcella Althaus-Reid,* edited by Lisa Isherwood and Mark D. Jordan, 124–40. London: SCM Press, 2010.

Keller, Catherine. "The Apophasis of Gender: A Fourfold Unsaying of Feminist Theology." *Journal of the American Academy of Religion* 76, no. 4 (December 2008): 905–33.

____. *The Face of the Deep: A Theology of Becoming.* London: Routledge, 2003.

_____. *From a Broken Web: Separation, Sexism, and Self.* Boston: Beacon Press, 1986.

_____. *God and Power: Counter-Apocalyptic Journeys.* Minneapolis: Fortress Press, 2005.

_____. "Introduction: The Process of Difference, the Difference of Process." In *Process and Difference: Between Cosmological and Poststructuralist Postmodernisms,* edited by Catherine Keller and Anne Daniell, 1–29. Albany: State University of New York Press, 2002.

_____. "The Love of Postcolonialism." In *Postcolonial Theologies: Divinity and Empire,* edited by Catherine Keller, Michael Nausner, and Mayra Rivera, 221-42. St. Louis: Chalice Press, 2004.

_____. *On the Mystery: Discerning Divinity in Process.* Minneapolis: Fortress Press, 2008.

_____. "Talking Dirty: Ground Is Not Foundation." In *Ecospirit: Religions and Philosophies for the Earth,* edited by Laurel Kearns and Catherine Keller, 63–76. New York: Fordham University Press, 2007.

Keller, Catherine, and Anne Daniell, eds. *Process and Difference: Between Cosmological and Poststructuralist Postmodernisms.* Albany: State University of New York Press, 2002.

Keller, Catherine, and Laurel C. Schneider, eds. *Polydoxy: Theology of Multiplicity and Relation.* London: Routledge, 2011.

Keller, Catherine, Michael Nausner, and Mayra Rivera, eds. *Postcolonial Theologies: Divinity and Empire.* St. Louis: Chalice Press, 2004.

Kim, Van Nam. *A Church of Hope: A Study of the Eschatological Ecclesiology of Jürgen Moltmann.* Lanham, MD: University Press of America, 2005.

King, Barbara J. King. "Jared Diamond, A New Guinea Campfire, and Why We Should Want to Speak Five Languages." National Public Radio, posted January 10, 2013, http://www.npr.org/blogs/13.7/2013/01/10/168878237/jared-diamond-a-new- guinea-campfire-and-why-we-should-want-to-speak-five-languag (accessed May 25, 2013).

King, Martin Luther, Jr. "Letter from Birmingham Jail." In *Why We Can't Wait*, 85-110. 1964. Reprint, Boston: Beacon Press, 2011.

Kwok, Pui-lan, Don H. Compier, and Joerg Rieger, eds. *Empire and the Christian Tradition: New Readings of Classical Theologians.* Minneapolis: Fortress Press, 2007.

Lee, Bernard. *The Becoming Church: A Process Theology of the Structure of Christian Experience.* New York: Paulist Press, 1974.

____. "Reconstructing Our American Story: Intentional Christian Communities." *Chicago Studies* 26, no. 1 (April 1987): 11–24.

Lyon, K. Brynolf. "Companions on the Way: Creating and Discovering the Congregational Subject." *Encounter* 63, no. 1–2 (Winter/Spring 2002): 147–57.

McLaren, Brian D. *Everything Must Change: Jesus, Global Crises, and a Revolution of Hope.* Nashville: Thomas Nelson, 2007.

Míguez, Néstor. "Contexto Sociopolítico de los Estudios Poscoloniales en AL." Paper presented at the Pressing On: Legacy of Marcella Althaus-Reid Conference, ISEDET, Buenos Aires, Argentina, July 9, 2013.

Míguez, Néstor, Joerg Rieger, and Jung Mo Sung. *Beyond the Spirit of Empire: Theology and Politics in a New Key.* Reclaiming Liberation Theology. London: SCM Press, 2009.

Moltmann, Jürgen. *The Church in the Power of the Spirit: A Contribution to Messianic Ecclesiology.* Translated by Margaret Kohl. Minneapolis: Fortress Press, 1993.

____. "The Diaconal Church in the Context of the Kingdom of God." In *Hope for the Church: Moltmann in Dialogue with Practical Theology*, edited and translated by Theodore Runyon, 21–36. Nashville: Abingdon, 1979.

____. "The Life Signs of the Spirit in the Fellowship Community of Christ." In *Hope for the Church: Moltmann in Dialogue with Practical Theology*, edited and translated by Theodore Runyon, 37-56. Nashville: Abingdon, 1979.

____. *The Spirit of Life: A Universal Affirmation.* Translated by Margaret Kohl. Minneapolis: Fortress Press, 1992.

____. *Sun of Righteousness, Arise!: God's Future for Humanity and the*

Earth. Translated by Margaret Kohl. Minneapolis: Fortress Press, 2010.

____. *The Trinity and the Kingdom: The Doctrine of God*. Translated by Margaret Kohl. 1981. Reprint, Minneapolis: Fortress Press, 1993.

Moore, Stephen D., and Mayra Rivera, eds. *Planetary Loves: Spivak, Postcoloniality, and Theology*. New York: Fordham University Press, 2011.

Morris, Randall C. *Process Philosophy and Political Ideology: The Social and Political Thought of Alfred North Whitehead and Charles Hartshorne*. Albany: State University of New York Press, 1991.

Müller-Fahrenholz, Geiko. "In the Fellowship of the Spirit of God." In *The Kingdom and the Power: The Theology of Jürgen Moltmann*, 80-106. London: SCM Press, 2000.

Murphy, Timothy. "The Pacifism of Duane Friesen: Engaged Realism, Process Thought, and Critical Assessment." *Process Studies* 42, no. 1 (Spring-Summer 2013): 110–31.

____. "Reconceiving Revolution: Towards Micro-Revolutions of Becoming." *Claremont Journal of Religion* 2, no. 2 (Spring 2013): 87-113. Accessed November 8, 2013. http://claremontjournal.com/wp-content/uploads/2013/06/Reconceiving Revolution-Towards-Micro-Revolutions-of-Becoming-by-Timothy-Murphy.pdf.

Nessan, Craig L. *Beyond Maintenance to Mission: A Theology of the Congregation*. Minneapolis: Fortress Press, 1999.

Nussbaum, Martha C. *Creating Capabilities: The Human Development Approach*. Cambridge: Belknap Press of Harvard University Press, 2011.

____. *Frontiers of Justice: Disability, Nationality, Species Membership*. Cambridge: Belknap Press of Harvard University Press, 2006.

Odin, Steve. *Process Metaphysics and Hua-yen Buddhism: A Critical Study of Cumulative Penetration vs. Interpenetration*. Albany: State University of New York Press, 1982.

Oh, Jea Sophia. *A Postcolonial Theology of Life: Planetarity East and West*. Upland, CA: Sopher Press, 2011.

Oord, Thomas Jay. *The Nature of Love: A Theology*. St. Louis: Chalice Press, 2010.

Ott, Daniel J. "The Church in Process: A Process Ecclesiology." Ph.D. diss., Claremont Graduate University, 2006.

Paeth, Scott R. *Exodus Church and Civil Society: Public Theology and Social Theory in the Work of Jürgen Moltmann.* Burlington, VT: Ashgate, 2008.

Petrella, Ivan. "Liberation Theology after Marcella." In *Dancing Theology in Fetish Boots: Essays in Honour of Marcella Althaus-Reid,* edited by Lisa Isherwood and Mark D. Jordan, 200-06. London: SCM Press, 2010.

Pittenger, Norman. *The Christian Church as Social Process.* Philadelphia: Westminster Press, 1971.

_____. *The Pilgrim Church and the Easter People.* Wilmington, DE: Michael Glazier, 1987.

Pixley, George. "The Bible's Call to Resist." In *Resistance: The New Role of Progressive Christians,* edited by John B. Cobb, Jr., 3–31. Louisville: Westminster John Knox Press, 2008.

_____. "Latin American Liberation Theology." In *Resistance: The New Role of Progressive Christians,* edited by John B. Cobb, Jr., 165–85. Louisville: Westminster John Knox Press, 2008.

"Power and Empire: A Process-Liberation Conversation." Conference, Center for Process Studies, Claremont, CA, October 11-13, 2011.

Rah, Soong-Chan. *The Next Evangelicalism: Freeing the Church from Western Cultural Captivity.* Downers Grove, IL: InterVarsity Press, 2009.

Rawls, John. *Political Liberalism.* Expanded ed. New York: Columbia University Press, 2005.

_____. *A Theory of Justice.* Cambridge: Belknap Press of Harvard University Press, 1971.

Rhodes, J. Stephen. "The Church as the Community of Open Friendship." *Asbury Theological Journal* 55, no. 1 (Spring 2000): 41–49.

Rieger, Joerg. *Christ and Empire: From Paul to Postcolonial Times.* Minneapolis: Fortress Press, 2007.

_____. "Contesting the Common Good and Religion in the Context of Capitalism: Abrahamic Alternatives." Paper presented at the Twelfth Transdisci-plinary Theological Colloquium, Drew Theological School, Madison, NJ, February 9, 2013.

_____. "Theology and Mission Between Neocolonialism and Post-colonialism," *Mission Studies: Journal of the International Association for Mission Studies* 21, no. 2 (2004): 201–27.

Rieger, Joerg, and Kwok Pui-lan. *Occupy Religion: Theology of the Multitude*. Lanham, MD: Rowman & Littlefield, 2012.

Rivera, Mayra. *The Touch of Transcendence: A Postcolonial Theology of God*. Louisville: Westminster John Knox Press, 2007.

Robbins, Jeffrey W. *Radical Democracy and Political Theology*. Insurrections: Critical Studies in Religion, Politics, and Culture. New York: Columbia University Press, 2011.

Rose, Philip. *On Whitehead*. Wadsworth Philosophers Series. Belmont, CA: Wadsworth, 2002.

Ruether, Rosemary Radford. *Gaia and God: An Ecofeminist Theology of Earth Healing*. New York: HarperCollins, 1992.

_____. "Talking Dirty, Speaking Truth: Indecenting Theology." In *Dancing Theology in Fetish Boots: Essays in Honour of Marcella Althaus-Reid*, edited by Lisa Isherwood and Mark D. Jordan, 254–67. London: SCM Press, 2010.

Russell, Letty M. *Church in the Round: Feminist Interpretation of the Church*. Louisville: Westminster John Knox Press, 1993.

Schneider, Laurel C. *Beyond Monotheism: A Theology of Multiplicity*. London: Routledge, 2008.

Sen, Amartya. *The Argumentative Indian: Writings on Indian History, Culture and Identity*. New York: Picador, 2005.

_____. *Development as Freedom*. Oxford: Oxford University Press, 1999.

_____. *The Idea of Justice*. Cambridge: Belknap Press of Harvard University Press, 2009.

Shore-Goss. Robert. "Dis/Grace-full Incarnation and the Dis/Grace-full Church: Marcella Althaus-Reid's Vision of Radical Inclusivity." In *Dancing Theology in Fetish Boots: Essays in Honour of Marcella Althaus-Reid*, edited by Lisa Isherwood and Mark D. Jordan, 1-16. London: SCM Press, 2010.

Smythe, Lewis. "The Role of the Church in Changing Persons and

Society." *Lexington Theological Quarterly* 6, no. 3 (July 1971): 81–91.

Sölle, Dorothee. "The Kingdom of God and the Church." In *Thinking About God: An Introduction to Theology*. Translated by John Bowden, 136–53. London: SCM Press, 1990.

Spivak, Gayatri Chatravorty. *A Critique of Postcolonial Reason: Toward a History of the Vanishing Present*. Cambridge: Harvard University Press, 1999.

———. *Death of a Discipline*. Wellek Library Lectures. New York: Columbia University Press, 2005.

Suchocki, Marjorie Hewitt. *Divinity and Diversity: A Christian Affirmation of Religious Pluralism*. Nashville: Abingdon Press, 2003.

———. "The Dynamic God." *Process Studies* 39, no. 1 (Spring 2010): 39–58.

———. *The End of Evil: Process Eschatology in Historical Context*. 1988. Reprint, Eugene, OR: Wipf & Stock, 2005.

———. *The Fall to Violence: Original Sin in Relational Theology*. New York: Continuum, 1994.

———. *God, Christ, Church: A Practical Guide to Process Theology*. Rev. ed. New York: Crossroad, 1989.

———. *In God's Presence: Theological Reflections on Prayer*. St. Louis: Chalice Press, 1996.

———. "Prayer in Troubled Times: A Process Perspective." Center for Process Studies lecture, Claremont School of Theology, Claremont, CA, October, 2010.

Sung, Jung Mo. *Desire, Market and Religion*. Reclaiming Liberation Theology. London: SCM Press, 2007.

———. *The Subject, Capitalism, and Religion: Horizons of Hope in Complex Societies*. New York: Palgrave Macmillan, 2011.

Taylor, Mark Lewis. "Spirit and Liberation: Achieving Postcolonial Theology in the United States." In *Postcolonial Theologies: Divinity and Empire*, edited by Catherine Keller, Michael Nausner, and Mayra Rivera, 39–55. St. Louis: Chalice Press, 2004.

Thatamanil, John. "The Invention of 'The Religious' and 'The Political': Genealogy of Religion, Interfaith Dialogue, and Political Theory."

Paper presented at the Twelfth Transdisciplinary Theological Colloquium, Common Good(s): Economy, Ecology, and Political Theology, Drew Theological School, Madison, NJ, February 10, 2013.

Whitehead, Alfred North. *Adventure of Ideas*. 1933. Reprint, New York: Free Press, 1967.

———. *Dialogues of Alfred North Whitehead*. Edited by Lucien Price. 1954, Reprint, Boston: David R. Godine, 2001.

———. *The Function of Reason*. 1929. Reprint, Boston: Beacon Press, 1971.

———. "Immortality." In *The Philosophy of Alfred North Whitehead*, edited by Paul Arthur Schilpp, 682–700. 1951. Reprint, La Salle, IL: Open Court, 1971.

———. *Modes of Thought*. 1938. Reprint, New York: Free Press, 1968.

———. *Process and Reality*. Corrected edition. Edited by David Ray Griffin and Donald W. Sherburne. New York: Free Press, 1978.

———. *Religion in the Making*. 1926. Reprint, New York: Fordham University Press, 2011.

———. *Science and the Modern World*. 1925. Reprint, New York: Free Press, 1967.

———. *Symbolism: Its Meaning and Effect*. 1927. Reprint, New York: Fordham University Press, 1985.

Williams, Delores S. *Sisters in the Wilderness: The Challenge of Womanist God-Talk*. Maryknoll, NY: Orbis Books, 1993.

Williamson, Clark M. "Companions on the Way: The Church." In *Way of Blessing, Way of Life: A Christian Theology*, 251–76. St. Louis: Chalice Press, 1999.

Williamson, Clark M., and Ronald J. Allen. *The Vital Church: Teaching, Worship, Community, Service*. St. Louis: Chalice Press, 1998.

Wink, Walter. *Engaging the Powers: Discernment and Resistance in a World of Domination*. Minneapolis: Fortress Press, 1992.

World Alliance of Reformed Churches. *Accra Confession: Covenanting for Justice in the Economy and the Earth*. Accra, Ghana: 24th General Council, 2004.

Yearbook and Directory of the Christian Church (Disciples of Christ),

2011. Edited by Howard E. Bowers. Indianapolis: Office of the General Minister and President, 2012.

Yearbook & Directory of the Christian Church (Disciples of Christ), 2014. Edited by Howard E. Bowers. Indianapolis: Office of the General Minister and President, 2014.

Yoder, John Howard. *Body Politics: Five Practices of the Christian Community before the Watching World*. Nashville: Discipleship Resources, 1992.

_____. *The Christian Witness to the State*. Institute of Mennonite Studies Series, no. 3. Newton, KS: Faith and Life Press, 1964.

_____. *The Original Revolution: Essays on Christian Pacifism*. 1971. Reprint, Scottdale, PA: Herald Press, 2003.

_____. *The Priestly Kingdom: Social Ethics as Gospel*. Notre Dame: University of Notre Dame Press, 1984.

Young, Iris Marion. *Inclusion and Democracy*. Oxford: Oxford University Press, 2000.

_____. *Justice and the Politics of Difference*. Princeton: Princeton University Press, 2011.

Young, Robert J. C. *Postcolonialism: A Very Short Introduction*. Oxford: Oxford University Press, 2003.

Made in the USA
Columbia, SC
13 July 2017